THE GAY FIRESIDE COMPANION

Published as a trade paperback original
by Alyson Publications, 40 Plympton St., Boston, Mass. 02118.

Distributed in the U.K. by GMP Publishers,
PO Box 247, London, N17 9QR, England.

First U.S. Edition: December, 1989

ISBN 1-55583-164-8

THE GAY
FIRESIDE
COMPANION

LEIGH W. RUTLEDGE

Alyson Publications, Inc.

To RICHARD DONLEY

FOREWORD
AND
ACKNOWLEDGEMENTS

Early in the discussions of finding an appropriate title for this book, someone suggested calling it *Leigh Rutledge's Encyclopaedia of Homosexuality*. I winced at the thought of my name in the title — maybe Fellini can get away with it, I cannot — and when I expressed my misgivings to a friend, he claimed, "But *why*? Honey, you *are* gay trivia!" That made me laugh. Labels and titles, of course, don't matter. Just so long as people enjoy the books, and learn a few things from them.

This current book is meant to be an offbeat reference book to be read for pleasure, an informative book that is meant to provide entertainment. One friend of mine likes to say that everything in my books must pass what he calls the "Did You Know" test — in other words, if you're reading one of the books with someone else in the room, you're going to want to look up and say, "Oh my God, listen to *this*!" or "Did you know such-and-such?" In reality, of course, there is no such test and I'm not consciously aware of any specific criteria as I put the books together. I just pick things that amuse, enrage, or astonish me, or that bear repeating or are worth remembering, or that answer questions I've always wanted an answer to, such as "Who actually invented the jockstrap?" or "What was absinthe?" or "What is specifically involved in a male-to-female transsexual operation?" One way or another, everything in these books reflects an almost obsessive curiosity about the world and gay life.

Unlike *The Gay Book of Lists* and *Unnatural Quotations* —

which some readers have told me they consumed in a single weekend, or even in a single long night — this book is meant to provide a little more leisurely reading. Whatever flaws the concept of a "fireside companion" may have, that is, in many ways, exactly what this book is meant to be: a book to curl up by the fire with, to curl up in bed with, to sit outside on the porch under the shade of a big tree reading.

One small word of caution: as will become readily apparent, none of the entries in this book is meant to be comprehensive or exhaustive. Turning to "Leonard Bernstein" or "Ronald Reagan," for example, as often as not one will find not the story of their lives, as in the *Encyclopaedia Britannica*, but whatever information about them has struck my eye. For those who have read my two previous books, it goes without saying that I have a bias for the curious and the little known. Consider this book then a kind of gay information "scavenger hunt."

For their help in providing me with information and assistance, I would like to take a moment to thank: the Academy of Motion Picture Arts and Sciences Library in Beverly Hills, the American Institute for Public Opinion Research, the Captains of ISMI, Chesebrough-Ponds, Inc., the Dallas Department of Health and Human Services, Richard E. Donley, H. Montgomery Hyde, Jockey International, Daniel Martinez, Lola Milani, J. Scott Paisley, Kay Roberts, Craig Rodwell, the Roper Center at the University of Connecticut, Edward Rutledge, the research department at the San Jose *Mercury News*, Chris Schick, Charlotte Simmons, Sam Staggs, Johnny Townsend, and Peter Urbanek. A big thanks also to Neil Woodward at Category Six Bookstore in Denver, who has proved time and again that a helpful relationship with a good bookseller is at least as important to a writer as the other intimate relationships in one's life.

As with *The Gay Book of Lists* and *Unnatural Quotations*, I would enjoy hearing from anyone who has comments, additions, corrections, questions, and even complaints about *The Gay Fireside Companion*. Those so inclined should write:

Leigh W. Rutledge
P.O. Box 5523
Pueblo, Colorado 81002

One final remark, this one about dates. All birth dates and death dates in this book have been double- and in some cases triple-checked. But anyone doing research quickly learns that so-called "unimpeachable" facts from so-called "unimpeachable" sources may vary widely. I found, for example, four different years of birth for actor George Maharis — all four of them from reference sources considered completely reliable. I finally chose the one that, given other information, seemed most reasonable. Wherever there have been ambiguities about similar facts, I have used the same practice.

Leigh W. Rutledege

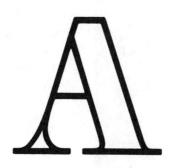

ABSINTHE, yellowish-green liqueur favored by — and commonly associated with — numerous nineteenth-century "aesthetes," including Oscar Wilde, who, according to friends, sometimes drank himself into a delirium with it, especially during his last days in Paris. At least one of Wilde's acquaintances tried to suggest that the playwright's "unnatural" desires stemmed from an overindulgence in absinthe. When another acquaintance criticized the poet Ernest Dowson for being a heavy absinthe drinker, Wilde remarked, "You mustn't mind that a poet is a drunk, rather that drunks are not always poets."

First produced in 1797, absinthe is distilled from an herb — wormwood — and then flavored with licorice, anise, fennel, and other ingredients. It has an unusually high alcohol content for a liqueur. Because of its supposed propensity to cause hallucinations, toxic reactions, and mental deterioration, its manufacture and sale were prohibited by most European countries in the early twentieth century, and importation into the United States was banned in 1915. An absinthe-like liqueur — lower in alcohol content and without the wormwood — is sold today under such brand names as "Pernod," "Pernod 45," and "Ricard."

ACADEMY AWARD, BEST ACTOR — FIRST ACTOR TO RECEIVE NOMINATION FOR A PERFORMANCE IN AN OPENLY GAY ROLE. Peter Finch, for his portrayal of a

Actor Peter Finch in *Sunday, Bloody Sunday:* He lost to Gene Hackman.

homosexual doctor in *Sunday, Bloody Sunday*, in 1971. He lost to Gene Hackman in *The French Connection*.

ACADEMY AWARD, BEST ACTOR — FIRST ACTOR TO ACTUALLY WIN FOR A PERFORMANCE IN AN OPENLY GAY ROLE. William Hurt, for his portrayal of Luis Molina, a homosexual window dresser imprisoned for "corrupting a minor," in the 1985 film *Kiss of the Spider Woman*.

ACADEMY AWARDS CEREMONY, MAN WHO STREAKED IN 1974. Ten years after his death, self-described gay performance artist Robert Opel probably holds the distinction of having been seen in the nude by more people than any other man in history. A former advertising man from West Hollywood, Opel became famous when, as a stunt, he "streaked" the Academy Awards ceremony in 1974, having first gained access to the backstage area with a fake press badge. Just as actor David Niven was about to introduce Elizabeth Taylor to present the night's final Oscar, for Best Picture, Opel suddenly emerged from the stage scenery and ran naked past the footlights. His figure was clearly visible to the more than one billion viewers watching the ceremony on T.V. There was scattered laughter and applause from the audience, but it was actor Niven who brought down the house when he quipped, "The only way that poor man could get a laugh was by showing off his shortcomings." Opel himself later remarked of the prank, "It wasn't streaking in front of a billion people that scared me. When I was hiding out in the scenery, I was tangled up in about a thousand high-voltage wires."

A few months later, Opel once again disrobed publicly,

this time at a Los Angeles City Council meeting attended by L.A.'s notoriously conservative police chief, Ed Davis. The meeting was being held to decide on a proposed city ordinance banning nude sunbathing at municipal beaches. To protest the ban, Opel walked into the council chambers stark naked. He was promptly arrested and charged with indecent exposure and disrupting a public meeting.

Opel eventually moved to San Francisco, where he opened the city's first "leather" art gallery — The Fey Way Gallery, in the South of Market district — devoted to the works of Tom of Finland, Chuck Arnett, Tom Hinde, and similar artists. It was in that gallery one night, in July 1979, that Opel and three friends were confronted by armed intruders demanding money and drugs. In the course of the robbery, Opel was taken into a back room and shot to death by one of the burglars. The thieves then fled, with a total booty of one camera, one backpack, and five dollars in cash.

Ironically, just shortly before his murder, Opel had staged a mock public execution of Dan White — convicted assassin of Harvey Milk and San Francisco Mayor George Moscone — at the city's U.N. Plaza. "I am Robert Opel," he proclaimed. "I am an artist, a cocksucker, and an anarchist ... Men like myself have been feared and persecuted because of our sexual preference. But I persist. Eventually, I believe, I will receive wider attention."

Opel was thirty-nine at the time of his death.

ADAMS, NICK (1931-1968), U.S. actor, born Nicholas Aloysius Adamshock, best known for his role as Johnny Yuma in the T.V. series *The Rebel* (1959-1962). After a brief stint in the Coast Guard, Adams hitchhiked to Hollywood in 1951 and got a part in a Coca-Cola commercial with James Dean, before either one of them was famous. He also supposedly tried to generate some much-needed income by hustling on the streets of Hollywood, where his allegedly huge endowment and smooth, charismatic features made him popular among regular customers on Santa Monica Boulevard and the Sunset Strip. He became friends with Dean — which later led to some feverish speculation about the exact nature of their relationship — and the two worked together again (al-

Nicholas Aloysius Adamshock, better known as Nick Adams: What's the old saying about a man's hands...

beit, Adams in a small role) in *Rebel Without a Cause* in 1953.

Adams wanted desperately to be a star and tried numerous extravagant publicity ploys to reach that goal. After James Dean's death in a car accident in 1955, Adams capitalized on the almost necrophiliac frenzy that broke out afterward and tried to publicly cast himself as Dean's artistic heir apparent: for a time, he even appeared in public dressed in the same tight blue jeans, white T-shirt, and red jacket that had become Dean's trademarks. Ironically, Dean's lines during his final scene in the film *Giant* had to be redubbed for technical reasons after his death, and Adams — known throughout Hollywood as an expert mimic — was secretly called in by the studio to do the job. The last words James Dean speaks in *Giant* are actually spoken by Nick Adams.

In the years that followed, Adams eked out a respectable niche for himself, even if it wasn't the kind of stardom he yearned for. Part of the problem was his reputation as hotheaded and arrogant, with more ambition than talent. Fellow actors complained about his penchant for trying to crowd them out of the camera frame, and directors labeled him impossible to work with because he refused to stick to the script. But he had parts in seventeen films during his sixteen-year career, including *Mr. Roberts*, *Picnic*, and *The Interns*. In 1963, he spent almost ten thousand dollars of his own money in a manic advertising campaign to win an Academy Award nomination for his performance in *Twilight of Honor*, a courtroom drama co-starring Richard Chamberlain. He succeeded in getting the nomination, but failed to win the Oscar.

Adams's best remembered role came in 1959, when he was cast as Johnny Yuma — a former Confederate soldier wandering the Old West, dispensing justice to pretty widows, fatherless boys, and down-on-their-luck ranchers — in the ABC T.V. series *The Rebel.* The show was a modest success, thanks in part to Adams's sexy persona, and the actor thought he was finally on the verge of something big. But the ratings quickly started to slide after the first season, and the show disappeared from the airwaves in 1962.

After the series' cancellation, and after failing to win the Academy Award, Adams's career took a nosedive. One of his last roles was in a low-budget Japanese horror film, *Frankenstein Meets the Giant Devil Fish*, in 1966. Unable to cope, he sought treatment with anti-anxiety drugs. He died in 1968 of an overdose of sedatives and alcohol, an apparent suicide at the age of thirty-six.

Although married and divorced with two children, Adams had a reputation for being aggressively bisexual. Some people have suggested he was simply one of Hollywood's restless mercenaries and didn't care who he slept with as long as there was something in it for him.

ADONIS, subtitled "The Art Magazine of the Male Physique." Early physique magazine "dedicated to man's desire to improve his face and figure." *Adonis* featured handsome, muscular young models in posing straps, or sometimes completely nude but only from the back. The magazine first started publishing in 1951.

Like other "physical culture" magazines from the period, its fleshy and provocative photos of near-naked men — often taken by such renowned male photographers as Bob Mizer of the Athletic Model Guild or Don Whitman of the Western Photographic Guild — were published under the then-necessary pretense of championing physical fitness and good health, while in actuality providing erotica for gay men. Models were often presented under such coy captions as "Ripening grain, ripening youth — the strength of America," or "Here is the finest flower of masculine perfection. Jim is in the Navy, so you can be sure the country is in good hands!" Perfunctory statistics on the

Adonis (1958) plus *Body Beautiful* (1958) eventually equalled *The Young Physique* (1964).

model's alleged body measurements — chest, waist, biceps, etc. — were also provided, as were occasional articles on fitness, bodybuilding, and good sleeping habits. *Adonis* also published a companion magazine, *Body Beautiful: Studies in Masculine Art.*

In 1958, *Adonis* and *Body Beautiful* were combined to create a single magazine, *The Young Physique.* By the mid-1960s, *Young Physique* — although still confined to photographs of male models in posing straps — was becoming more and more openly gay. The model copy became more suggestive ("Richie has his own Greenwich Village apartment, where he likes to entertain lots of new friends, including fellow physical culturists. Why don't *you* drop in on Richie sometime?" or "Gino's perfect thighs are the result of daily workouts with his friends — on the barbells, that is !"). In an apparent attempt to more boldly announce its real intentions, one memorably campy 1964 cover featured a rear shot of a dark-haired young man — labeled "Pink Narcissus" — looking coyly over his shoulder at the reader and dressed in lavender leotards, shiny pink boots, and a white fur jacket.

Like most early physique

magazines, *Adonis, Body Beautiful,* and *The Young Physique* were openly sold in many drugstores. However, with the liberalization of attitudes in the late sixties, gay erotica became more explicit, and the physique magazines gave way to increasingly "hardcore" photography.

The first *Advocate:* The September, 1967 issue included a story about the fifteenth anniversary of ONE, the nation's oldest surviving homophile organization.

THE ADVOCATE, national gay newsmagazine. The first issue came out in 1967, was twelve pages long, and cost twenty-five cents. It was started in Los Angeles by Dick Michaels — a reporter for a large chemical newsmagazine — and two other men, who wanted to report "what the straight press wouldn't print, and what gay people needed to know about what was happening in their world." The initial printing — surreptitiously done by a friend, late one night in the basement of a network television studio — was five hundred copies. Current circulation is 75,000 copies.

AIDS as King Tut's curse: Just how desperate can a tabloid get?

AIDS, MOST MEMORABLE EXPLANATION FOR. Asserting that ancient Egypt was "a hotbed of homosexual activity," one supermarket tabloid, *The Globe,* announced in 1983 that AIDS was actually "the curse of

Tutankhamen," and that the disease was unleashed on the world when archaeologists first opened King Tut's tomb in 1922. The *Globe* quoted one archaeologist who contended that the disease had been brought to the U.S. in the late 1970s, during a highly publicized tour of artifacts from the young pharaoh's tomb.

AIDS, U.S. PUBLIC OPINION POLLS ON.

—1983—

• Do you think AIDS is God's punishment against homosexuals for the way they live? (ABC News/*Washington Post*)
   Yes: 13%
   No: 75%
   No opinion: 12%

• (Asked of people who said they had homosexual friends) As a result of the AIDS epidemic, are you less comfortable than you were before with your homosexual friends and acquaintances? (Gallup for *Newsweek* magazine)
   Yes: 21%
   No: 78%
   Don't know: 1%

• How worried are you that you or someone you know will contract AIDS? (Gallup for *Newsweek* magazine)
   Very: 7%
   A little: 15%
   Not very: 23%
   Not at all: 42%

• Which of the following factors do you think can cause a person to contract AIDS? (Roper)
   Homosexual contact: 75%
   Receiving a
      blood transfusion: 50%
   I.V. drug use: 42%
   Giving blood
      to a blood bank: 23%
   Being Haitian: 20%
   Having hemophilia: 15%
   None of the above: 1%
   Don't know: 8%

—1985—

• How, if at all, has the AIDS epidemic affected your attitudes about homosexuals? (Roper for *U.S. News and World Report*)
   More sympathetic: 16%
   More negative: 28%
   No change: 53%

• In which of the following ways can the disease AIDS be spread? (CBS News/*New York Times*)
   Sharing a drinking glass
      with someone who has
      AIDS: 47%
   Toilet seats: 28%

• Should it be a crime for someone with AIDS to have sex with another person? (*Los Angeles Times*)
   Yes: 51%

• Do you support mandatory tattooing to identify people who test positive to the AIDS virus? (*Los Angeles Times*)
   Yes: 14%

• Would you demand increased funding for AIDS research if the disease primarily affected heterosexuals? (*Los Angeles Times*)
   Yes: 40%

• How worried are you that you or someone you know will contract AIDS? (Gallup for *Newsweek* magazine)
   Very: 14%
   A little: 27%
   Not very: 27%
   Not at all: 31%

• Do you think that the fear of AIDS has caused unfair discrimination against all homosexuals? (Gallup for *Newsweek* magazine)
   Yes: 46%
   No: 43%
   Don't know: 11%

• Which of the following precautions have you, or someone you know, taken to try and reduce the chances of getting AIDS? (Gallup for *Newsweek* magazine)
   Avoiding people you know
      or suspect to be
      homosexual : 13%
   Avoiding places where
      homosexuals may be
      present: 28%

—1986—

• Which of the following precautions have you, or someone you know, taken to try and reduce the chances of getting AIDS? (Gallup for *Newsweek* magazine)
   Avoiding people you know
      or suspect to be
      homosexual: 18%
   Avoiding places where
      homosexuals may be
      present: 33%

• Which of the following measures should be taken with people who have AIDS? (Gallup for *Newsweek* magazine)
   Quarantine: 54%
   Require them to become
      part of government
      tracking system: 33%
   Require them to
      leave their jobs: 4%

—1987—

• (Asked of parents who belonged to a support group for parents and friends of gays) As a result of the AIDS epidemic, are you more cautious about physical contact with your homosexual child than before? (*Psychology Today*)
   Yes: 3%

• (Asked of the same group) Do you agree that AIDS occurs among homosexuals as a "punishment for their sins?"

(*Psychology Today*)
Yes: 1%

• (Asked of the same group) Would you avoid a child of yours who contracted AIDS? (*Psychology Today*)
Yes: 2%

• Should people with the AIDS virus be required to carry a medical card revealing their condition? (Gallup)
Yes: 60%
No: 24%
No answer: 16%

• Should employers be allowed to fire people who have the AIDS virus? (Gallup)
Yes: 33%
No: 43%
No answer: 24%

• Do most people with AIDS have only themselves to blame? (Gallup)
Yes: 45%
No: 13%
Don't know: 42%

• How likely do you think it is that AIDS will infect and kill a large share of the nation's population? (American Medical Association)
Very likely: 48%
Possibly: 32%
Not likely/Don't know: 20%

—1988—

A CBS News/*New York Times* poll showed that, of 1,606 people questioned, 64% had little or no sympathy for "people who get AIDS from homosexual activity." Even more — 74% — had little or no sympathy for people who contracted the disease through IV-drug use.

AIDS EPIDEMIC, EIGHT YEARS IN THE HISTORY OF (1981-1988).

—1981—

July 3: *The New York Times* reports the recent outbreak of a rare cancer, Kaposi's sarcoma, in forty-one previously healthy gay men, aged twenty-six to fifty-one. Dr. Alvin E. Friedman-Kien of New York University Medical Center says he has tested nine of the men and "found severe defects in their immunological systems." The article appears on page twenty of the *Times*.

August 24: As more cases of Kaposi's sarcoma are diagnosed in gay men in New York City, novelist and screenwriter Larry Kramer writes an impassioned plea in the *New York Native* for donations to aid research for the disease at New York University. "The men who have been stricken," writes Kramer, "don't appear to have done anything that many New York gay men haven't done at one time or another. We're appalled that this is happening to them and terrified that it could happen to us." Kramer's appeal is immediately attacked in some gay quarters as alarmist and unnecessarily provocative.

August 28: The Centers for Disease Control in Atlanta report that cases of Kaposi's sarcoma and pneumocystis pneumonia — a rare parasitical form of pneumonia — are rapidly increasing across the country. Ninety-four percent of the cases have been diagnosed in gay men. One researcher speculates that the diseases may be linked to the men's "sexual lifestyle, drug use, or some other environmental cause."

December 1: *The Plain Truth*, a publication of the Worldwide Church of God, seizes on the recent outbreak of unusual opportunistic infections among gay men and publishes an article entitled "The New Silent Epidemic: Promiscuity's Latest Penalty" — the first of countless such volleys from religious groups in the years to come.

—1982—

January 4: Gay Men's Health Crisis Inc., a non-profit organization to help people with AIDS, is founded in New York City by Edmund White, Larry Kramer, Dr. Lawrence Mass, Nathan Fain, Paul Popham, and Paul Rapoport, all of whom have lost friends to the disease and are worried about the lack of services for people with it. GMHC holds its first major benefit, at the Paradise Garage, in April, raising almost $30,000 in donations. Within two years, GMHC will be taking in nearly a million dollars in contributions, and will have become the prototype for AIDS social services organizations across the country.

April 13: U.S. Representative Henry Waxman (D-California) convenes the first Congressional hearings on the recent outbreak of unusual opportunistic infections among gay men. During the hearings, Waxman states, "There is no doubt in my mind that if these same diseases had appeared among Americans of Norwegian descent, or among tennis players, rather than gay males, the responses of both the government and the medical community would have been different."

April 29: An indignant San Francisco reader criticizes *The Advocate* for running a recent series on Kaposi's sarcoma and

Congressman Henry Waxman:
As early as 1982 he called attention to the fact that homophobia was holding back AIDS research.

the other "new" diseases attacking some gay men. The reader complains, "Two hundred cases of a dozen diseases amongst twenty million gay people in this country is hardly something to write a series on, unless you're a doctor who needs business or someone who has a morbid imagination."

May 6: Gay entertainer Hibiscus (real name: George Harris) — founder of the Cockettes and the Angels of Light — becomes the first gay celebrity to die from AIDS.

June 18: A bulletin from the CDC suggests, for the first time, that AIDS may be transmitted by some kind of infectious agent, such as a virus.

August 1: The CDC reports that AIDS has now been identified in three groups other than gay men: drug users, hemophiliacs, and Haitian immigrants. The number of diagnosed cases of AIDS in the U.S. stands at 505, with a mortality rate of about forty percent. Dr. James Curran of the CDC predicts that the most likely new targets of the disease will be "people like us — doctors, hospital staffers, oral surgeons, people who handle blood." However, the predicted explosion of cases in medical personnel never comes.

September 1: President Reagan vetoes a recent federal spending bill that calls for $500,000 to help the Centers for Disease Control in the fight against AIDS. The White House dismisses the half-million-dollar appropriation as "too expensive." Reagan's veto is later overridden by Congress.

October 1: The *Saturday Evening Post* publishes an article titled "Being Gay Is A Health Hazard," which routinely and repeatedly refers to AIDS as "the gay plague."

November 8: Two men with AIDS, Michael Callen and Richard Berkowitz, publish an article titled "Two Gay Men Declare War on Promiscuity" in the *New York Native*. "We, the authors, have concluded that there is no mutant virus and there will be no vaccine," the two men write. "Our lifestyles created the present epidemic of AIDS among gay men ... Deep down, we know why we're sick." At the same time, an article by Michael Lynch in the Canadian gay newspaper *The Body Politic* rejects the idea that AIDS poses a serious health threat to gay men, and castigates both the straight and gay press for "panic-mongering." The article asserts that the AIDS epidemic is actually part of a conspiracy to re-equate homosexuality with disease.

December 1: The U.S. House of Representatives overwhelmingly votes an additional $2.6 million to the CDC for more research into AIDS.

December 10: The *San Francisco Chronicle* reports the case of a twenty-month-old infant believed to have contracted AIDS through a blood transfusion. The article's headline: "MYSTERY OF S.F. BABY WITH 'GAY' DISEASE." That same day, the CDC reports that an "AIDS-like syndrome" has been found in two dozen infants, most of them the children of IV-drug users or Haitian immigrants.

—1983—

January 6: In response to mounting concerns that AIDS can be transmitted by blood transfusions, three of the country's largest blood-banking associations propose to unilaterally exclude gay men from donating blood. However, the proposal is rejected and replaced by a screening policy that includes asking potential donors whether they have any of the early symptoms of AIDS.

January 13: The CDC reports that 891 cases of AIDS have now been diagnosed in the U.S., with a continuing mortality rate of about forty percent. Almost half of those cases have been in New York City. Dr. Harold Jaffe, assistant director of the AIDS Task Force for the CDC, is quoted as saying, "With most diseases, the more you learn about them, the less scared you are. With this disease, the more I learn, the more scared I am."

February 3: Novelist Edmund White tells *Rolling Stone* magazine that he continues to go to gay bathhouses for sex. Dismissing the calls of some gay leaders for an end to sexual promiscuity, at least until the cause of AIDS can be ascertained, White remarks, "It's cruel to say, but a lot of the people who are the loudest on this issue are men in their forties who, perhaps by the harsh standards set by our community, no longer have the sort of attractiveness that's required in settings where one is likely to have multiple, anonymous encounters."

March 1: A twenty-seven-year-old airman first class is threatened with discharge from the Air Force after it is learned he has AIDS. An Air Force review board recommends discharging the airman for "misconduct" and depriving him of all future medical benefits. Only after the American Civil Liberties Union threatens to file a lawsuit on the soldier's behalf does the Air Force reverse itself

March 28: A front page headline in this morning's *New York Times* reads, "Virus Kills 30 of Austria's Lippazaner Horses." The *Times* has yet to do a front page story on AIDS, even though nearly five hundred people in the U.S. have died from it.

April 7: The five states with the most number of AIDS cases are: New York, with 633; California, with 285; Florida, with 82; New Jersey, with 81; and Texas, with 26.

April 18: In an article for *Newsweek* magazine, a New York physician complains that trying to find effective medical treatments for people with AIDS is like "throwing darts at a dartboard — blindfolded."

April 20: Alleging that "the diseases now being transmitted by homosexuals ... threaten to destroy the public health of the state of Texas," conservative state legislators in Austin move to recriminalize homosexual acts between consenting adults. Another bill, introduced at the same time, seeks to ban homosexuals, or those who "promote the homosexual lifestyle," from taking jobs in teaching, food handling, law enforcement, and "any other position of public leadership or responsibility." Texas eventually reinstates its laws against sodomy in August 1985; the law provides for punishment of homosexual sodomy only.

April 23: Dr. Jane Teas, a doctor at the Harvard School of Public Health, suggests in a letter to the British medical journal *Lancet* that there may be a connection between AIDS and a similar disease found in pigs, African Swine Fever. Swine Fever, she notes, causes immunosuppression in pigs, along with a variety of other symptoms similar to those in people with AIDS. Dr. Teas speculates that the Swine Fever virus may have somehow moved from pigs into the bloodstreams of Haitians, where it adapted and became AIDS. Although her theory is heralded by some New York gay activists and writers, the scientific establishment remains skeptical. Adding to the controversy is speculation that the CIA first introduced the Swine Fever virus into the Caribbean region, as part of an unsuccessful attempt to decimate the agricultural industry of Cuba.

April 27: NBC Nightly News broadcasts a report that a virus, the Human T-cell Lymphotopic Virus, Type III — HTLV-III, for short — may be the cause of AIDS. The report is widely denounced as premature and unfounded.

May 3: The White House disconnects its direct-dial telephone numbers in order to halt a barrage of calls asking the Reagan Administration for additional funding for AIDS research. The day had been set aside nationally, in advance, to lobby the Administration for more AIDS funding. Asked about the abrupt phone disconnection, one White House spokesman dismisses the phone-in effort as "just an organized campaign" — leading one commentator to retort, "That's more than might be said for the White House's own program on AIDS."

May 6: An article in the *Journal of the American Medical Association* rejects growing speculation that AIDS is transmitted by a virus, and instead puts the blame on "profound promiscuity" among gay men. The article demurely concedes, however, that, "We cannot, at this time, explain why AIDS is thought to be occurring in Haitians, hemophiliacs, and others."

May 6: A physician on ABC's *Good Morning America* tells viewers that although AIDS is "still confined to male homosexuals, Haitians, and hemophiliacs," it could soon spread to "normal people."

May 22: "The panic is here," announces Pat Gourley of the Gay and Lesbian Community Center of Denver, Colorado. "I know lots of people who worry about every bruise they get, who worry about a swollen lymph node, the night sweats, even a slight fever. Every gay man I know worries about AIDS — I mean, *profoundly* worries."

May 23: New York City's ABC affiliate, WABC, advertises an upcoming special on AIDS with a splashy newspaper ad that reads, LAST YEAR, A KILLER CAME OUT OF THE CLOSET AND INTO YOUR NEIGHBOR-HOOD.

June 2: U.S. Congressman Larry McDonald, a conservative anti-gay Democrat from Georgia, proposes that a federal "user tax" be imposed on people with AIDS to help finance federal AIDS research. McDonald explains that people with AIDS have brought the disease on themselves, so they — not the American taxpayer — should have to pay for the search for a cure. (Three months later, McDonald is one of 269 people killed when the Soviet Union shoots down Korean Airlines Flight 007.)

June 17: The New York State Funeral Directors Association announces that its members will no longer embalm the bodies of people who have died from AIDS, until the federal government issues guidelines on the subject. Funeral homes in other parts of the country are also refusing to handle the bodies of people with AIDS, and in some cases morticians are bilking survivors for extra money before proceeding with embalming and interment.

June 19: In a highly publicized sermon to his followers in Lynchburg, Virginia, Moral Majority leader Jerry Falwell calls AIDS "the judgment of God," and explains that, "You can't fly into the laws of God and God's nature without paying the price." His remarks ignite a national controversy among religious leaders, including New York's Episcopal Bishop Paul Moore, Jr., who tells the press, "AIDS is not God's vengeance upon the homosexual community. The God whom Jews and Christians worship is a loving, merciful God who does not punish children like a wrathful father." Moore also stresses that AIDS must not be used as a political weapon to "roll back the hard-earned progress of the gay community."

June 21: For the first time since Ronald Reagan was elected president, the White House opens its doors to representatives of the gay community. A member of Reagan's staff agrees to meet with members of the National Gay Task Force to discuss the federal government's response to the AIDS epidemic. Gay political leaders are encouraged by the meeting.

June 27: To allay widespread fears that AIDS is spread by casual contact, Secretary of Health and Human Services Margaret Heckler visits the Warren Magnuson Clinical Center in Bethesda, Maryland, where she is photographed shaking hands with people with AIDS and sitting at their bedsides.

July 1: The Club Bath chain reports that business at its New York and San Francisco bathhouses is down by more than fifty percent. Mark Chataway, of Gay Men's Health Crisis in New York, remarks, "Before AIDS, going to the baths had an aura almost like smoking. People knew it wasn't too good for them, but it was socially acceptable. Now it has the aura of shooting heroin."

July 1: A national toll-free AIDS hotline, set up by the Department of Health and Human Services, begins taking its first phone calls. Response is so overwhelming that, in the first few days, an estimated one thousand callers per hour cannot get through.

July 1: The American Red Cross reports a sixteen percent drop in blood donations nationwide and attributes the decline to public fears and misinformation about AIDS. "There is no association between AIDS and donating blood," says Dr. Alfred Katz of the Red Cross's blood services division. "We can't say that loudly enough."

July 18: City officials in Tulsa, Oklahoma order a city park swimming pool closed and drained after its use by a local gay rights group for a private party. Officials cite their fears about the spread of AIDS as the reason for the action.

July 21: Dr. Robert Selig of the CDC tells *U.S.A. Today* that federal statistics probably represent only one-half of the actual number of AIDS cases in the U.S.

July 26: San Francisco General Hospital opens a special ward devoted to the needs of people with AIDS, the first ward of its kind in any U.S. hospital.

Initial capacity for the ward: twelve to fifteen beds.

August 1: Robert Bazell, science correspondent for *NBC News*, publishes an article on AIDS in *The New Republic*, in which he scoffs at the idea there will be as many as six thousand diagnosed cases of the disease in the next twelve months (he is wrong), and in which he asserts, "If AIDS were magically to disappear and many gay men were to resume widespread promiscuity, there is a good chance that some other horrible disease would find its way into the gay population and then spread to others."

August 1: The U.S. House of Representatives convenes subcommittee hearings on the federal government's response to the AIDS epidemic. One 34-year-old gay man with AIDS, Roger Lyon, tells the committee, "I came here today in the hope that my epitaph would not read that I died of red tape." The committee eventually concludes that the Reagan Administration has been irresponsible in its reaction to the epidemic, and that federal funding to fight AIDS has been "inadequate" and "unnecessarily delayed." Ten congressmen — all of them conservative Republicans loyal to the president — file an angry dissent from the committee's findings.

August 16: An American physician living in the Bahamas, Dr. Lawrence Burton, announces he has discovered the cause of AIDS: a commercial brand of lubricant used by homosexuals during anal intercourse. Burton claims to have placed a dab of the lubricant on the anuses of healthy mice twice a day, and that after twenty-one days, the mice began to develop swollen lymph nodes as well as various infections. His "findings" are greeted with overwhelming skepticism.

September 1: The CDC concludes that "poppers" are not the cause of AIDS, but says they may still be a contributing factor in the development of certain opportunistic infections contracted by people with the disease.

September 15: During the last minutes of a two-day medical conference, French scientist Luc Montagnier, a virologist at the Pasteur Institute in Paris, presents data on why he believes that an unusual virus — known in the U.S. as HTLV-III — is the cause of AIDS. Because his presentation is scheduled late at night on the last day of the conference, many scientists and researchers have already gone back to their hotel rooms, and after Montagnier's presentation is over, few people come up to ask questions about his findings.

December 5: Larry Kramer tells an interviewer he has had thirty-seven friends die from AIDS. "Can't something be done?" he asks. "The rest of the city, my straight friends, go on with life as usual and I'm in the middle of an epidemic."

—1984—

January 30: The CDC reports there have now been 3,339 cases of AIDS diagnosed nationwide. Nationally, about eight new cases of AIDS are being diagnosed every day.

February 1: The *Southern Medical Journal* publishes an editorial suggesting that AIDS is "the due penalty" for those men who have "abandoned the natural function of the woman and burned in their desire toward one another."

February 10: Poet Allen Ginsberg is quoted in the *Washington Blade* as saying that if AIDS is the natural result of gay sexual excesses, "then probably it's not such a horrible thing to happen to the gay species,

since it wakes everybody up to the quality of their affairs, and the value of more permanent affairs."

February 14: Seattle Mayor Charles Royer signs an executive order prohibiting discrimination against sexual minorities by city agencies and employees, after it is discovered that the city's policemen are circulating among themselves lists of local people suspected of having AIDS. "I wouldn't touch a person with AIDS," says one Seattle police officer. In a related incident, a Seattle fireman refuses to assist a gay male couple because, in his words, "of hepatitis and AIDS with you guys."

February 24: Composers Ned Rorem and Elliott Carter, along with Metropolitan Opera conductor James Levine and other distinguished musicians, perform a special concert in memory of Paul Jacobs, pianist for the New York Philharmonic. Jacobs recently died of AIDS. The concert consists entirely of the music he loved most.

March 1: The *American Journal of Medicine* reports a cluster of AIDS cases — forty men in Los Angeles, New York City, San Francisco, and other cities — all traceable back to one man with AIDS, who apparently had the disease in 1980. The finding helps bolster the hypothesis that AIDS is spread through some sort of contagion. However, whether or not all forty men were actually infected by the man remains unproveable.

March 16: Thirteen homeless people with AIDS are forced to move out of a San Francisco motel, after the San Francisco *Examiner* publishes stories naming the motel and referring to its residents with AIDS. Four days later, the San Francisco AIDS Foundation announces it will open its own shelter for homeless people with AIDS, but refuses to disclose the shelter's location, to protect the people using it.

March 19: The CDC reports the first clear-cut case documenting that AIDS can be transmitted through a blood transfusion.

April 1: An editorial column in today's Shenandoah, Pennsylvania *Evening Herald* condemns homosexuality as the cause of AIDS and asserts, "No amount of smoke-screening by you queers can hide the fact that it's your own kind who are responsible for the AIDS explosion."

April 23: At a press conference in Washington, D.C., Secretary of Health and Human Services Margaret Heckler announces that the "probable" cause of AIDS — a virus known to American researchers as HTLV-III — has been discovered. (Later, the virus comes to be known simply as "HIV," for Human Immunodeficiency Virus.) At the same news conference, Heckler confidently predicts that a vaccine against AIDS will be available in two years.

May 11: Assistant U.S. Secretary of Health and Human Services Dr. Edward Brandt is forced by the Reagan Administration to cancel his appearance at a National Gay Task Force dinner. Brandt, who is openly sympathetic to the gay community and its battle against AIDS, initially accepted an invitation to attend the banquet and present a humanitarian award to a group helping in the fight against AIDS. However, the Reagan Administration pressures Brandt to cancel his appearance, after at least one national "pro-family" group demands that he be fired if he attends the function. (Brandt resigns from his job five months later.)

June 1: The nation's first AIDS discrimination lawsuit is filed, by a Detroit insurance agent who claims that the company he worked for fired him after learning he had been diagnosed with AIDS. The suit seeks $5 million in damages, but the man dies before the case can reach the courts. In a bizarre twist of events, the company that fired him later tries to collect $100,000 in death benefits from a life insurance policy they took out on the man before terminating his employment.

July 15: The World Health Organization reports there have been a total of 451 cases of AIDS diagnosed in western Europe so far: 180 in France, 79 in West Germany, 54 in Great Britain, and 80 more cases in seven other countries.

August 13: A severely ill 29-year-old man with AIDS is refused admission to a hospital in San Luis Obispo, California, on the grounds "it would not be suitable in our city" to treat him. Instead the hospital sends him, without any medical supervision, to San Francisco, two hundred miles away. The man dies shortly afterward, and San Francisco health authorities angrily accuse the San Luis Obispo hospital of hastening his death. (A few months later, in Boston, an emergency ward patient with AIDS is ordered by a doctor to leave the hospital, for fear the man will infect other patients and members of the emergency room staff.)

August 15: One of the nation's fiercest and most visible AIDS activists, Bobbie Campbell, dies from AIDS in San Francisco, at the age of thirty-two. Campbell, who once humorously dubbed himself "the AIDS poster boy" and who was described by friends as the "Douglas MacArthur" in the fight against AIDS, traveled widely to raise public awareness of the disease.

October 15: Dr. James Curran of the CDC predicts that by 1985 AIDS will be the leading cause of death among IV-drug users and hemophiliacs.

October 17: Scientists reveal that the AIDS virus has been found not only in blood and semen, but in saliva and teardrops as well. The revelation leads to increased public fears that the disease may be readily transmitted by casual contact. However, public health officials discount such ideas and argue that AIDS is very unlikely to be spread through tears or through saliva droplets emitted in talking, sneezing, or casual kissing.

October 18: One gay man's plan to convert his Palm Springs resort hotel into a residence for people with AIDS is condemned by the city's mayor as "the worst thing that's ever happened" to the city. "You don't take a hospital and put it right in the middle of a resort area," argues the mayor. "This could *hurt* Palm Springs." Despite later threats by the mayor to organize demonstrations and petition drives against the plan, the new residence center welcomes its first two guests with AIDS in early December.

November 8: An article in the most recent issue of *Nature* suggests that the AIDS virus has been present in the population of Zaire since 1977, and that at least five percent of the country's population may be infected.

November 16: The West German government announces it will seek legislation making it a crime, punishable by up to three years in prison, for anyone diagnosed with AIDS to have sex with another person.

—1985—

January 1: After almost four years into the AIDS epidemic, the president and Mrs. Reagan have yet to use the word "AIDS" in public, or show that they even know — or care — that there is an epidemic. Says one AIDS activist, "Our president doesn't seem to know AIDS exists. He is spending more money on the paint to put the American flag on his missiles than he's spending on AIDS."

January 28: *Newsweek* magazine reports a huge nationwide increase in autologous blood donations, in which prospective hospital patients are storing up their own blood for future use in surgery, to avoid contracting AIDS through regular blood transfusions. Also, acting under the mistaken assumption that women cannot contract AIDS, some surgical patients are requesting blood transfusions from female donors only. In response to the growing hysteria, a doctor at Sloan-Kettering points out there have been only 106 cases of AIDS linked to blood transfusions, out of ten to twelve million units of blood transfused every year. "Statistically," he explains, "you're much more likely to get run over on your way to the hospital."

February 1: Dr. Bruce Voeller, president of the California-based Mariposa Foundation, announces the discovery of a substance, nonoxynol-9, which "blows the AIDS virus apart and inactivates it very quickly." The CDC, which collaborated in Voeller's research, confirms the report. Nonoxynol-9 is found in most commercial spermicides, and Voeller tells the press that the use of a condom in combination with a jelly or cream containing at least a five percent concentration of nonoxynol-9 may help "put the brakes" on the AIDS epidemic.

February 1: Delta Airlines announces new regulations prohibiting people with AIDS from flying on its aircraft. The regulations allow airline employees to remove, by force if necessary, any passenger known to have the disease. Ten days later, under intense pressure from medical authorities and civil rights groups, Delta is forced to rescind the ban.

February 4: The Reagan Administration releases its 1986 budget request, calling for only $85.5 million in AIDS-related funding — a $12 million cut from the previous year.

February 10: With guns drawn, vice-squad officers in Atlanta force their way into and raid the city's two gay bathhouses. Nine patrons and one employee are arrested. The raids come after city officials file lawsuits against the bathhouses, citing them for promoting the spread of AIDS. Fourteen months later, Georgia Governor Joe Harris outlaws the operation of gay bathhouses in the state altogether.

March 2: The U.S. Public Health Service approves the use of the first test to screen donated blood for contamination by the AIDS virus. However, the test remains highly controversial, since, among other things, it yields a high rate of false positives, perhaps as much as thirty percent.

March 10: William Hoffman's play about AIDS, *As Is*, opens at New York's Circle Repertory Theater, to rave reviews in both the gay and mainstream press. Seven weeks later, it moves to Broadway. The play is later nominated for three Tony Awards, including one for Best Play of the Year.

March 15: A report in the *Journal of the American Medical Association* confirms that AIDS is not spread by casual contact, but points out it *can* be spread by heterosexual intercourse.

March 18: Syndicated gossip columnist Liz Smith reveals in her column in the New York *Daily News* that after a recent theater performance in New York City, noted critic John Simon exclaimed, "Homosexuals in the theater! My God, I can't wait until AIDS gets all of them!" In a later interview, Simon acknowledges making the remark (though claims he was slightly misquoted), and adds, "It was something I said in anger ... Obviously, this is not something I believe. It is not something I'm proud of."

March 24: An interfaith forum of Jewish, Catholic, Lutheran, Baptist, and Episcopal leaders in New York City declares that AIDS is not a punishment from God for homosexuality, and condemns what one Baptist official calls the "un-Christian, damnable, judgmental, Swaggart-Falwell kind of epidemic" of AIDS hysteria and anti-homosexual prejudice in America.

April 1: The publishers of *Burke's Peerage* in London announce that to keep future generations of British nobility from being contaminated by the AIDS virus, they will henceforth exclude the names of all people with AIDS, or their relatives, from its annual listing of eligible marriage partners.

April 14: At an international conference on AIDS in Atlanta, researchers estimate that as many as two million Americans have now been exposed to the HIV virus, and predict that a growing number of heterosexuals will be diagnosed with AIDS in the coming years. At the same conference, doctors reveal that the AIDS virus, by its mere presence in the brain, can cause severe neurological problems, advancing to a state of dementia, similar to Alzheimer's Disease, in some people. In some patients, AIDS dementia may become the dominant manifestation of the disease.

April 21: *The Normal Heart,* a play about AIDS by Larry Kramer, opens at New York's Public Theater.

May 10: The Young Americans for Freedom, a conservative, anti-gay, political youth group, calls for the immediate closing of all gay bathhouses and gay bars, as well as all other places where gays assemble, in order to halt the spread of AIDS.

May 17: Dr. James Curran of the CDC is quoted as saying that, "A single sexual contact for a gay man in New York or San Francisco, or many other American cities, now means a substantial risk of getting infected" with the AIDS virus.

May 18: The 76-member governing board of the Southern California American Civil Liberties Union votes unanimously to oppose the shutting down of gay bathhouses across the country, unless closure can be supported by "clear and convincing medical and epidemiological evidence" that such establishments encourage the spread of AIDS. The resolution follows closely on a similar vote by the northern California chapter of the ACLU.

May 19: More than half-a-million dollars is raised for the AIDS Medical Foundation at a star-studded "Comic Relief" benefit held at New York's Shubert Theater. Among the celebrities who perform at the benefit: Steve Martin, Joan Rivers, Elaine May, and Mike Nichols. Among the 1500 people who pay $500 a ticket to attend the show: Claudette Colbert, Phil Donahue, Dustin Hoffman, Richard Gere, and New York City Mayor Ed Koch.

May 20: The number of people diagnosed with AIDS in the U.S. has now passed the ten-thousand mark. The CDC predicts that the figure will double within the next twelve months.

June 1: A small, poverty-stricken town in Florida — Belle Glade (population 20,000) — makes national headlines when it is revealed that the town has thirty-seven diagnosed cases of AIDS, a per capita rate more than five times the national average. Public health officials are at a loss to explain why the disease is so prevalent in the town, but some feel there must be a link between Belle Glade's poverty and unsanitary conditions and the high rate of AIDS. Others predict that mosquitoes are spreading the disease. However, researchers later discover that AIDS has been routinely spread in the town through sex and through contact with infected blood.

June 14: In a newly published study, one-third of the physicians and nurses at a major metropolitan hospital acknowledge that people with AIDS receive inferior hospital care compared to people with other diseases. Additionally, nine percent of the physicians and nurses surveyed believe that "homosexuals who contract AIDS are getting what they deserve." Thirty-one percent say they feel more negatively about gay people since the onset of the epidemic.

June 26: John Lorenzini, director of The Persons With

AIDS Alliance, chains himself to the door of the Federal Building in San Francisco to protest the indifferent attitude of the Reagan Administration to the AIDS epidemic. He is forcibly removed and arrested. Several months later, Lorenzini repeats the protest, this time with a companion. Eventually, a small permanent camp of protestors chains themselves — and their cots and their tents — to the building, in an ongoing protest against the federal government's slow response to AIDS.

June 27: At the annual Gay and Lesbian Freedom Parade in Columbus, Ohio, antigay protestors hire a private plane to fly overhead with a banner reading, "AIDS — GOD'S CURSE ON HOMOS!"

July 15: Lawyers for Johnson and Johnson, manufacturers of "Band-Aids" adhesive-brand bandages, order the San Diego AIDS Project to cease and desist an AIDS fundraising campaign called "Ban-Aids." The campaign uses a logo of a stick-on bandage with the words "BAN-AIDS" over it.

July 22: Australia's two main domestic airlines announce they will henceforth refuse to carry any passengers with AIDS.

July 23: Actor Rock Hudson, in Paris to undergo medical treatment for what was originally described as liver cancer, reveals he in fact has AIDS and is undergoing treatment with an experimental new drug, HPA-23. Two weeks earlier, Hudson had appeared frail and ill at a publicity press conference for close friend Doris Day; at the time, spokesmen for the actor said he was suffering only from the "aftereffects of the flu and a couple of sleepless nights." After undergoing treatment in Paris, Hudson is flown back to the U.S. on a chartered 747. He is admitted, in serious condition, to UCLA Medical Center.

July 26: U.S. Senators Pete Wilson (R-California) and Alfonse D'Amato (R-New York) hold a first-of-its-kind Capitol Hill briefing on AIDS for other Republican senators. However, not a single senator shows up for the gathering. A few, however, do send members of their staffs.

August 2: Suspecting he may have contracted AIDS after drinking from the same bottle as a gay man, an eighteen-year-old in Coventry, England beats the gay man to death. Because of what are seen as "exceptional" circumstances in

Sen. Pete Wilson: What if you hold an AIDS hearing and no senators show up?

the case, the eighteen-year-old is sentenced to only three months in prison for the murder.

August 14: Los Angeles becomes the first city in the nation to ban discrimination against people with AIDS in housing, employment, education, and health care. The San Francisco Board of Supervisors follows suit with a similar set of ordinances on November 5.

August 26: Ryan White, a Kokomo, Indiana boy with hemophilia, is barred from attending local schools after he is diagnosed with AIDS. Despite a later court victory allowing Ryan to return to classes — but only if he uses a separate bathroom at school, eats with disposable utensils in the cafeteria, and does not take gym class — the White family is forced from Kokomo by angry residents who slash their automobile tires, pelt their home with eggs, and, finally, fire a bullet through their living room window. The Whites eventually move twenty-five miles away, to Cicero, where Ryan is admitted without incident to the local school.

August 30: The Defense Department announces it will now test all military recruits for exposure to the HIV virus and that it will bar those who test positive from entering the armed forces.

September 11: Washington, D.C. Fire Chief Theodore Coleman orders city fire stations to stop listing the names and addresses of people with AIDS on firehouse chalkboards. In one station, the names are listed under the heading, "IMPORTANT NOTICE! LOOK OUT! AIDS PATIENTS!"

September 17: President Reagan uses the word "AIDS" for the first time in public, while answering a question about the disease during a White House press conference.

September 23: This week's cover story in *Time* magazine is titled "The New Untouchables," and deals with the growing wave of prejudice and violence against people with AIDS. The article includes stories about people with AIDS left to lie in their own excrement in some big-city hospitals; hairdressers, barbers, and food handlers with AIDS being routinely fired from their jobs; and the incident of a woman employee at the Gay and Lesbian Community Services Center in Los Angeles who, as she was leaving work one evening, was doused with acid by a group of teenagers who screamed, "Die, you AIDS faggots!"

September 26: Elizabeth Taylor is named national chairperson of the newly formed American Foundation for AIDS Research. The appointment comes shortly after Taylor helped organize a celebrity dinner in Los Angeles, which raised more than $1.3 million for AIDS research. Asked why she has become chairperson of the foundation, Taylor replies, "It seemed to me that not too many people were doing anything. I thought maybe for one time in my life fame could be an advantage."

September 27: Colorado Governor Richard Lamm is lambasted by medical authorities and gay rights groups after remarking, "There are only two types of AIDS patients. Either you're dying or you're dead," and suggesting that expensive medical treatment for people with AIDS is a waste of money since the disease is always fatal.

September 29: Episcopal and Catholic authorities report that many Christians are refusing to take communion for fear of contracting AIDS from the communion cup.

September 30: New York City mayoral candidate Diane McGrath calls for the immediate closing of all gay bars, gay porno theaters, and gay bathhouses, and tells the press, "The AIDS virus has no civil rights."

October 1: The government of Bangladesh announces it is considering a ban on shipments of used clothing from the United States, until tests can unequivocally prove that the clothes do not harbor the AIDS virus.

October 2: Rock Hudson dies from AIDS at his home in Beverly Hills. He was fifty-nine. Hudson's close friend Elizabeth

Taylor tells the press, "I love him. He is tragically gone. Please God, he has not died in vain."

October 24: Two New York City men, one of whom was believed to have AIDS, tie themselves together at the waist with a silk sash, toast each other with champagne, and then jump together, to their deaths, out the window of their 35th-floor apartment.

December 7: Soviet officials acknowledge for the first time that there have been cases of AIDS — fewer than ten, they say — inside the Soviet Union.

December 8: Despite assurances from medical authorities that AIDS is not spread by saliva, a Flint, Michigan man who tested positive to exposure to the HIV virus is charged with "assault with intent to murder," and is released on $10,000 bail, after he allegedly spit on four policeman. The charge is later dismissed.

December 17: University of California researchers announce, "there is no doubt whatsoever" that condoms block the transmission of the AIDS virus. One of the researchers states, "For gay men, condóms must now become as sexy as jockstraps."

December 24: Dedication ceremonies are held in New York City for an AIDS hospice opened there by Mother Theresa. At the Christmas Eve dedication, Mother Theresa says of people with AIDS, "Each one of them is Jesus in a distressing disguise."

—1986—

January 19: A 26-year-old Army private, Michael W. Foster, hangs himself with his boot laces after being told by military authorities that he has tested positive for HIV-antibodies. Foster received no counseling with his test results, but was instead routinely confined for medical surveillance at Walter Reed Army Hospital. His body is discovered hanging in an unused hospital stairwell. The suicide prompts the military to re-evaluate its policies regarding HIV-positive soldiers and to provide counseling as part of the HIV-antibody test.

February 3: The new Secretary of Health and Human Services, Otis Bowen, proposes that all new immigrants to the United States be screened for exposure to the HIV virus. The proposal effectively adds AIDS to the list of conditions that can be cited by immigration officials as reason to deny immigrants permanent residence in the U.S.

February 11: A new study financed by the Pentagon concludes that AIDS is probably transmitted by sneezing, coughing, toilet seats, door knobs, and air conditioning, and recommends that the federal government hold in reserve a plan to eventually identify people with AIDS with a kind of "Star of David" on their clothing, such as Jews were forced to wear in Nazi Germany. When news of the conclusions is leaked by the San Francisco *Examiner*, everyone involved with the study quickly tries to distance themselves from it.

February 13: A joint study by the CDC and New York's Montefiore Medical Center overwhelmingly concludes that AIDS is not spread by casual contact. The study involved more than one hundred people who lived, for three months or more, in close contact with a family member with AIDS. In some cases, family members shared toothbrushes, razors, combs, and drinking glasses, and nearly all of them exchanged routine hugs and kisses. Only one person — a five-year-old girl who acquired the disease in utero from her mother — showed any sign of infection with the HIV virus.

March 1: While trying to formulate an AIDS education program in England, British health authorities try to acquire copies of *The Advocate* and the *New York Native* to learn more about the disease and how American education efforts work. However, because the importation of such publications would violate British customs laws, the authorities are forced to smuggle in copies of the newspapers in secret diplomatic pouches.

March 1: The president of Ansell-Americas, manufacturers of Lifestyles condoms, enthusiastically exclaims to the press, "AIDS is a condom marketer's dream!"

March 18: Conservative columnist William F. Buckley calls for mandatory tattooing of "everyone detected with AIDS." Buckley proposes that homosexuals with AIDS be tattooed on the buttocks, and that IV-drug users with AIDS be tattooed on the upper forearm, as a warning of their condition to others.

May 30: Fashion designer Perry Ellis dies of what is officially described as "viral encephalitis." However, reliable reports begin to circulate that Ellis in fact died of AIDS, and that the real cause of his death is being obscured for fear of damaging future profits from his popular line of clothing.

June 23: Despite overwhelming medical testimony that AIDS cannot be spread by casual contact, the U.S. Justice Department rules that employers are within their legal rights to fire employees with AIDS, if the firing is based on fears — no matter how irrational — that the disease may spread to other workers. In 1987, the U.S. Supreme Court effectively reverses the ruling by including contagious diseases among the handicaps protected by federal anti-discrimination laws.

June 23: The U.S. Navy court-martials a sailor for refusing to submit to HIV-antibody testing as recently ordered by Department of Defense guidelines. The sailor is found guilty of "insubordination," sentenced to forty-five days in jail, and is issued a "bad conduct" discharge from the armed services.

June 30: A San Francisco gay man files suit against the San Diego Police Department after he is forced against his will to undergo an HIV-antibody test in jail. Police allege that during a confrontation at the San Diego Gay Pride parade, the man bit two police officers. After the man refuses to be tested at a nearby hospital, he is taken to jail, where police forcibly administer the test themselves. The man is charged with battery and resisting arrest.

July 16: The CDC reports that although blacks make up only twelve percent of the general population, they account for more than one-quarter of all reported cases of AIDS. And nearly sixty percent of all children with AIDS are black. Authorities predict that the problem of AIDS in the black community will get substantially worse in the years to come.

July 20: Gay porn star Beau Mathews dies of AIDS at his West Hollywood home, at the age of twenty-nine.

July 26: Controversial New York attorney Roy Cohn, a former counsel for Senator Joseph McCarthy, dies of AIDS, at the age of fifty-nine. For months, Cohn had denied rumors he had AIDS. He also publicly denied he was gay.

July 28: Claiming a lack of "compelling need" for such legislation, California Governor George Deukmejian vetoes a bill to protect people with

AIDS from discrimination in housing and employment.

July 29: Two Florida prison inmates are charged with conspiracy to commit murder after they allegedly pour AIDS-tainted blood serum into the coffee cup of a corrections officer. "I'm familiar enough with AIDS to know there's not a big risk," the officer tells the press, but admits that when he learned the coffee he'd been drinking was tainted, "I more or less went into shock."

August 1: A midwestern telephone company begins trying to market disposable telephones to hospitals who treat people with AIDS.

August 26: Former professional football player Jerry Smith, of the Washington Redskins, acknowledges in an interview in *The Washington Post* that he has AIDS. Smith is the first professional athlete to make such an announcement. "I want people to know what I've been through," he says, "and how terrible this disease is. Maybe it will help people understand. Maybe it will help in development with research. Maybe something positive will come out of this." Smith dies from AIDS less than two months later.

September 2: The country's first hospital devoted entirely to the diagnosis, research, and treatment of AIDS — the Institute for Immunological Disorders — opens its doors in Houston, Texas. Fifteen months later, it is forced to close, claiming it has suffered heavy financial losses from treating so many indigent people with AIDS.

October 4: United Press International reports that Stephen Barry, former personal valet to Prince Charles of England, has died from AIDS.

October 7: The Los Angeles County Board of Supervisors votes unanimously to ban the sale of "poppers," which have been linked by some researchers to the development of Kaposi's sarcoma in people with AIDS. Connecticut, New York, Utah, Massachusetts, Tennessee, and Wisconsin, along with several municipal governments, have also restricted the sale of "poppers."

October 22: U.S. Surgeon General C. Everett Koop issues a 36-page document, *The Surgeon General's Report on Acquired Immune Deficiency Syndrome.* The report, which addresses a wide variety of AIDS-related issues, is praised

U.S. Surgeon General C. Everett Koop surprised many with his strong leadership of the battle against AIDS.

by some gay leaders as "moderately progressive," and Koop himself, a deeply religious conservative who has voiced anti-gay sentiments in the past, surprises the gay community when he writes, "At the beginning of the AIDS epidemic many Americans had little sympathy for people with AIDS. The feeling was that somehow people from certain groups 'deserved' their illness. Let us put those feelings behind us. We are fighting a disease, not people." Because of what is seen by some Reagan Admin-

istration officials as the report's "liberal" bias, it goes largely undistributed, and tens of thousands of copies are left to languish in government warehouses. In the coming months, Koop becomes more highly visible and takes on an activist role in trying to dispel myths about AIDS and defuse public fears surrounding the disease. He also outlines controversial ways — including the need for early sex education about both homosexual and heterosexual relationships — to help prevent the spread of the disease. As a result, Koop is eventually vilified by many of the right-wing, "pro-family" groups that once praised and supported his appointment.

November 1: A poll conducted in San Francisco reveals that nearly twenty percent of the gay and bisexual men in that city claim they are celibate as a result of the AIDS epidemic.

November 1: The World Health Organization predicts that by 1990 there will be 3.5 million diagnosed cases of AIDS worldwide, and that over 100 million people will have been exposed to the HIV virus.

November 3: An Indiana judge rules that a divorced construction worker may no longer visit his two-year-old daughter, after the man tests positive to HIV-antibodies. The judge calls the man "a danger to the ... child's well-being."

November 6: By 71% to 29%, voters in California defeat Proposition 64, the so-called "LaRouche Initiative." The initiative would have allowed state health authorities to quarantine people with AIDS, or anyone exposed to the HIV virus, and could have prohibited them from working in schools, restaurants, and the health care field. Supporters of the initiative campaigned with the slogan, "Spread panic, not AIDS!" Eighteen months later, a similar ballot initiative is also defeated by a wide margin by California voters.

November 12: Rock Hudson's last live-in lover, Marc Christian, files a multi-million-dollar lawsuit against Hudson's estate, claiming his life was recklessly endangered because neither Hudson nor his personal secretary, Mark Miller, ever informed Christian that the actor had AIDS. Christian, who lived with Hudson during the last two years of the actor's life — and who received nothing in Hudson's will — told reporters, "I found out he had AIDS on the six o'clock news like everyone else ... I was scared of dying." In February 1989, a Los Angeles jury awards Christian over $20 million in damages, despite the fact he has consistently tested negative to HIV-antibodies.

December 6: The Roman Catholic Archdiocese of Los Angeles withdraws its support, and the use of it facilities, for an AIDS education program aimed at local Latinos. The diocese is angered because the program promotes the use of condoms to help prevent the spread of AIDS.

December 16: Actor Douglas Lambert dies of AIDS in London, at the age of fifty.

December 28: "New Right" leader Terry Dolan dies of AIDS at the age of thirty-six. A closeted homosexual, Dolan allied himself with numerous conservative and religious groups, to help push the New Right's pro-family, anti-gay agenda during much of the Reagan era.

January 14: San Francisco's NBC affiliate, KRON, becomes the first major market television station in the country to air condom commercials. In the first week that the ads appear, the station receives 153 letters supporting the decision, 49 letters opposing it.

February 4: Pianist and entertainer Liberace dies of AIDS, at the age of sixty-seven. Liberace's death certificate initially lists the cause of death as heart failure due to degenerative brain disease; but a local county coroner challenges the certificate and reveals that Liberace in fact died of AIDS. The controversy leads to renewed speculation over exactly how many AIDS-related deaths are going unreported in the country. One public health official estimates that in California alone perhaps as many as twenty percent of all deaths from AIDS go uncounted.

March 16: The CDC reports there have now been 32,825 cases of AIDS diagnosed nationwide.

March 20: The U.S. government approves the use of the first major new drug in the fight against AIDS: AZT (azidothymidine). AZT has proven successful in inhibiting the ability of the HIV virus to replicate itself inside human cells. However, both the government and the drug's manufacturer, Burroughs Wellcome, stress that it is not a cure. Cost for a one-year prescription to AZT: $10,000.

March 23: Federal health officials reveal that as many as twelve thousand people who received blood transfusions between 1978 and 1985 may have been infected with the HIV virus. In what is termed "the new panic over AIDS," AIDS hotlines across the country are overwhelmed with calls from terrified people, and some HIV-antibody testing sites become booked solid, in advance, for the next three months.

March 24: More than 250 gay activists stage a demonstration in New York City to protest "foot dragging" by the Food and Drug Administration in approving new drugs for the treatment of AIDS. Seventeen demonstrators are arrested when they sit down in the middle of Broadway during morning rush-hour traffic.

April 17: Real estate agents for Rock Hudson's 7,000-square-foot home overlooking Beverly Hills are forced to reduce their asking price from $7 million to $2.9 million, because of the fear of AIDS among potential buyers. The property has been on the market for six months, with no bids.

May 1: The People's Republic of China announces it will henceforth require all long-term foreign residents to submit to HIV-antibody testing or otherwise supply a health certificate stating they do not have AIDS. Later, the Chinese begin an intensive AIDS education program blaming outsiders for bringing the disease into the country; the campaign warns the Chinese people to avoid sexual relations with all foreigners. One by-product of the campaign: foreign exchange students, especially those from African countries where the disease is most prevalent, become targets of increasing violence, abuse, and discrimination.

May 4: In a speech approved by the White House, Secretary of Education William Bennett sharply criticizes safe-sex education efforts as "condomania," and suggests that AIDS is a "good thing" if it discourages "teen sex."

May 7: U.S. Congressman Stewart McKinney, a liberal Republican from Connecticut, dies of AIDS at the age of fifty-six, amid press stories he was bisexual. Shortly before his death, McKinney asked that his condition be publicized in the hope it might help others to deal with the AIDS crisis. His widow and five children later establish a foundation in his memory, to help pay the medical expenses of indigent people with AIDS. One of the foundation's first actions is to propose a residence, in McKinney's congressional district, for homeless people with the disease.

May 31: Speaking at an AIDS fundraising dinner in Washington, D.C., President Reagan is booed when he reiterates his support for widespread mandatory HIV testing. A later Reagan remark that the best way to prevent the spread of AIDS is through sexual abstinence provokes Elizabeth Taylor to tell the press, "His advice is really not very sensible. It's really amazing how our president confronts this national tragedy."

June 1: The morning after President Reagan is booed at an AIDS fundraiser in Washington, D.C., Vice-President George Bush is booed at the opening of an international conference on AIDS when he announces his own support for widespread mandatory HIV testing. Not realizing he can still be heard over the microphone, Bush turns to a friend and asks disgustedly, "Who was that, some gay group out there?"

June 2: At a party to celebrate the 70th anniversary of *Forbes* magazine, millionaire publisher Malcolm Forbes gives close friend Elizabeth Taylor a personal check for $1 million to help AIDS research.

June 2: On an HBO comedy special, comedian Sam Kinison lispingly mocks gay men for "falling in love" with "other guys' smelly, hairy asses," then sarcastically thanks homosexuals for "giving us the Black Plague of the Eighties!" Kinison tells his audience, "It's really nice now to have to go to a public restroom and have to use your foot for everything; open the door, flush the toilet, turn on the sink, no hands, man." Kinison adds that given a choice between giving money to help AIDS research or adding a couple of "tittie channels" to his cable service, he'll choose the "tittie" channels. Later, on a cut of his comedy album *Have*

You Seen Me Lately?, Kinison rants, "Safe sex? *Get off our back!* Because a few fags fucked some *monkeys* ... because of this shit, they want us to wear rubbers ... They say, 'Heterosexuals die of it, too.' Name *one!*" Kinison later tries to defend his routines in an interview in the *Los Angeles Times*: "I think people get anger out of their system by seeing me. You can't ignore anger. If the gay community thinks there isn't a major resentment by the American public for the disease they've caused, they're nuts."

June 5: Speaking at the Third International Conference on AIDS, an official of the World Health Organization warns that the disease could eventually create political and economic chaos in Third World nations, especially in those African countries — such as Uganda and Zaire — where ten percent of the pregnant women are believed to have been exposed to the virus.

June 9: Conservative political activist Paul Gann announces he has contracted AIDS, apparently through multiple blood transfusions he received in 1982. As a result of his diagnosis, Gann calls for sweeping political measures to help stem the spread of the epidemic, including a mandatory death penalty for anyone who knowingly spreads the disease. "You know," he tells the press, "it seems as though those who have AIDS, or who might have AIDS, want to keep it all a big secret so they can keep on doing what they want and keep spreading the disease to other victims. I want to put a stop to that!" Later, he concludes, "We have worried too much about people's civil rights. That is what is causing this disease to spread. We are not worrying enough about the innocent bystanders that are being exposed." Gann dies from AIDS two years later.

June 26: The Illinois General Assembly passes what some gay activists call the "broadest and most coercive" AIDS legislation in the country. The legislation calls for mandatory HIV-antibody testing for: all hospital patients between thirteen and fifty-five, all couples applying for a marriage license, all convicted sex offenders, all prison inmates either beginning or ending a prison sentence, and anyone convicted of crimes related to IV-drug use. The bill also gives the Public Health Department broader powers in quarantining people who have,

or are suspected of having, AIDS. Because of the failure of some parts of the legislation — for example, marriage-license applications in Illinois drop by more than twenty percent in the months following passage of the measure — the legislature repeals parts of the bill in 1989.

July 2: Director and choreographer Michael Bennett, best known for his hits *A Chorus Line* and *Dreamgirls*, dies of AIDS, at the age of forty-four.

July 5: New York State Senator James Donovan(R) tells the *New York Post* that teenagers should be given rosary beads instead of condoms to help prevent the spread of AIDS. "The best way I know to fend off immoral behavior," says the senator, "is prayer."

July 11: Dr. Tom Waddell, former Olympic athlete and founder of the Gay Games, dies from AIDS. He was forty-nine.

July 23: President Reagan announces the formation of a new, thirteen-member presidential commission on AIDS. Even before the commission begins its work, it is widely denounced as a "joke" by many gay activists and as an "embarrassment" by medical authorities. Criticism of the panel centers on the fact it does not include a single expert on AIDS, nor any people with AIDS, nor even a representative for people with AIDS. The commission *does* include such outspoken conservatives as: Republican fundraiser Richard DeVos; Cory SerVaas, publisher of *The Saturday Evening Post* and a staunch political ally of tele-evangelist Pat Robertson; homophobic New York Archbishop John Cardinal O' Connor; Congresswoman Penny Pullen, an associate of Phyllis Schlafly; and Teresa Crenshaw, a southern California sex therapist who was one of the only medical figures in California to support the 1986 "La Rouche Initiative." Despite pressure from within his own administration not to do so, Reagan does appoint one openly gay man, geneticist Dr. Frank Lilly, to the commission. However, the makeup of the panel still leads one national newsmagazine to compare it to "something out of the Twilight Zone," and even some members of Reagan's own administration privately regard the commission as a "fiasco."

August 7: U.S. Attorney General Edwin Meese encourages law enforcement officers to always wear rubber gloves whenever dealing with members of groups at a high risk for AIDS.

August 10: *Newsweek* magazine runs a cover story on AIDS — "The Face of AIDS: One Year in the Epidemic" — which features the photos of hundreds of men, women, and children who have died from the disease between August 1986 and July 1987. Brief, captional biographies accompany each photo. Praise for the article is widespread. However, a Florida woman — leader of a group trying to keep children with AIDS out of Florida's schools — tells the press, "*Newsweek's* cover story made it look like there were all these grandmothers and women with AIDS, but you opened it and you could tell they were all queers."

August 24: Robert Moore, president of the International Banana Association, threatens legal action against PBS if the network goes ahead with using a banana for a condom demonstration on an upcoming special on AIDS.

August 28: The Arcadia, Florida home of three hemophiliac brothers, all of whom have tested positive to HIV-antibodies, is firebombed and

Newsweek magazine's "Face of AIDS": Like the Quilt, it showed the people behind the numbers.

destroyed. The incident stems from a local controversy over whether the boys should be admitted to public schools. The day after the firebombing, the boys' mother announces that the family will move elsewhere.

September 1: A health clinic in Seattle, Washington begins marketing a greeting card that contains a gift certificate for one HIV-antibody test. The card is being sold at local gift shops and retails for $30.

September 21: Singer Dionne Warwick is given an award by the Department of Health and Human Services for her "exceptional service as a leading health ambassador" in the fight against AIDS. Warwick recently donated more than $1 million, from the royalties of her hit single "That's What Friends Are For," to AIDS research. Warwick recorded the single with Elton John, Gladys Knight, and Stevie Wonder.

October 2: A Traverse City, Michigan city commissioner is forced to resign after he asserts that homosexuals are the cause of AIDS and recommends that "a quick cut of the scalpel" to gay men would bring the epidemic to a quick conclusion.

October 11: Half-a-million gay men, lesbians, and gay rights

The Quilt: First displayed in October of 1987, it vividly emphasized the extent of the AIDS epidemic.

supporters march on Washington, D.C. to demand increased funding for AIDS-related projects and an end to federal laws that discriminate against gay men and lesbians. The centerpiece of the march is the unfurling of the AIDS Quilt, begun by Cleve Jones and the NAMES Project in San Francisco. The Quilt contains almost two thousand panels memorializing the names and lives of people who have died from AIDS, and covers a space larger than two football fields.

October 14: Under a new law overwhelmingly passed by the U.S. Senate, federally financed educational materials about AIDS must stress sexual abstinence as the best way to combat the disease. The new law also denies federal money to AIDS education programs that "promote or encourage, directly or indirectly" homosexual activity. Only two senators, Weicker of Connecticut and Moynihan of New York, vote against it.

October 20: The United Nations holds its first General Assembly session on AIDS — more than six years after the epidemic first began.

October 28: A St. Louis microbiologist, Dr. Memory Elvin-Lewis, makes national headlines when she reveals that a patient she'd had twenty years earlier — a sixteen-year-old boy known only as Robert R. — apparently died of AIDS in 1969, making him the first known case of the disease in the U.S. "The case has always stayed in our minds," Elvin-Lewis tells the press. "We were frustrated and saddened by our inability to help him." Robert R. was afflicted with a variety of opportunistic infections, including chlamydia, lung infections, and Kaposi's sarcoma. But Elvin-Lewis and her associates were unable to discover or treat the underlying cause of the boy's problems. After Robert R.'s death, she maintained specimens of the boy's tissues and body fluids in a freezer: "I wanted to save everything I could, in the hope that someday new techniques would enable us to figure out what had really happened." Tests on those samples lead doctors to assert a "ninety-nine percent certainty that this boy had AIDS."

November 19: According to the most recent reports, the average survival time for a person with AIDS is now four hundred days after diagnosis.

November 30: A California teacher with AIDS, Vincent Chalk, wins the nation's first legal battle in which a public school teacher with the disease fought to stay in the classroom. Chalk had been removed from his job working with hearing-impaired youngsters after school officials learned he had AIDS. On the day of his reinstatement, Chalk is greeted by his students with flowers, hugs, and kisses.

December 15: Burroughs-Wellcome, manufacturers of the drug AZT, announces it is reducing the price of a one-year prescription to the drug from $10,000 to $8,000. By mid-1989, there will be more than 20,000 people on AZT worldwide — bringing annual sales of the drug to over $160 million.

—1988—

January 11: The CDC reports that the number of AIDS cases in the U.S. has passed the fifty-thousand mark. One new case of AIDS is being diagnosed in the U.S. every seventeen minutes. There is about one AIDS-related death in the U.S. every hour.

February 2: School officials in Radford, Virginia cancel performances by a traveling theater group after learning that the troupe recently performed a play about AIDS, which included several people with the disease on-stage. "My belief," says the Radford superintendent of schools, "is that the community would not support the use of school facilities by people who have worked with individuals who have AIDS."

February 12: Nevada becomes the first state to require mandatory HIV testing for all boxers. State boxing regulators cite fears that, with so much blood and saliva typically expelled during a boxing match, fighters might contract AIDS in the ring or transmit the disease to spectators.

February 29: According to recent figures released by the World Health Organization, the countries with the most reported cases of AIDS are: the United States, with 55,167; France, with 3,073; Uganda, with 2,369; Brazil, with 2,325; West Germany, with 1,760; and Tanzania, with 1,608. However, the Organization warns that some central African countries such as Uganda are grossly under-reporting the number of diagnosed cases.

April 1: The CDC reports that twelve percent of all American-made condoms fail reliability standards and leak. Twenty-one percent of all foreign-made condoms have failed similar testing. "Condom use," concludes the CDC, "cannot completely eliminate the risk of transmission" of AIDS.

May 2: Republican Iowa state legislator Virgil Corey tells the *Des Moines Register* that the state government shouldn't try to prevent the spread of AIDS in Iowa's prisons. "It's probably a good way to thin out the population," Corey remarks, "so we don't have to build new prisons."

June 1: Rock star Ted Nugent tells an interviewer he doesn't worry much about AIDS because, "I can't imagine any girl I've ever touched being downwind of a faggot or a dope user ... My girls are real clean, and most of 'em are real young, so no problem."

June 7: As part of an AIDS education program in a wealthy Atlanta suburb, high school students are shown a videotape that labels gay people "perverts" and asserts that AIDS can be transmitted by casual kissing and toilet seats. The tape also claims that numerous cases of AIDS have been spread — from doctor to patient, and from patient to doctor — through legalized abortions. In response to complaints from local health authorities, the tape is withdrawn.

June 25: Eleven months after it was first established, President Reagan's Commission on AIDS releases it final report and recommendations. To the surprise of many, the commission — which has undergone several personnel changes since its inception — calls for a "progressive approach" to the AIDS crisis, and lists 180 recommendations to deal with the epidemic, including the need for federal legislation prohibiting discrimination against people with AIDS, laws making it a crime for health workers to violate the confidentiality of a person's HIV status, and increased funding for AIDS-related research and support services. The report's final chapter attacks the Reagan Administration's "distinct lack of leadership" throughout the epidemic. Despite assurances from President Reagan's domestic policy adviser, Gary

Bauer, that, "We're certainly not just going to file the report or stonewall it for the next six months," that is exactly what the Administration does: the report and its recommendations are ignored by the White House.

July 1: Customs officials at a London airport detain a U.S. tourist with AIDS and interrogate him for two-and-a-half hours before allowing him to enter the country. In the process of searching the man's luggage, one customs officer ruins over $1,000 in AZT and other medication the man brought with him. The interrogation and search end only after the International Red Cross intervenes.

August 14: At an outdoor rally for President Reagan on the day before the Republican National Convention begins in New Orleans, thirty AIDS activists are surrounded by pro-Reagan supporters and then kicked, beaten, and knocked to the ground. The confrontation begins when the activists hold up signs protesting the Reagan Administration's record on AIDS. Some at the Republican gathering begin chanting, "Die faggots!" Police disperse the angry crowd, and then abruptly

— and, according to eyewitnesses, arbitrarily — arrest five of the gay demonstrators.

August 15: Delegates at the Republican National Convention vote down a proposed plank in the party platform calling for antidiscrimination legislation to protect people with AIDS. The plank is vetoed despite George Bush's support for such legislation. Instead, the Republican Party's plank on AIDS only reminds the country that, "The Reagan–Bush Administration launched the nation's fight against AIDS."

August 24: Actor Leonard Frey, best known for his roles in *The Boys in the Band* and *Fiddler on the Roof*, dies from AIDS, at the age of forty-nine.

August 28: French journalist and philosopher Guy Hocquenghem dies from AIDS, in Paris, at the age of forty-two.

October 9: The Soviet Union reports the country's first fatality from AIDS, a 29-year-old female prostitute from Leningrad.

October 11: Over one hundred and fifty protestors are arrested at a massive demonstration in front of the offices of the Food and Drug Administration in Washington D.C. More than a thousand people joined the demonstration, which demanded that the federal government make experimental drugs more accessible to people with AIDS. The demonstration lasts nine hours. Eight days later, the FDA announces it will reduce the time usually taken to approve new drugs to treat people with AIDS.

November 1: The Smithsonian Institute asks for several panels from the AIDS memorial quilt, to put on permanent display in the Institute's Division of Medical Sciences.

December 20: Former ABC News anchorman Max Robinson dies from AIDS, at the age of forty-nine.

December 21: The World Health Organization, which originally predicted that between fifty million and one hundred million people worldwide would contract AIDS by the year 1991, now revises that figure to about seven million. The Organization credits the changes in sexual behavior and IV-drug use for a slowing down in the transmission of the disease.

ALCATRAZ, EARLY ESCAPE ATTEMPT BY TWO GAY CONVICTS. In 1937, two gay men, 25-year-old Teddy Cole and 37-year-old Ralph Roe, made national headlines when they escaped from the supposedly inescapable federal prison on Alcatraz Island. Cole, a convicted murderer and kidnapper, and Roe, serving a 99-year sentence for bank robbery, were lovers. The two men took advantage of a heavy fog one morning to launch their escape, first by crawling out a prison factory window and then climbing a ten-foot-high cyclone fence. They were last seen alive diving from one of the island's towering bluffs into the San Francisco Bay.

Despite an intensive search by the police and Coast Guard, no trace of them was ever found, and prison officials later concluded, perhaps self-servingly, that the two men must have drowned: authorities pointed out that the tide was particularly high the day of the escape, the water temperature was barely fifty degrees, and the nearest land was over a mile away. There were, however, some published reports, several months later, that Cole and Roe had been spotted in South America, where it was said, they were living together.

Alexander the Great: Do his remains rest under a Moslem mosque?

ALEXANDER THE GREAT'S BODY — DISAPPEARANCE OF. After Alexander the Great's death in Babylon in 323 B.C., one of his generals, Ptolemy, took the body back to Alexandria, Egypt, where it lay for more than three hundred years, sheathed in gold and encased, according to some eyewitnesses, in a sarcophagus of pure glass. The body — which was regarded by the Alexandrians as perhaps their most precious possession, because of the legends associated with it — was still there at the time of Julius Caesar: Caesar himself paid homage to it, as did his successor, Augustus.

Shortly afterward, however, all trace of it disappeared. The traditional site of its interment, the "Soma" — the burying place of all the Ptolemaic kings, at the center of the city — eventually became the site of a Moslem mosque, and for centuries there has been speculation that Alexander's mummified remains, and the crystal coffin that contained them, are buried somewhere beneath it. E.M. Forster, in his book *Alexandria: A History and a Guide*, provided one tantalizing clue. He mentioned the story of a member of the Russian Consulate who, in the mid-19th century, became lost in the labyrinthine catacombs beneath the mosque. Peering through a hole in some rubble, the Russian claimed to have seen "a human body in a sort of glass cage with a diadem on its head and half bowed on a sort of elevation or throne. A quantity of books or papyrus were scattered around." Because of logistical problems, the mosque's catacombs have not, to this day, ever been fully excavated or explored.

ARMED FORCES, U.S. — DISCHARGE OF HOMOSEXUALS, 1974-1983. According to a 1984 report by the U.S. government's General Accounting Office, 14,311 members of the Army, Navy, Air Force, and Marines were discharged for homosexuality between 1974 and 1983. The Navy accounted for more than half — 8,151 — of those discharges. The number of per-year discharges for homosexuality more than doubled over the period, from 875 in 1974 to 1,796 in 1983. In 1983 alone, the cost of investigating charges of homosexuality in the military exceeded $370,000.

ARNOLD OF VERNIOLLE, TRIAL FOR SODOMY IN 1323. A thirty-year-old French Catholic subdeacon, Arnold was found guilty in 1323 of having committed sodomy with three local youths. According to testimony, Arnold often took the youths — aged fifteen, sixteen, and eighteen — on picnics, where they would spread a blanket, drink wine, then sometimes wrestle together and afterwards perform sodomy. On one occasion, all three of the youths went to Arnold's study, where one of them performed sodomy on another while Arnold and the third watched. For these acts, an ecclesiastical tribunal sentenced Arnold to be bound in iron chains for the rest of his life and force-fed a diet of bread and water; the tribunal labeled this punishment "a salutary penance." No records exists of how long Arnold survived under these conditions. (Arnold's case is dealt with at length in Michael Goodich's book *The Unmentionable Vice: Homosexuality in the Later Medieval Period.*)

ARTHUR, CHESTER — GAY GRANDSON OF. Chester Arthur — the twenty-first president of the United States — had a gay grandson, Gavin, who worked for many years with both Magnus Hirschfeld and Alfred Kinsey in their studies of homosexuality. An early gay activist, Gavin was also a close friend of Havelock Ellis. Despite his somewhat privileged upbringing, Gavin spent much of his life panning gold, ranching in Colorado, and working in the merchant marine. In 1966, he published a book about homosexuality, *The Circle of Sex.* He died in San Francisco in 1972, at the age of seventy-one.

ARVIN, NEWTON (1900-1963), famed U.S. literary critic and biographer. Arvin's critical biography of Herman Melville won the National Book Award in 1951. He also wrote widely praised biographies of Hawthorne, Longfellow, and Whitman.

A reclusive intellectual, Arvin was tormented by his homosexuality most of his life, and tried committing suicide on three occasions, once by swallowing an overdose of Nembutals after longingly watching a group of young male athletes skating together on a frozen pond one winter afternoon. His best-known love affair was with Truman Capote in the late 1940s. Speaking of his homosexuality, Arvin once wrote, "I feel as if I were — indeed I am — going about in disguise, though luckily it is a disguise I have worn so long that no doubt it looks as if it fitted me. I am an impostor. Won't I some time be caught and exposed?"

Exposure finally *did* come, in 1960. In later years, Arvin, a gentle and soft-spoken man, wanted nothing so much as to be left alone with his books and his critical work. His only apparent sexual outlet was masturbation, and he became an almost obsessive collector of gay pornography. In 1960, the office of one of his suppliers was raided, and authorities found Arvin's name and address among the confiscated papers. Soon afterward, the police broke into and ransacked Arvin's home. There they found his enormous collection of pornography — including several hundred stories and explicit nude photographs — and charged him with being "a lewd and lascivious person in speech and behavior," a charge that carried a potentially weighty prison term.

Because of Arvin's stature as a literary critic, his arrest made national headlines. His friends rallied to his support, but a nervous breakdown followed and Arvin, who was sixty at the time, was admitted to Northhampton State Hospital for psychiatric treatment. Although he was not fired from Smith College, where he had taught for many years, school officials never allowed him back into the classroom.

Arvin eventually received a one-year suspended sentence from the courts, but only after he was coerced into giving police the names of at least fifteen other men he thought might also be collectors of pornography. He died three years later, in 1963, of pancreatic cancer.

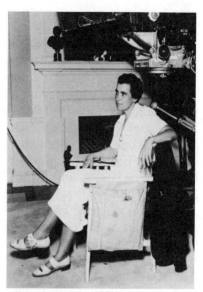

Dorothy Arzner: One of the earliest women film directors.

ARZNER, DOROTHY (1900-1979), U.S. film director, a lesbian, and one of the only women film directors in Hollywood history. Her father owned a small Hollywood cafe, where she worked as a waitress and first made contact with various influential people in the movie industry. Her first job in the studios was as a script girl. Later, she became a film editor, and gained attention for her superb, stylized editing of the bullfighting sequences in Rudolph Valentino's *Blood and Sand*. She was given her first directing assignment in 1927: a now-forgotten movie entitled *Fashions for Women.*

Arzner's best-known films include *The Wild Party* (1929); *Working Girls* (1931); *Christopher Strong* (1933), which featured Katharine Hepburn in an unusual role for the time, as a headstrong, individualistic, and independent woman; *Craig's Wife* (1936), with Rosalind Russell in her first big success, as a housewife who cares more about material possessions than she does about her husband; and *The Bride Wore Red* (1937), with Joan Crawford. Arzner retired from Hollywood in 1943, though she continued making Army training films, for the WACs, for several years.

ASS, slang expression for the buttocks. It is derived from the commonly used British term arse. Arse — and its now-obsolete variant, ears — go back in written English at least to the eleventh century. They were in turn apparently derived through the centuries from the ancient Greek orrhos and the Hittite arras, both of which referred to either the rectum or the buttocks.

B

THE BAEKELAND MURDER (1972). On November 17, 1972, 26-year-old Tony Baekeland — a would-be painter and writer who had never discovered much purpose to life — suddenly found himself at the center of one of the most publicized crimes of the decade. He was charged with having stabbed to death his wealthy, socialite mother, Barbara, in her fashionable London apartment near Buckingham Palace. When police arrived on the scene, they found Barbara Baekeland lying dead on the kitchen floor, with a single stab wound through her heart; a bloody kitchen knife was on the counter above her. Her son, Tony — who at first tried to blame someone else for the killing — was in the bedroom, nonchalantly ordering Chinese food over the telephone.

When first questioned, Tony denied having had anything to do with the crime; he claimed his elderly grandmother was the actual killer. But his statements were so inconsistent, and he kept rambling on so incoherently, that police finally took him down to the station for questioning. Shortly afterward, Tony confessed to the stabbing, and was charged with murder.

The Baekelands were a prominent and extremely well-to-do family. The family patriarch, Leo Baekeland, had been a multimillionaire industrialist, famous as the inventor of the first successful plastic, Bakelite, in 1909, and as the founder of the modern plastics industry. His grandson, Brooks — Tony's father — had a reputation as a rigidly disciplined adventurer and explorer whose exploits, including a parachute jump into the Andes, often found their way into the pages of the *National Geographic*; friends called him "an intellectual Errol Flynn." Brooks's wife, Barbara, was beautiful, flamboyant, and elegant. She was also — according to those who knew her intimately — narcissistic, impulsive, and emotionally immature. She proudly counted novelists, filmmakers, and royalty among her many acquaintances. The family friends included novelist James Jones and poet Robert Graves.

On the night of the killing, Tony and his mother had, according to the maid, been arguing. Their arguments — ferocious, passionate, sometimes violent — were by then legendary to everyone who knew the family. Mostly, Tony and his mother argued about the fact that Tony was gay; Barbara Baekeland couldn't deal with it. She loved everything about her son — his wit, his sense of style, his loyalty to her — but she could never reconcile herself to his homosexuality. For a long time, she even tried to "cure" him by finding willing girls to take him to bed. These hoped-for seductions backfired bit-terly — her husband, Brooks, eventually wound up leaving her for one of the girls — and Barbara became more and more emotionally unstable. She sometimes talked of suicide.

Most of the family's friends knew about the troubled relationship between mother and son. What many of them didn't know was that, in 1968, Barbara finally took matters into her own hands and decided to seduce the boy herself. In a grotesque attempt to cure Tony of his homosexuality, Barbara coerced him into having sex with her when he was twenty-two and they were staying alone together in a house on Mallorca. The episode added a new twist to an already volatile relationship, and the fury of emotion between them became explosive. Even before the murder, there had been fights when Tony threatened her with a knife. The fight on November 11, 1972 ended with him finally killing her.

In June 1973, eight months after the stabbing, Tony was convicted of "manslaughter under diminished responsibility," and was sent to a psychiatric hospital outside London for prolonged treatment. But the cycle of tragedy didn't end there.

In 1981, he was pronounced rehabilitated by hospital authorities, and was released to the custody of his maternal grandmother — the grandmother he had at first accused of his mother's murder — in New York City. He made a poor adjustment to the outside world, and began to despise the 87-year-old woman, who was confined to a wheelchair. According to testimony, he spent the first week at her apartment listening to loud music all day and reading the Bible or chanting over his mother's ashes at night. Soon, he began hearing voices.

After barely a week, he woke up one morning, and decided to kill the old woman. He picked up a telephone and knocked her out of her wheelchair with it. Then he ran to the kitchen, found a knife with a six-inch blade, and returned to stab her five times in the chest. When police arrived, they found the old lady slumped in a corner and covered with blood. Miraculously, she survived. Tony was charged with attempted murder and incarcerated at Rikers Island.

The attack made front-page headlines across the country, both because of the Baekeland family name, and because of Tony's murderous history. But there was still one last headline to be written. On March 20, 1981, while awaiting trial for the assault on his grandmother, Tony killed himself in prison: he pulled a plastic bag over his head, tied it closed with a drawstring, and suffocated himself. His father, Brooks — who had had almost nothing to do with Tony since Barbara's murder in 1972, and who had once described Tony as "the personification of evil" — said in a statement to the press, "It was a beautiful ending — in plastic, too!"

BARS, GAY — TOTAL NUMBER IN THE U.S. As of January 1, 1989, there were an estimated 1,750 gay bars in the United States.

BEDBUGS, HOMOSEXUAL BEHAVIOR IN. According to studies, some species of male bedbugs mate with a female only after having engaged in homosexual activity with one another. In the process, one male bedbug mounts and ejaculates semen into another male; the second bedbug then takes his own sperm, plus the recently deposited sperm of the other male, and impregnates the female.

BENNETT, WILLIAM (b. 1943), former Secretary of Education under President Reagan, later appointed "Drug Czar" under President Bush. One of the most consistently conservative members of either administration, Bennett told *The Washington Times* in 1982 that homosexuals *should* be allowed to teach in public schools, and that homosexuality was grounds for dismissal only if a teacher "proselytizes." "I was taught by some," Bennett added. "It shouldn't be prohibited." Pressed by the interviewer, who insisted that homosexuals should be kept out of the classroom because they are "practicing sinners," Bennett replied, "Well, most of us are practicing sinners, too." (See also *AIDS EPIDEMIC, EIGHT YEARS IN THE HISTORY OF — May 4, 1987*)

BERNSTEIN, LEONARD (b. 1918), U.S. composer and conductor. In 1988, Bernstein publicly addressed the long-standing rumors of his homosexuality, as well as his image as a "bleeding heart" liberal. "Most people do think of me as just another pinko faggot, a bleeding heart, a do-gooder," he commented; then added after a pause, "But that's what I am."

BICEPS, BIGGEST IN THE WORLD. The largest biceps in the world reportedly belong to bodybuilder Gary Aprahamian of Queens, New York. Measured "cold" — that is, not immediately after a workout — Aprahamian's biceps measure twenty-five and one-half inches. His chest measures sixty-one inches.

BLACKSTONE, WILLIAM (1723-1780), renowned English jurist, one of the most influential commentators in the history of English law. In his famous *Commentaries on the Laws of England*, in 1769, Blackstone termed homosexuality a crime "the very mention of which is a disgrace to human nature," and made a renewed call for it to be "strictly and impartially punished."

More than two hundred years later, in 1986, Blackstone's comments were quoted by Chief Justice Warren Burger of the U.S. Supreme Court, as one justification for upholding the constitutionality of Georgia's anti-sodomy laws. However, in a dissent from the majority, Justice Harry Blackmun countered by quoting Oliver Wendell Holmes, Jr., who once wrote, "It is revolting to have no better reason for a rule of law than that so it was laid down in the time of Henry IV. It is still more revolting if the grounds upon which it was laid down have vanished long since, and the rule simply persists from blind imitation of the past."

BLITZSTEIN, MARC (1905-1964), U.S. composer, gay, best known for his Depression-era "labor opera," *The Cradle Will Rock*, which premiered in 1937. Blitzstein wrote the opera — about life in a fictitious Steeltown, U.S.A. — to be staged by Orson Welles and John Houseman, as part of the Federal Theatre project, a federally-funded program of the Works Progress Administration. Welles and Houseman were captivated by Blitzstein's opera for purely theatrical reasons — it was, Houseman recalled in his memoirs, "unlike anything either of us had ever tried before" — but federal authorities were scandalized by the work's radical politics and socialist message, and confiscated all of the play's scenery, costumes, and musical scores shortly before its scheduled premiere. After Welles and Houseman defiantly announced that, scenery and costumes or not, the premiere would take place

as scheduled, a dozen uniformed federal security guards took over the theater. The W.P.A. then effectively banned the theater's orchestra from performing the work, while Actors' Equity forbade the play's actors from appearing in it on stage.

Determined now to go ahead with the opera no matter what, Welles and Houseman quickly bought a used upright piano for a hundred dollars, and found an abandoned theater on Seventh Avenue, just hours before the premiere was to begin. Their intention was to have Blitzstein himself play and sing the entire opera on stage. By the time of the work's premiere, there had been so much publicity that over twenty-five hundred people showed up at the theater; the audience filled the seats, the aisles, and the mezzanine. Eager to see what had become of the opera, most of the work's original performers and stagehands were also in the audience.

At 9:01, the curtain rose on Blitzstein, alone on stage with the piano. As he played the overture to the banned opera, he described the work's setting to the massive audience. Then, he began to sing the actual libretto. After a few minutes, however, he suddenly realized he was not singing alone. One of the opera's original cast members — a girl named Olive Stanton — had spontaneously stood up from where she was sitting in the audience and had begun singing her part. Soon, other cast members, emboldened by her, took up their roles and began singing as well, from where they were sitting scattered throughout the audience. "Our actors," Houseman wrote in his memoirs, "had been forbidden by their union to appear *on stage*. There was no rule against their appearing *in the house*. And that's what they did! They acted all over that theater — in the aisles, in stage boxes, between rows of seats ... Improvising with amazing ingenuity — unrehearsed, undirected — they played each scene in a different and unexpected part of the house." The audience response was amazing; when the opera was finished, the applause and cheering went on for almost an hour, and the next morning, the story — about the "opera that couldn't be stopped" — was on the front page of every newspaper in New York City. Almost immediately after the incident, Welles and Houseman were fired from the W.P.A.

for insubordination.

In 1952, Blitzstein premiered another of his operas, *Regina,* based on Lillian Hellman's play *The Little Foxes.* Hellman was originally scheduled to do the on-stage narration for the opera, but because she had recently testified in front of the House Un-American Activities Committee — and had refused to cooperate with it — she was afraid of being booed off the stage. "I don't think they will hiss you," Blitzstein told her, "and if they do, I won't have it. I'll just come out and say I don't want my music played before such people, and we'll give them their money back and send them home." "I laughed" Hellman recalled in her book *Scoundrel Time,* "because I could hear him doing it, enjoying it." Hellman appeared as the opera's narrator as scheduled and, far from being booed, she was given a standing ovation by the audience. The opera itself was a moderate success.

Blitzstein had long contemplated writing a musical work about Sacco and Vanzetti — the two anarchists executed for murder in 1927, amid international controversy over their guilt or innocence — and in 1964, he rented a house on

Martinique to work on an opera on the subject. One night, at a local bar, he picked up two young Portuguese sailors on shore leave and took them home. The sailors, after having sex with him, robbed him and then beat him to death. He was fifty-nine. Both sailors were later apprehended, convicted of murder, and sent to prison.

BOOKSTORE, GAY — OLDEST IN U.S. The oldest bookstore in the U.S. is Oscar Wilde Memorial Bookstore, 15 Christopher Street, New York City. It was founded in 1967 by Craig Rodwell. When the store first opened — originally on Mercer Street — it was subject to a variety of bomb threats, broken windows, and threatening phone calls. In 1973, the store moved to its current location on Christopher Street. Rodwell has since installed shatter-proof windows.

THE BOYS IN THE SAND (1971), gay porn film directed by Wakefield Poole, a former dancer and choreographer and a former member of the Ballet Russe de Monte Carlo.

Generally regarded as the first quality gay porno film, *The Boys in the Sand* opened on December 29, 1971 in New York City, and grossed nearly $25,000 during its first week. Within the first month, it had grossed over $100,000, and was ranked number forty-six on *Variety*'s list of the top-grossing films for the period: higher than *Kotch, Minnie and Moskowitz*, and Elizabeth Taylor's new film, *X, Y, and Zee*.

The Boys in the Sand continued to play at the same theater, the 55th Street Playhouse, for nineteen consecutive weeks, before opening, with equal success, in other major U.S. cities. The film turned its star, Casey Donovan, into an instant gay celebrity. Poole made a sequel, *The Boys in the Sand II* — also with Casey Donovan — in 1984, thirteen years after the original. (See also *PORN STAR, GAY — FIRST AND MOST FAMOUS.*)

BRESLIN, JIMMY — HOMO-PHOBIA OF. In 1979, the noted New York City newspaper columnist wrote an editorial attacking *The Village Voice* for running a recent special supplement on "Gay Life." "Once, the *Voice* had Norman Mailer writing about J. Edgar Hoover," Breslin complained. "Now the paper consists of impenetrable sentences about the agonies of a gay in Elyria, Ohio, who is so proud that he is gay that he doesn't do another blessed thing in the whole world except be gay." Breslin added, "Because of places like the *Village Voice*, a regular person doesn't dare order cheese in a restaurant in Manhattan. The gays have taken over cheese just as they take over bars and entire city blocks. There are so many gays typing out nonsense about eating cheese with their lovers that I now am afraid when I ask a waiter in Manhattan for a slice of Brie he's going to kiss me."

BROTHERS AND SISTERS, GAY AND LESBIAN — CELEBRITIES WHO HAVE. Among the celebrities who have gay or lesbian siblings are: David Soul (a lesbian sister), singer Ronee Blakley (a gay brother), Grace Jones (a gay brother), and controversial talk-show host Morton Downey, Jr. (a gay brother). Downey's brother has been diagnosed with AIDS. Despite that — or, perhaps in his mind, because of it — Downey himself is outspokenly opposed to homosexuality. "The anus," he is fond of telling his audiences, "is an exit, not an entrance."

BRUCE, LENNY (1926-1966), controversial and ground-breaking U.S. comic and satirist. Bruce allegedly got out of the Navy in 1942 by dressing as a woman and promenading up and down his assigned ship during midnight watch. "A number of guys who saw it didn't report it," Bruce wrote later, "out of fear that they'd be given a Section Eight themselves. Finally one night I was doing my nautical Lady Macbeth when four guys, including the chief master-at-arms, jumped me. I yelled, 'Masher!'" Interrogated by four Navy psychiatrists, Bruce denied being a homosexual, and said he enjoyed intercourse with women. Asked if he enjoyed wearing women's clothes, he replied, "Sometimes. When they fit." Shortly afterward, he was given an honorable discharge.

In his autobiography, *How to Talk Dirty and Influence People*, Bruce briefly discussed homosexuals as an object of humor during the Fifties and Sixties. "From *Charlie's Aunt* and *Some Like It Hot* and Milton Berle," he wrote, "the pervert has been taken out of Krafft-Ebing and made into a sometimes-fun fag. Berle never lost his sense of duty to the public, though. Although he gave homosexuals a peek out of the damp cellar of unfavorable public opinion, he didn't go all the way; he left a stigma of menace on his fag — 'I sweah I'w kiw you.'"

BUCKINGHAM, BOB, muscular and good-looking police constable who became lovers and close friends with English novelist E.M. Forster (1879-1970). The two first met in 1930, at a party for the annual Oxford-Cambridge boat race, when Buckingham was twenty-eight. Forster, at fifty-one, was arguably the greatest English novelist of the twentieth century; Buckingham was from a poor family, and had worked as a boxer and a boot salesman before becoming a policeman. Immediately fascinated by one another, they began a friendship that lasted forty years. For Forster, Buckingham probably represented the fulfillment of his long-held desire, "to love a strong young man of the lower classes and be loved by him, and even hurt by him."

Although they had sex during the early years of their relationship, Buckingham was primarily heterosexual, and he eventually married. Forster was initially jealous of the new bride — and she of him — but the three adapted to the exigencies of the situation, and

wound up forming a close, satisfying friendship. In fact, the Buckinghams named their first child after Forster. It was Buckingham's wife who nursed Forster during his final illness, and it was in the Buckinghams' home that Forster died, at the age of ninety-one, on June 7, 1970.

BURTON, SIR RICHARD — BURNING OF DIARIES AND LAST MANUSCRIPT OF. It was a peculiar marriage from the start. Sir Richard Burton (1821-1890) was a darkly handsome explorer, an amateur sexologist who spoke more than twenty-five languages and who delighted in collecting material on the sex customs of far-flung places. He was particularly fascinated by homosexuality and wrote several *apologias* of it; his most famous work was an explicit translation of the highly erotic *Arabian Nights*, with all of the homosexual passages left intact. Burton's wife, Isabel, on the other hand, was an ardent Catholic, and an aristocrat, who adored her husband but only just tolerated his work. From all accounts, theirs was not a particularly passionate marriage: Burton liked to think of Isabel as his "brother."

Richard Burton: He collected information about sexual customs in many cultures — only to have his work destroyed after his death.

When Burton died in 1890, he left behind forty years' worth of scrupulously kept personal diaries, in which he detailed some of his own homosexual exploits, as well as information on homosexuality gathered from around the world. He also left the unpublished manuscript of his last book, a translation of the Arabian sex manual *The Scented Garden*. Just

before his death, he had been putting the finishing touches on the manuscript and was preparing several essays, including one on homosexuality, to accompany it. "I have put my whole life and all my life-blood into that *Scented Garden*," he told a friend. "It is the crown of my life."

Left with these potentially scandalous papers after his

death, Isabel was stricken by a conflict of conscience. In the end, her Catholicism won out: she built a small bonfire with most of her husband's papers — including the precious diaries and the manuscript of *The Scented Garden*—and reduced them all to ashes, an act for which, according to one writer, "neither her friends nor posterity could forgive her." Then, as if to add insult to injury, she turned around and gave her husband—who loathed Christianity — not one, but *two* Catholic funerals, in hopes of redeeming his soul.

BUSH, GEORGE (b. 1924), U.S. president. Discussing his political relationship with Ronald Reagan, Bush told a crowd during the 1988 presidential campaign, "We have had triumphs, we have made mistakes, we have had sex." After a shocked silence, a deeply embarrassed Bush corrected himself; he had meant to say, "We have had setbacks."

BUTRICK, MERRITT (1959-1989), U.S. actor, best known for his role as Captain Kirk's son in the movies *Star Trek II: The Wrath of Khan* and *Star Trek III: The Search for Spock.* He died of complications from AIDS, in Los Angeles, March 17, 1989, at the age of twenty-nine. In his brief eight-year career, he also appeared in the films *Zapped, Head Office,* and *Shy People.*

BUTTON, DICK (b.1929), former U.S. Olympic skating star who dominated U.S. and international competition for several years, from 1948 until 1952.

In 1978, Button, then in his late forties, was brutally attacked, along with five other gay men, by a gang of teenagers wielding baseball bats, a hammer, and a couch leg one summer night in Central Park. According to one of the teenagers, the gang had gone into the park to "get us some faggots." One gay man was beaten in the head fifteen times. Button, though lucky to have escaped with his life, suffered serious nerve damage and permanent hearing loss in one ear as a result of the attack. Three of the youths were later apprehended; they were eventually convicted of assault.

Widely regarded as one of the most influential skaters in the history of the sport, Button won the world championship in men's figure skating five years in a row, from 1948 to 1952. He also won the gold medal in men's figure skating in both the 1948 and 1952 Winter Olympics, and in 1948 became the only man to simultaneously hold the Olympic, world, European, North American, and United States championship titles. He currently appears as a guest commentator for *ABC Sports.*

BUTTON FLY — INVENTION OF. The button fly on trousers was developed in Turkey sometime shortly before 1700. According to one historian, "The Turks introduced the fly to Europe between the eighteenth and nineteenth centuries. Its purpose was not only to facilitate urination, but also to facilitate fornication and rape." The button fly remained standard on pants, until the introduction of the zipper in 1893. It is still

The fashionable boy of the 1890s: His multi-purpose button fly came courtesy of the Turks.

preferred today — especially on blue jeans — by many men.

CAMP LINES, MEMORABLE AND QUOTABLE FROM THE MOVIES.

"If I'd been a ranch, they would've named me the Bar-Nothing."

Rita Hayworth, *Gilda* (1946)

❐

"Oh I'm so tired of just being pretty."

Kim Novak, *Picnic* (1955)

❐

"I always so terribly wanted to meet a young man — and now, three of them at once! You're lovely, doctor. Of course, the two end ones are unbelievable."

Anne Francis,
Forbidden Planet (1956)

❐

"I hate dot qveen!"

Zsa Zsa Gabor, *Queen of
Outer Space* (1958)

❐

"Honey, you're a mess. You better stop eating those chocolates."

Marlene Dietrich to Orson
Welles, *Touch of Evil* (1958)

❐

"Usually one must go to a bowling alley to meet a woman of your stature."

John Gielgud, *Arthur* (1981)

❐

"Don't you know that a man being rich is like a girl being pretty? You might not marry a girl because she's pretty, but — my goodness — doesn't it help?"

Marilyn Monroe, *Gentlemen
Prefer Blondes* (1953)

❐

"'I love you' is such an inadequate way of saying I love you."

Joan Crawford,
Possessed (1947)

❐

"Oh Mama, all they want is my body!" Carroll Baker, *Harlow* (1965)

"No, I tell you no. I won't have you bringing strange young girls in for supper — by candlelight, I suppose, in the cheap erotic fashion of young men with cheap erotic minds ... Go on, go tell her — you'll not be feeding her ugly appetites with *my* food. Or my son."

Mother, in *Psycho* (1960)

☐

"I am She Who Must Be Obeyed."

Helen Gahagan, *She* (1935)

☐

"Mother, my mother — what is the phrase? — she isn't quite herself today."

Anthony Perkins,
Psycho (1960)

☐

"Oh Thou my God, save Thy servant that trusteth in Thee: save him from this big-mouthed cooz with the motor-driven ass."

Anthony Perkins,
Crimes of Passion (1984)

☐

"I like big muscles, and red corpuscles — I like a beautiful hunk of man."

Jane Russell, *Gentlemen Prefer Blondes* (1953)

☐

"Look, if you think you're gonna get back in my panties, forget it. There's one asshole in there already."

Kathleen Turner,
Crimes of Passion (1984)

☐

"My mother — a waitress!" Ann Blyth, *Mildred Pierce* (1945)

"She suffers from something called dementia precox, which is to say she's mad as a hatter, poor child."

Katharine Hepburn,
Suddenly, Last Summer (1959)

❐

"He's no good, but he's what I want."

Judith Anderson, *Laura* (1944)

❐

"Peggy Sue, do you know what a penis is? Please, Peggy Sue — *stay away from it!*"

Barbara Harris, *Peggy Sue Got Married* (1986)

❐

"Too much of a good thing can be wonderful."

Mae West, *I'm No Angel* (1933)

❐

"Look at me when you talk to me! I'm not some sort of garbage pail you can slam a lid on and walk away from! Let me tell you about hell, about being a silly woman who needs to feel she belongs to someone — even someone as empty as you are, Frankie!"

Eleanor Parker, *The Oscar* (1966)

❐

The insurance ran out on the 15th. I'd hate to think of you having a smashed fender or something while you're not, uh, fully covered."

Fred MacMurray to
Barbara Stanwyck,
Double Indemnity (1944)

❐

"All right, Mr. De Mille. I'm ready for my close-up." Gloria Swanson, *Sunset Boulevard* (1950)

"Dorothy, didn't you notice? His pocket was bulging!"

Marilyn Monroe, *Gentlemen Prefer Blondes* (1953)

❒

"You kinda get turned on by a guy who treats you nice, like the *schlep* you were out with tonight. But a guy who wipes his feet on you — that you dig!"

Stephen Boyd,
The Oscar (1966)

❒

"You think new curtains are enough to please me!"

Ann Blyth,
Mildred Pierce (1945)

❒

"No wire hangers! What's wire hangers doing in this closet, when I told you no wire hangers — ever?!"

Faye Dunaway, *Mommie Dearest* (1981)

❒

"You have a point — an idiotic one — but a point."

George Sanders,
All About Eve (1950)

❒

"Your hair is like a field of daisies. I should like to run barefoot through your hair."

Franchot Tone,
Bombshell (1933)

❒

"Fasten your seat belts — it's going to be a bumpy night." Bette Davis, *All About Eve* (1950)

"There I was, with a perfectly strange plumber — and no polish on my toe nails!"

Marilyn Monroe, *The Seven Year Itch* (1955)

❐

Judge: "Young lady, are you trying to show contempt for this court?" Mae West: "Mmm, no, I'm doing my best to hide it."

My Little Chickadee (1940)

❐

"I wouldn't worry too much about your heart. You can always put that award where your heart ought to be."

Bette Davis, *All About Eve* (1950)

❐

"I'm sorry I spoiled your day by asking you to be my wife."

Laurence Harvey, *Walk on the Wild Side* (1962)

❐

"Oh I'm bored. And I've only just gotten up!"

Capucine, *Walk on the Wild Side* (1962)

❐

"I *am* big! It's the pictures that got small!"

Gloria Swanson, *Sunset Boulevard* (1950)

❐

"She might have fooled me, but she didn't fool my mother."

Anthony Perkins *Psycho* (1960)

❐

"You're just like me — you can't make love to anyone you like."
George Peppard,
The Carpetbaggers (1964)

❐

"Nature, Mr. Allnut, is what we're put in this world to rise above."
Katharine Hepburn,
The African Queen (1951)

❐

"You, you're forty-two. There are many good minutes left for you."
Milton Berle to Eleanor Parker, *The Oscar* (1966)

❐

"Don't fuck with me, fellas — this ain't my first time at the rodeo!"
Faye Dunaway,
Mommie Dearest (1981)

❐

"She's always just a little out of breath and sees beauty in everything — like shit."
Elizabeth Taylor, *X, Y and Zee* (1972)

❐

"Mistreat me, make love to me, anything. Only get it over with. Then throw me out."
Carroll Baker,
The Carpetbaggers (1964)

❐

"Toto, I have a feeling we're not in Kansas anymore."
Judy Garland,
The Wizard of Oz (1939)

CAPOTE, TRUMAN (1924-1984), U.S. author. Composer Ned Rorem described him as "a toad puffed up with hot air ... All that Truman touches turns to fool's gold." *Time* magazine, in 1976, called him "Jackie Susann with an education." And Gore Vidal, a one-time friend who later sued him for libel, dismissed him as having "the mind of a Kansas housewife: likes gossip, and gets all shuddery when she thinks about boys murdering people." He concluded, "I can't read Capote. I'm a diabetic." Vidal also once commented, "Every writer ought to have at least one thing he does well, and I'll take Truman's word that a gift for self-publicity is the most glittering star in his diadem." Other attacks — especially those motivated by Capote's androgynous flamboyance, his short (5'3") and chubby build, and his distinctive, high-pitched voice — often came from total strangers, many of whom seemed personally galled that such an eccentric, obviously "faggy" individual was accorded so much attention in the media. Virtually everyone loved to mimic his improbable, lisping voice — a cheap and easy parlor trick, rather like gaily imitating someone with a harelip.

In contrast, thirty years before his death, Capote had been called "the hope of modern literature" by W. Somerset Maugham, and after the publication of his first novel, *Other Voices, Other Rooms* in 1948, he became the toast of literary New York. The word "masterpiece" was so frequently, and often so carelessly, ascribed to everything he wrote that it eventually became a meaningless accolade. Of course, his seemingly effortless rise to fame, and his sudden position as high society's favorite spoiled child, provoked the almost immediate resentment of several other writers of his generation. Revealingly, Gore Vidal — whose disparagement of Capote has often had more than a slightly obsessive edge to it — remarked in an interview, "I had — and have — perfect contempt for those writers of book-chat who were not able to see how very bad Capote's work was — and, obviously, how good mine was!"

But Vidal and other naysayers to the contrary, Capote was one of the most powerful and suggestive American writers of the twentieth century. It was not only that his style was fluid and elegant; it was that his work was invariably infused with a deep sense of compassion and humanity. At times, this led some of his work to become too "cute," and he was often accused of overt sentimentality. Yet it is difficult to read *A Christmas Memory* or *A Beautiful Child* — his poignant and unnerving account of an afternoon spent with Marilyn Monroe — and not be touched by the tender insights and haunting lyricism of his style.

His work was admirable for many reasons: for the smooth, hypnotic texture of each line; for the suggestiveness of its often spare but perfectly chosen images. Describing a macabre luncheon date with Joan Crawford, or the pangs of a sensitive boy growing up in the South, or merely the sight of the enigmatic Garbo silently window-shopping at Tiffany's, he perfected a form that he also virtually invented: the taut, quasi-journalistic prose poem. If he was a sentimentalist, then it was a sincere sentimentality, heartfelt without sordidness. It has sometimes been suggested that perhaps because he was so obviously "different" himself, he wished to prove to the world that we are all more similar than different, and all, in our own ways, looking for exactly the same things. Nowhere was this more evident than in his most famous and disturbing book, *In Cold Blood*, which some people scorned for its non-censorious, supposedly sympathetic portrait of two young, cold-blooded killers. Capote himself was widely quoted as saying, "I'm an alcoholic. I'm a drug addict. I'm a homosexual. I'm a genius. Of course, I could be all four of these dubious things and still be a saint."

Capote once said that the most frightening things in his life were "betrayals, abandonments." Small wonder. His beautiful, narcissistic mother and his fun-loving father virtually abandoned him after his birth in 1924: a small son was an encumbrance to his mother's pursuit of *la dolce vita* and to his father's pursuit of one get-rich scheme after another. Little Truman was left to be raised in part by relatives in a small town in Alabama. (His mother ultimately committed suicide with an overdose of drugs — see MOTHERS, FASCINATING OF FAMOUS GAY MEN.)

Capote started writing when he was ten, and entered a local short-story contest with "Old Mrs. Busybody," a story that, prophetically, served up a local scandal as fiction. According to relatives, he started drinking when he was fifteen, and kept a suitcase full of whiskey, bourbon, and blackberry brandy in his bedroom closet.

He was only twenty when his first story was accepted for publication. A short time later, he won an O. Henry Prize for his story "Shut a Final Door." His self-described literary influences were Dickens, Colette, Willa Cather, Proust, and Guy de Maupassant.

He was a famous writer by the time he was twenty-three, having won national acclaim for *Other Voices, Other Rooms*. But the clear, commanding quality of his writing wasn't the only reason he attracted attention: the jacket of *Other Voices, Other Rooms* had a controversial photo of him lounging androgynously on a sofa, with a seductive, ethereal look on his beardless baby-face. "He looks as if he were dreamily contemplating some outrage against conventional morality," wrote one critic — and Capote probably was. Although he was in his early twenties, he looked no older than fifteen. He was blond and pretty, with sensitive, intelligent eyes. "I was a beautiful little boy," he later remarked, "and everyone had me — men, women, dogs, and fire hydrants. I did it with everybody." And everybody, it seemed, wanted to "do it" with him. He was invited everywhere, was fawned over by all of the flashy lions of the *beau monde*. He was befriended by movie stars and pursued by royalty; he was seen in public with the Kennedys, and was photographed dancing in nightclubs with Marilyn Monroe. In a sense, there was some of the absurd tragedy of "The Elephant Man" in all of this: for all of his beardless beauty and literary brilliance, Capote was still something of an oddity — small, lisping, devastatingly precocious, and exotic — and many people wanted to know him simply because so many other people wanted to know him. On the other hand, his charm was widely regarded as irresistible. Shortly after Capote's death, his long-time friend John Huston remarked, "He was one of the most charming people I ever knew. I venture to say that no one could resist Truman's charms when he chose to apply them."

Capote's celebrity increased with each successive publication: *The Grass Harp*, a novel proclaimed by one critic as "a parable of human freedom;" *The Muses Are Heard*, a colorful account of Capote's travels in the Soviet Union; *Breakfast at Tiffany's* (Capote, incidentally, had a strong aversion to the film version); as well as travel pieces and essays on such diverse topics as Spain, Greta Garbo, Brooklyn Heights, Colette, Marlon Brando, and paperweight collecting. And, of course, there was *In Cold Blood*, which he spent six years researching and which he described as "a non-fiction novel." One of his most beloved works was — and still is — *A Christmas Memory*, one of the most evocative and haunting Christmas stories in the English language.

His appearances on talk shows, where he provoked curiosity with his flamboyant airs and savage wit, helped to make his name a household word. And, while not exactly front-page material, his public feuds with people like Gore Vidal and Norman Mailer still created headlines. (Mailer, incidentally, denounced *In Cold Blood* as "a failure of the imagination" — even though, several years later, he wrote his own "non-fiction novel," *The Executioner's Song*, which, in some critics' minds, bore more than a passing resemblance to *In Cold Blood*.)

In 1966, with *In Cold Blood* still at the top of the bestseller lists, Capote organized one of the most talked about social spectacles of the sixties: a masked ball, deemed "the party of the century," at the Plaza Hotel in New York City. The event was considered so newsworthy that the entire guest list, of 540 people, was published in *The New York Times*. It was said that many people of note who *weren't* invited actually fled the country for a time to make it appear that they would have been invited had they been available. "You know," Capote said later, "I sit up at night aghast at the people I forgot to invite."

In a way, the masked ball at the Plaza Hotel was to coincide with Capote's own literary "masked ball" — the *roman a clef* of the century, *Answered Prayers*. The title came from a quote of St. Therese ("More tears are shed over answered prayers than unanswered ones"), and few books, especially ones that never completely materialized, have ever aroused more speculation, publicity, apprehension, and expectation. *Everyone*, only slightly veiled, was to make an appearance in it: from Maria Callas to Ayn Rand, from Nor-man Mailer to the Rockefellers, from Jackie Onassis to Elizabeth Taylor. It was to be a sweeping epic, his masterpiece, a kind of Wagnerian "Ring Cycle" of New York high society. "I'm constructing it in four parts," he told one reporter, "and actually it's like constructing a gun. There's the handle, the trigger, the barrel and, finally, the bullet. And when that bullet is fired from the gun, it's going to come out with a speed and power like you've never seen — WHAM!" Having seen not a word of it, people were already comparing it to Proust and Flaubert. Some celebrities were mortified that their innermost secrets would be revealed in print, and suddenly Truman was not as popular as he had once been. "I *told* them I was a writer," he said defensively.

He published a few chapters of it in *Esquire* magazine. But in 1977, he said he had stopped work on it, because he was "suffering a creative crisis and a personal one at the same time." The personal crisis, as the public was all too aware, involved drugs and alcohol. Dead drunk and incoherent, Capote had to be led from the podium while trying to give a commencement address. On television, a talk-show host was forced to cut him off in mid-sentence, when he started rambling insensibly. He found his way into the headlines half-a-dozen times: he collapsed in public; he was arrested for drunk driving; he was hospitalized. Of drugs and alcohol, he acknowledged, "I put them together like some sort of cocktail." Some of his problems were aggravated by illnesses that manifested themselves late in his life. He had epilepsy, and suffered from phlebitis. The epilepsy was treated with Dilantin, which contributed to his erratic behavior.

His last major publication was *Music for Chameleons* in 1980, an anthology of short pieces that Capote claimed represented a major transition for him as a writer. It was, he said, a new style for him: "severe, minimal." Some critics thought the book was as polished and vivid as anything he had previously written. But the press, who had come to regard him more and more as a kind of walking "media event," often focused on the book's gossip potential rather than its literary value. For example, Capote revealed in the book that he'd once had a sexual fling with Errol Flynn.

("Frankly," he wrote, "if it hadn't been Errol Flynn, I don't think I would've remembered it.") He wrote about the afternoon when Marilyn Monroe confessed to him she enjoyed dancing naked in front of a mirror because she liked to watch her breasts bounce up and down. And he talked about the people he despised most — Werner Erhardt, Billy Graham, Sammy Davis, Jr. — and the people he thought were "saints" — Pat Nixon, the deposed empress of Iran, et al. It sometimes seemed as if the only things people wanted anymore from Capote were the bitchy tidbits of gossip, the scathing put-downs, the laughable vocal gestures; and, in many ways, he fed on and encouraged their frivolous expectations.

On August 25th, 1984, Capote was found dead at the Bel-Air home of his close friend Joanne Carson, Johnny Carson's ex-wife. "He was my protector and my best friend," Carson told reporters over the telephone. "What am I going to do without him?" Capote had recently begun writing *Answered Prayers* again, and was reportedly working on it the night before his death.

In *Music for Chameleons*, he wrote: "So I began to think of what I would have inscribed on my tombstone — except that I shall never have one, because two very gifted fortune-tellers, one Haitian, the other an Indian revolutionary who lives in Moscow, have told me I will be lost at sea, though I don't know whether by accident or by choice ... Anyway, the first inscription I thought of was: AGAINST MY BETTER JUDGMENT. Then I thought of something far more characteristic. An excuse, a phrase I use about almost any commitment: I TRIED TO GET OUT OF IT, BUT I COULDN'T."

. "I believe in an afterlife," he later wrote. "That is to say, I'm sympathetic to the notion of reincarnation." If given a choice, he wanted to be reincarnated "as a bird — preferably a buzzard. A buzzard doesn't have to bother about his appearance or ability to beguile and please; he doesn't have to put on airs. Nobody's going to like him anyway; he is ugly, unwanted, unwelcome everywhere. There's a lot to be said for the sort of freedom that allows."

CARR, ROBERT (1590-1645), earl of Somerset and lover of King James I of England. Known for his handsome and

James I: Only one of many politicians who has worried what an old lover might say.

muscular good looks, Carr started out as a court page, but was soon advanced by James to the position of earl of Somerset. However, he became increasingly arrogant and soon alienated the king, who began to favor young George Villiers, the future duke of Buckingham, instead.

In 1615, when he was twenty-five, Carr was tried for complicity in the murder of a nobleman, Sir Thomas Overbury. James was so worried that in the course of the trial Carr might make some outburst revealing his homosexual relationship with the king, that two men were hired to flank Carr throughout the proceedings, ready to throw cloaks over him should he speak out on that subject. He didn't. Carr was eventually found guilty and sentenced to death for his part in Overbury's murder; however, James — by his own admission, a sentimental man, especially over a pretty face — had him pardoned, and allowed him to "retire into obscurity."

CASTLEHAVEN, SECOND EARL OF (1595-1633), English nobleman whose infamous trial and conviction for sodomy in 1633 was immediately used by some to "prove" that licentious behavior, especially homosexuality, was on the increase in England. Castlehaven was convicted of sodomizing one of his male servants, as well as enjoining his wife and daughter to have sex with other servants so that he could watch. The charges were considered so shocking that the entire indictment against him was drawn up in Latin. He was eventually beheaded for his "crimes." Two of his young male servants were also subsequently convicted of buggery, and were hanged.

CHAMP, 1960s physique magazine, whose stated purpose was "to awaken the youth of

Champ magazine of 1962: An early showcase for gay artists.

America to the importance and need of developing a sound body." The magazine was started by male photographer Bob Anthony, and began publishing in 1960. *Champ* not only featured the usual pictures of handsome young men in posing straps, but also showcased the original drawings of several early gay artists. These drawings often had absolutely no relevance to bodybuilding or physical fitness, but were among some of the first contemporary gay erotic art to be published on a wide scale.

An editorial in one of the magazine's first issues underlined its intentions: "In the young champs you see in this issue," wrote the editor, "notice the purity of muscular delineation, the admirable contours, perfect symmetry, pleasing proportions which glitter more than showy clothes or man-made garments — garments only distract from the true, aesthetic appreciation of true male physical perfection."

CHASE, CHEVY (b. 1943), U.S. comedian and entertainer. Appearing on Tom Snyder's late-night *Tomorrow* show in 1980, Chase lispingly mocked actor Cary Grant and remarked, with a limp-wristed hand gesture, "He really was a great physical comic, and I understand he was a homo. What a gal!" Grant immediately slapped Chase with a $10-million slander suit. However, Grant eventually let the matter drop. "I shouldn't have said that," Chase commented some time later, "because it's been such a pain in the neck."

CHEST, MALE — BEST IN THE WORLD. In 1985, *People* magazine asked a panel of "experts" — Harvey Fierstein, Arlene Dahl, former Playmate Barbi Benton, and female bodybuilder Lori Bowen-Rice

Richard Gere: He tied for third.

— to pick the best male chest in the world. Olympic gold medalist swimmer Steve Lundquist placed first. "That's the kind of chest to wrap new Ralph Lauren sheets around," Harvey Fierstein remarked. John Kennedy, Jr. placed second, and Sylvester Stallone, Richard Gere, and football player Herschel Walker all tied for third.

CIGARETTES, EFFECT ON ABILITY TO ACHIEVE AN ERECTION. A 1982 study by researchers at Florida State University found that smoking high-nicotine cigarettes had a significantly adverse effect on the ability of most males to achieve and maintain an erection; among other things, high-nicotine cigarettes noticeably lengthened the time it took test subjects to become fully aroused. However, no noticeable changes in sexual response were observed in men who smoked low-nicotine cigarettes. Other studies have found that cigarette smoking also adversely affects the amount of semen ejaculated during orgasm.

CINCINNATI GAY PRIDE WEEK PARTY, ATTACK ON (1979). On June 30, 1979, forty gay people arrived at a previously reserved city park swimming pool in Cincinnati, Ohio, for a private party celebrating the city's Gay Pride Week. They were greeted with signs reading, "Fags Enter At Your Own Risk" and "Queers Stay Away." The pool had been filled with trash. Fifty local residents began pelting the group with rocks, bottles, and boards while screaming "fag," "queer," and other epithets. Police arrived, watched the attack in progress for a few minutes, then quickly drove on. One would-be swimmer was forced to take refuge in his car, but was quickly surrounded; his vehicle was heavily damaged by the mob, and the man was res-cued only when a television camera crew arrived. Police never returned to the scene, despite persistent calls from some neighbors that a riot was in progress.

CIRCUMCISION, the operation of cutting away all or part of the foreskin of the penis. The origin of the practice is unknown, although some researchers believe it probably dates back to the Stone Age. The operation was widely performed, usually just before puberty, in ancient Egypt. It was also common in other parts of Africa, as well as among the Maya, the Aztecs, the Incas, and in some parts of Polynesia. In almost all cases, it was performed with a specially consecrated stone knife, usually as part of a ritual with broader religious and social significance.

Circumcision was practiced uniformly among the Jews, as a ritual of purification and as a sign of a covenant between them and God. Later, the early Christian church ruled that its members were not obligated one way or the other to circumcise their male children. However, in the early 130s, the Roman emperor Hadrian denounced circumcision as a mutilation of the genitals and ordered a universal ban on it.

By the mid-twentieth century, circumcision had become so widespread that, in 1966, researchers Masters and Johnson reported that of three hundred male volunteers participating in their sex studies, only thirty-five — or about eleven percent — were uncircumcised. The modern practice, in many U.S. hospitals, of automatically circumcising male infants, arose in part from statistical evidence — now challenged — that Hindus, who never perform circumcision, have the highest rate of cancer of the penis in the world, while among Jews cancer of the penis is virtually unknown. In 1971, the American Academy of Pediatrics concluded there were no valid medical indications for circumcision, and in recent years there has been a growing trend away from the practice. Current estimates are that about half, or slightly less than half, of the world's male population is circumcised.

The myth that a circumcised penis is more sexually sensitive than an uncircumcised one (or that an uncircumcised penis is more sexually sensitive than a circumcised one) is universally regarded by researchers and sexologists as just that: a myth. Despite that, however, one sexologist reported that some men seem "almost willing to go to war over the superiority of their foreskins, or lack of them." In some cases, circumcised adult males have gone so far as to seek surgical reparation of their foreskins. In other cases, men have sued their parents — unsuccessfully — for allowing circumcision to have been performed on them as infants.

One interesting footnote: much of the world's supply of interferon — a natural body protein thought to be useful in fighting certain kinds of cancer — is extracted from discarded foreskins collected at hospitals.

THE CITY AND THE PILLAR (1948), novel by Gore Vidal. Shortly after the book's publication, *The New York Times* refused to accept advertising for it, because of its theme of male homosexuality, and Orville Prescott, the *Times*'s daily reviewer, disgustedly announced he would never review a book by Vidal again. True to his word, Prescott refused to review any new book by Vidal for the next sixteen years. Numerous other publications also refused to advertise or review the novel. "As we all know," Vidal later said wryly, "I invented homosexuality in 1948 with *The City and the Pillar*."

COCKROACHES — CONVERSION TO HOMOSEXUALITY REPORTEDLY CAUSED BY PESTICIDE. In 1986, researchers in Gainesville, Florida, announced they had developed a pesticide that effectively controlled and eliminated cockroaches by changing the males to homosexuals. The new chemical, Gencor, reportedly caused significant hormone changes in male cockroaches, turning them into homosexuals and thus eliminating future generations of individual colonies. The researchers claimed the pesticide was close to one hundred percent effective within seven months of application.

A sixteenth-century codpiece: Did it leave too little — or too much — to the imagination?

CODPIECE (*fl.* 16th century), a flap, cover, or pouch for the male genitals, usually worn with tight-fitting breeches. Originally just a flap of clothing to make urination easier, the codpiece soon evolved into an oversized pouch for containing the penis and testicles. It became a fashionable and conspicuous part of men's wardrobes, and was eventually viewed as a status symbol. By the early 1500s, codpieces were so padded and spectacular as to often suggest a permanent erection. Wealthy men often wore theirs encrusted with precious gems. Military men and statesmen demanded that their portraits be painted with the codpiece conspicuous, so as to suggest great virility and prowess. However, fashions changed, and by 1580, codpieces were mocked as indecent and undignified. (For a time, the term "codpiece" also came to be used briefly as a synonym for the penis or the penis and testicles together.)

CONDOMS, or "rubbers." No one is completely certain when, or by whom, the condom was first invented. Some historians believe that a form of condom may have been used by the men of ancient Rome. (The word "condom" may in fact come from the Latin word *condus*, meaning "a collector.") Others maintain that the renowned Italian anatomist Gabriel Fallopius invented the condom in the wake of a sixteenth-century syphilis epidemic. And still others attribute the invention to a seventeenth-century English physician, Dr. Conton, who supposedly sought to prevent unwanted pregnancies among the mistresses of King Charles II.

Regardless of who actually developed them, condoms were probably first worn not so much for contraception, but as a means of preventing the spread of venereal disease. By the end of the seventeenth century, the Chinese and the Italians — Casanova among them — regularly used condoms made of linen and silk. In Asia, some condoms were made from tortoise shells and leather. Comfort was a major problem with the earliest condoms:

according to one seventeenth-century writer, the early condoms were so uncomfortable that they were "gossamer against infection, steel against love."

Eventually, condoms made of sheep gut were developed. Then, with the advent of vulcanized rubber in 1844, the latex condom was born. The first rubber condoms covered only the head of the penis, and were known by a variety of slang terms: "Russian thimbles," "English caps," "French letters," et al. The modern full-length condom dates back to design refinements made in the 1920s by American manufacturers.

CONNORS, DAVE (1945-1985), gay porn star, seen in such films as *One in a Billion, Dirt Bikes,* and *One, Two, Three.* Connors — who once described himself as "a little country boy out here in the big city trying to make good" — only started making gay porn films when he was in his thirties, but quickly gained recognition for what one video critic described as "an improbable endowment that looks like the product of some cock-obsessed special effects department in Hollywood." "I spent fifteen years of my life hiding from the fact that I'm heavily endowed," he told *Stallion* magazine in 1984, "and there have been times when I've had to be rude and obnoxious to people because of it ... People have used any ploy and every ploy to get me into bed." He added, "There aren't many people out there who are bigger — in twenty years of gay activity, I've met a handful who were as large as I am — but, only one who dwarfed me." Connors died from AIDS in 1985.

CRANE, CHERYL (b. 1944), lesbian daughter of film actress Lana Turner, and author of the book *Detour*, in which she detailed her life growing up in Hollywood as well as her ongoing nineteen-year relationship with another woman in San Francisco.

Crane first made national headlines in 1958 when, at the age of fourteen, she stabbed to death one of her mother's boyfriends, Johnny Stompanato — a former mafia bodyguard — after Stompanato started physically abusing Lana one night. "I'll cut you up and I'll get your daughter too!" Stompanato reportedly screamed at Lana. In an attempt to defend her mother, Cheryl grabbed a nine-inch butcher knife from the kitchen and stabbed Stompanato in the stomach; he died a short time later. After one of the most heavily publicized trials of a celebrity family in Hollywood history, a jury ruled the act was "justifiable homicide." Cheryl has also said that before that, she had been sexually abused by her mother's fourth husband, actor Lex Barker.

Cheryl first told her mother she was a lesbian when she was thirteen years old. "I said, 'Oh, mother, I'm in love.' And she said to me, 'Oh, how cute, what's his name?' I said, 'It's not a he, it's a she.' And instead of her going, 'Oh, my God!' you know, which a lot of parents would do, she said, 'Oh, darling, don't worry about that, you'll outgrow it.' And I didn't. So in my family, I guess with all the other traumas going on, it was a very minor detail.' She and her mother are now, in her words, "great friends." (See also *TURNER, LANA.*)

CRISWELL, former teacher and mortician turned professional psychic in the 1960s. Criswell became best known in 1968, when he published a volume of his predictions. At the time, he predicted that "perversion" would be widespread in the U.S. by the early 1970s and that by 1973 there would be completely homosexual cities; the U.S. Supreme Court, he said, would uphold the constitutional right of such cities to exist. He also predicted that sometime between May 1988 and March 1989, the U.S. Secretary of State, a closeted homosexual, would be caught in acts of "perversion." Criswell once asserted that 86% of his predictions are accurate, and also claimed to know the future of mankind through the year 1999, at which time, according to him, the planet Earth will leave its orbit and plummet into the sun.

DALLAS FILM CLASSIFICA-TION BOARD, founded in 1964, the only community film review board in the nation. The Board screens new motion pictures and adds its own set of rating letters — for violence, nudity, sexual content, and drugs — to films that have already been rated "R" by the Motion Picture Association of America. The Board's classification system carries the force of law: theater owners who do not prominently display the Board's classifications are subject to heavy fines.

In 1977, the Board added a new rating letter to its system of film classifications: "P" for perversion. The letter "P" is given to any film that deals with or touches on the subject of homosexuality. The film must then be advertised, both in the newspapers and at the box office, with the letter clearly and prominently visible. At the time the new rating letter was added, one board member told the press, "The Board is terrified that if a youngster sees anything resembling homosexuality on the screen, Dallas will suddenly turn into the Sodom and Gomorrah of the Southwest."

B. DALTON BOOKSELLERS, national chain of bookstores with over three hundred franchise locations. In 1978, B. Dalton's banned the display on bookshelves of both *The Joy of Gay Sex* and *The Joy of Lesbian Sex*. The ban came after police confiscated copies of the books from stores in Lexington, Kentucky, and Toronto, Canada. In Kentucky, the books were confiscated under a new anti-pornography law that forbade the display of any sexually oriented material in places that might be frequented by minors.

Dante: Hell has a special place for homosexuals.

DANTE (1265-1321), Italian poet. In 1312, Dante published *The Inferno*, the first volume of his masterpiece, *The Divine Comedy*. In it, he condemned homosexuals to the seventh circle of hell and prescribed their punishment: running for all eternity, and without ever having the right to stop, beneath a rain of fire over their naked bodies. Dante said that homosexuality inspired "not contempt, but sorrow" in him.

DAVIS, BETTE (b. 1908), U.S. actress. Davis became irritated when an interviewer asked her in 1982 if she thought she had such a large gay following because she was so "flamboyant." "Certainly, I've been one of the artists they admire very much," Davis replied. "It was always said that Judy Garland and I had the biggest following, but I don't think it's fair to say it's because I'm flamboyant. I'm *not* flamboyant. Joan Crawford was flamboyant."

DE HORY, ELMYR (1906-1976), international art forger who was gay. Perhaps the greatest art forger of the twentieth century, de Hory painted dozens of fake Picassos, Matisses, and Modiglianis, which for years deceived many of the best art dealers and museums in the world. The total market value of his counterfeit output was once estimated at over $60 million, and some of his forgeries are believed to still be hanging in reputable galleries and prestigious collections. Since his death, he has been acknowledged by art historians as "a genius of sorts."

His mother was from a

family of wealthy Jewish bankers; his father was a diplomat, the Hungarian ambassador to Turkey and several South American countries. Born in Budapest, de Hory began to show some artistic talent in his mid-teens and was sent to study at the prestigious Akademie Heimann in Munich, where he received rigorous training in drawing. From there, he went to Paris where he studied with the famous French painter Fernand Leger. De Hory had ambitions to become a renowned painter himself, but despite an occasional exhibition, his work was generally greeted with indifference, and he relied on a steady stream of money from his wealthy parents to make ends meet.

When the Nazis occupied Hungary, the de Hory family fortune was confiscated, and Elmyr suddenly found himself broke and struggling in Paris. Then one afternoon, a wealthy friend and art collector, Lady Malcolm Campbell, visited his studio and noticed what she thought was an unsigned Picasso hanging on the wall. It was actually a drawing that de Hory himself had dashed off in ten minutes one rainy afternoon when he was bored. De Hory did nothing to disabuse Lady Campbell of the work's authenticity, and when she offered him a large sum of money to buy it, he sold it to her. Later, after he learned she'd resold the work to a reputable London art dealer for a sizable profit, he immediately went to work and produced several more "Picassos," which he then sold to a dealer in Paris for $400. His career as an art forger had begun.

For the next two decades, de Hory produced paintings, drawings, and gouaches "by" Matisse, Renoir, Picasso, Modigliani, Dufy, and Braque. To sell his forgeries, he employed a variety of disguises and false identities. When word got around to "watch out for a suave fifty-year-old Hungarian with a monocle in his eye and a Matisse under his arm," de Hory simply changed his name and his appearance, and began marketing his wares in a new location.

He was once literally chased out of a gallery in Beverly Hills by a dealer who spotted the works as forgeries, but generally he managed to deceive experts around the world. He sold a forged Matisse to the Fogg Art Museum at Harvard University (only after years of painstaking investigation did they finally conclude it was a fake); another "Matisse" was praised internationally as a masterpiece, and sold for more than $60,000. De Hory was amazed when he would pick up an art book and discover one of his forgeries reproduced as an "exceptional" Picasso or Modigliani.

Eventually, de Hory linked up with two gay lovers, Fernand Legros and Real Lessard, who were Paris art dealers. Legros was a good-looking and unscrupulous huckster who persuaded de Hory to paint dozens of forgeries, which he and Lessard then peddled around the world for tens of thousands of dollars. Because the works often needed letters of authenticity before museums would buy them, they once sent one of de Hory's best Picassos to Picasso himself. Picasso, of course, didn't remember painting it; but then again, he didn't remember *not* painting it either. Finally, when he was told it had been valued at $100,000, the great artist remarked, "Well then, it must be real," and he authenticated the work.

The successful forgery ring was finally exposed in 1967 when a Texas millionaire, who had bought forty-four of the fakes, learned he was being defrauded and decided to press charges. (One journalist later called him, "the man who owns what may be the largest private collection of fake paintings in the world.") For nine years after that, de Hory managed to elude authorities and stay out of prison. Finally, in 1976, his arrest seemed imminent. Rather than face imprisonment at the age of seventy, the master of forgery committed suicide with a lethal overdose of barbituates.

DEAN, JOHN (b. 1938), Watergate conspirator and former presidential counsel to Richard Nixon. According to widely published reports at the time, Dean decided to help prosecutors in the Watergate investigation because he was terrified of being raped if he were sent to prison. Dean worried that his trim body and boyish looks would make him a prime target for prison rape.

"DEAR ABBY" AND "ANN LANDERS," daily syndicated advice columns written by Abigail Van Buren and Ann Landers, respectively, and carried by different newspaper syndicates. Ann Landers started her column in October 1955; Abigail Van Buren followed with an advice column of her own in January 1956. The two women are sisters, and between them, "Abby" has always been more openly sympathetic towards gay people. In fact, she has received awards for her contributions to the general public's understanding of gay men and lesbians.

A brief sampling of some of the more interesting items that have run in their columns through the years:

DEAR ANN (1981): A woman wrote for advice after discovering her 68-year-old husband in a storage room having sex with a young homosexual employee. She and her husband were only four months away from their fiftieth wedding anniversary. She'd had no previous inkling of her husband's homosexual interests. What should she do?

ANN'S REPLY: "Fifty years together is a long time — and you said they were good years." She advised the woman to tell her husband what she had seen, and then to seek counseling together.

DEAR ANN (1984): A mother wrote for advice about her thirteen-year-old son. He enjoyed dressing up in silk and satin garments and high-heeled shoes, and had recently cut up an old pair of blue jeans and re-tailored them into a denim miniskirt. "The boy does not look feminine," the mother wrote. "I see no signs of homosexuality." How should she handle the situation?

ANN'S REPLY: The boy should undergo a psychiatric evaluation to determine the underlying causes of his cross-dressing. Ann added, however, that according to experts, "cross-dressers are not usually homosexual, nor do they present a danger to society. Anguish, perhaps, but not danger."

DEAR ABBY (1987): A letter writer was going to stay with a gay friend during an upcoming week's vacation in San Francisco. Her son warned her she could contract AIDS through saliva and casual contact. Should she undergo an AIDS antibody test when she returned?

ABBY'S REPLY: "Your son is mistaken." Abby then gave her readers a brief lecture on how one can and cannot contract AIDS.

DEAR ABBY (1985): A gay man in Ohio wrote to complain that all of the female secretaries in his office were chasing after him — one even groped him —

despite the fact he was completely open about his homosexuality. What was the best way to handle the situation? He signed his letter, "Reluctant Sex Object in Ohio."

ABBY'S REPLY: Abby had no advice for the man, except to remind him that, "there is nothing more tempting than forbidden fruit."

DEAR ANN (1976): A reader asked if Ann supported the American Psychiatric Association's decision to drop homosexuality from its list of mental illnesses.

ANN'S REPLY: While she supported the idea of civil rights for gay people, she still believed that homosexuals and lesbians "suffer from a severe personality disorder." Granted, she said, "some are sicker than others, but sick they are and all the fancy rhetoric of the American Psychiatric Association will not change it."

DEAR ABBY (1983): A nineteen-year-old college student wrote to refute some psychotherapists' claims that gay men "choose" to be gay. "I have been attracted to males ever since fifth grade," he wrote, "and nowhere in my sexual development do I recall 'choosing' to like men instead of women.

Mine is a life of shame, loneliness, depression, and frustration, and believe me, Abby, I did not choose it."

ABBY'S REPLY: "I believe you, and I know that you speak for many, but you need not continue in a life of loneliness, depression, and frustration. Homosexual counseling is available, and I recommend it. You desperately need to accept yourself and respect yourself. And you are as entitled to happiness and a full life as any other human being. God bless." (In a similar reply a few years earlier, Abby had written that homosexuality was "a matter of one's disposition and hormonal makeup. This is a natural way for them to go. One doesn't choose homosexuality; it chooses them.")

DEAR ANN (1987): Two teenage brothers from Grand Rapids, Michigan, told Ann they didn't wear any underwear. Their mother told them it was unhealthy, their father called it indecent. Who was right — they or their parents?

ANN'S REPLY: "I say, wear underwear in the interest of personal hygiene."

DEAR ABBY (1974): A correspondent asked if Damon and Pythias, of ancient Greek legend, were gay. (According to the legend, the two were faithful Syracusan friends. When Pythias, condemned to death, was temporarily freed to go home and arrange his affairs before the execution, Damon stayed in prison in his place to assure his return. When Pythias came back, the tyrant Dionysius was so impressed with their loyalty to one another that he pardoned him.)

ABBY'S REPLY: She consulted twelve university experts for their opinions. Some said yes, Damon and Pythias were gay; some said no. The head of the University of Chicago's English Department passed on one colleague's comment: "I think Damon was okay, but I'm not so sure about Pythias."

DEAR ANN (1983): A 27-year-old gay man wrote to tell Ann that S&M was "sick, sick, sick." He related the story of one of his best friends who "was mixed up with it": the friend "deteriorated," underwent a major personality change, and "is still looking for a better trip and is becoming increasingly weird and miserable."

ANN'S REPLY: "Thanks for writing to inform the unsophisticated, which most of us are."

DEAR ANN (1989): A Rochester, New York, woman wrote to say how "infuriated" she was over all the publicity the AIDS memorial quilt was receiving. Her 44-year-old brother had just recently died of cancer. "There was no quilt for him," she wrote. "AIDS is avoidable," she added. "Most cancer is not." She was angry that many people with AIDS — "homosexuals who are promiscuous and reckless" — seemed to be treated like national heroes.

ANN'S REPLY: "I can understand your feelings, but please don't let your grief blind you to the facts. The reason AIDS has been given so much publicity is because it is a new disease for which there is no cure, while the cure rate for some types of cancer is fifty percent." Ann pointed out that unless a cure or a vaccine for AIDS is found soon, "it could bankrupt the health care system in this country."

DEATH IN THE AFTERNOON (1932), non-fiction study of bullfighting by author Ernest Hemingway. In a few brief lines, Hemingway returned to one of his most obsessive themes — homosexuality — and skewered many famous homosexuals. He condemned what he called, "the prissy exhibitionistic, aunt-like, withered old maid moral arrogance of a Gide; the lazy, conceited debauchery of a Wilde who betrayed a generation; the nasty, sentimental pawing of humanity of a Whitman" (See also *THE SUN ALSO RISES*.)

DECRIMINALIZATION OF HOMOSEXUALITY — EARLY CALL FOR IN U.S. In 1865, *The Mysteries of Man; or, Esoteric Anthropology*, a general sex education guide, was published in New York City. The book was notable for a paragraph on homosexuality, in which the author made an unusually progressive call — especially for 1865 — for the decriminalization of homosexual acts between consenting adults. "Among the crimes punished with death under the Mosaic law," he wrote, "were bestiality, sodomy, and incest. All are more or less unnatural, but I see no good reason for continuing the penalty, or for making them in any way the subjects of human retribution. Under the Mosaic dispensation there were, I believe, fourteen offenses punished with death. Many of these are not now reckoned offenses, and for most of the others the punishment is modified. I see no reason for punishing a man for an act which begins and ends with himself, or with a consenting party. Moreover, such laws are useless, as not one case in a thousand, from its very nature, can ever be brought to justice."

French actor Alain Delon

DELON, ALAIN (b. 1935), enormously good-looking French actor first discovered at the 1957 Cannes Film Festival, when he was twenty-two, and best known for his roles in such films as Luchino Visconti's *Rocco and His Brothers* and *The Leopard*, and Michelangelo Antonioni's *Eclipse*. The product of a broken home, Delon was expelled from numerous Catholic schools before enlisting in the French Navy, at the age of seventeen, and serving as a parachutist in Indochina. Five years later, he made his film debut. A brief stay in Hollywood, in the mid-1960s, resulted in his appearance in a handful of U.S. films, including *The Yellow Rolls-Royce* and a Dean Martin comedy-western, *Texas Across the River.*

In 1984, a French biography of the star alleged that he was not only intimately connected with the Marseilles underworld, but that he was also bisexual. Despite Delon's attempts to get an injunction against the book, its first printing sold out in a matter of weeks.

DIAPERS, AS SEXUAL FETISH FOR GAY MEN. For those gay men who are sexually aroused by diapers, plastic or rubber panties, wet pants, bedwetting, infantilism, little-boy fantasies, humiliation, spanking, discipline, "water sports," and more, there is an international club, DPF ("The Diaper Pail Fraternity"), in Sausalito, California. The club was founded in 1980 as a way for like-minded individuals to meet, correspond, and exchange information on their fantasies and fetishes. DPF publishes a newsletter and membership roster, and also acts as a clearinghouse for tapes, videos, erotic stories, and various products — including bedwetter pants, training panties, and diapers — related to the fetish interests of its members. Information is available by writing to Suite 164, 3020 Bridgeway, Sausalito, California 94965.

DIARIES, PRIVATE — GAY MEN WHO KEPT.

Joe Orton (1933-1967), English playwright. Orton began keeping a diary on December 20, 1966 and continued making entries until eight days before he was beaten to death with a hammer by his lover, Kenneth Halliwell, on August 9, 1967. The diary detailed many of his sexual escapades (thirty-eight in all) with public restroom habitués, willing young Moroccan boys — "Nothing ages one more than the sight of one's juniors, if they're beautiful in the nude" — and various strangers, including an Irishman right after the funeral of Orton's mother in late December 1966 ("He had a very tight arse. A Catholic upbringing, I suspect"). Aside from describing Orton's numerous sexual adventures, the eight-month-long diary also chronicled his sudden literary fame in London, as well as his disintegrating relationship with Halliwell. Orton was also fond of including bits of funny conversation he'd overheard on the buses or the streets, and absurdly funny scenes of everyday life he'd witnessed around him. The diary was published in 1986.

Saki (1870-1916), British writer. Born Hector Hugh Munro. One of the acknowledged masters of the short story, Saki began keeping a diary in January 1904, after he'd been given a tiny blank notebook — measuring only one inch wide by three inches long — by a friend. Saki wrote his minute diary entries in purple ink, and made various brief notations about the weather, what stories had been sent to which publications, and how much he was being paid for his work. The margins of the diary were also filled with enigmatic, short squiggles, which, it has since been deduced, were part of a code denoting his various sexual encounters. According to his biographer, A.J. Langguth, "Hector's average in his best months was an encounter every second day; when he was busy or traveling, every third day."

James Whale (1896-1957), Hollywood film director. According to Kenneth Anger, in *Hollywood Babylon II*, Whale — director of *Frankenstein* and *The Bride of Frankenstein* — enjoyed reading extracts from his explicitly homoerotic diary to guests lounging around his pool. Not all of the guests, says Anger, were amused.

Noel Coward (1899-1973), English playwright, actor, and composer. Coward began keeping a diary in 1941, and continued until December 31, 1969. At first, the entries consisted of mere terse descriptions of his daily activities: "Lunched at the White House," "Long gossip with Mrs. Churchill about Sarah and Vic," "My cold is worse and the weather is vile." With time, the entries grew longer and more energetic, at times full of soul-searching about his career and his advancing age. However, Coward meticulously kept any mention of his own romantic or sexual involvements out of its pages, although he did note with interest the publication of the Wolfenden Report on homosexuality in 1957, and the eventual decriminalization of homosexual acts in England.

Ludwig Wittgenstein (1889-1951), Austrian-English philosopher. Wittgenstein noted many of his homosexual fantasies and activities in his diary, all in a secret code of his own devising. The code was deciphered shortly after his death. Only a small part of the diary has survived: just a year before his death, Wittgenstein ordered the destruction of all but two of its volumes.

Sir Roger Casement (1864-1916), British public servant who gained renown as a martyr in the revolt against British rule in Ireland. After attempting to obtain German aid for the 1916 Irish rebellion, Casement was sentenced by the British to be hanged for treason. Although Casement had engaged in some treasonous activities against the British, the actual charges against him were considered to be trumped-up, the evidence was flimsy, and there were calls from all around the world — including from U.S. President Woodrow Wilson — for his reprieve. To squelch the demands for clemency, the British government typed up and secretly circulated within the international community extracts from Casement's explicitly homoerotic diaries. Some typical entries: "Steward showed enormous exposure after dinner — stiff down left thigh. I wanted awfully," and "I to meet enormous at 9. Will suck and take too," and "Huge tram inspector ... Stiff as sword and thick and long." The British gambit worked: calls for Casement's reprieve stopped soon after, and he was hanged on August 3, 1916.

Denton Welch (1915-1948), English author. "What do these little bits amount to?" Welch wrote of his diary just a year before his death. "Nothing to anyone else but me, of course; but I write them down just because they bring for a moment the hint of comfort that is always slipping away." When he was twenty, Welch was involved in a near-fatal car accident that left him crippled and, for much of the rest of his life, bedridden. In the years that followed, he wrote short stories and novels, and in 1942 he began his diary. "Denton Welch," William Burroughs once wrote, "makes the reader aware of the magic that is right under his eyes, for most of the experiences he describes are of a commonplace variety: a walk, a tea ... rain on a river, a visit to an antiques store, a picture on a biscuit tin..." Though the diary makes no direct reference to Welch's homosexuality, it does contain numerous homoerotic references, such as this description of a muscular teenage boy working in a cornfield: "The boy looked into me with that deep, sulky, suspicious, adolescent look. His biceps and shoulders were like silky balls melting together. How I longed to be strong and lusty." Welch died in 1948 at the age of thirty-three. His journals were published by Dutton in 1984.

Jean Cocteau (1889-1963), French artist, writer, and filmmaker. The existence of Cocteau's diary, covering the last thirteen years of his life, was kept secret until 1983, when the first volume was published in France. Cocteau began the diary July 16, 1951; it ended the year of his death. The diary contains Cocteau's impressions on art, Mediterranean landscapes, America, and even flying saucers, as well as his meditations on dreams, existentialism, semantics, and fame. Perhaps surprisingly, his homosexuality is never once mentioned or even alluded to.

Andre Gide (1869-1951), French author. Considered by many to be the premiere diarist in literary history, Gide began his *Journal* in 1889, when he was twenty, and published its last volume in 1950, when he was eighty-one. Comprising more than one million words, the diaries are a record of his life experiences, his impressions and emotions, his search for God, his moral crises, and his search for meaning in a world that seemed to him increasingly consumed by conformity and machines — all stretching over a period of some sixty years. According to one critic, "In its depth of self-knowledge, its humanity, and its perfection of style, his *Journal* is Gide's lasting memorial." "Rousseau says that he wrote his *Confessions* because he believed he was unique," Gide once said. "I am writing mine for exactly the opposite reasons, and because I know that a great many will recognize themselves in them."

Andy Warhol (1928-1987), U.S. artist. Warhol began keeping a diary in late 1976, initially to keep track of his business expenses for the IRS. It soon evolved into a breezy chronicle of his life amid New York's demimonde, full of gossip (Bianca Jagger passing her panties around to be sniffed at a dinner for the Metropolitan Museum), and conversations ("I learned," Warhol once said, "that you actually have more power when you shut up"), and endless invitations ("Got the invitation to President Carter's inaugural. It was addressed to 'Mr. and Mrs. Andy Warhol.' Don't you love it?"). Warhol continued to make entries in the diary until his death from a heart attack in 1987. The mammoth, 800-page work was published in 1989.

DICKINSON, EMILY — CENSORING OF PERSONAL LETTERS. Dickinson's letters to her future sister-in-law, Susan Gilbert, were heavily bowdlerized for publication, first in 1924 and then again in 1932, out of fear that posterity would interpret the relationship between the two women as having been lesbian in nature. Lines such as "Be my own again, and kiss me as you used to," and "The expectation once more to see your face again makes me feel hot and feverish, and my heart beats so fast," were routinely deleted by the book's editor, Martha Dickinson Bianchi, Susan Gilbert's own daughter and Emily Dickinson's niece. Because of the passionate nature of one communication, Bianchi reduced an eighteen-line letter to a brief, inconspicuous three-line note.

DILDOES. Dildoes were commonly used not only in ancient Egypt but in ancient Greece as well. The Greek models — called *olisbos* — were made from wood or padded leather, and had to be frequently oiled (usually with olive oil) before use. The finest models apparently came from the port city of Miletus, and there were complaints during times of shortages, as reflected in Aristophanes's play *Lysistrata*, where one woman wails to another, "There isn't one to be seen these days to console us poor grass widows!"

In ancient China, dildoes were made of glass or ivory, often with a syringe-like device inside that allowed warm milk or other sensuous substances to be squirted from the tip. However, the Chinese sex manuals of the time warned against overenthusiastic use of dildoes, since their hard surfaces might cause damage to delicate tissues.

In medieval times, one particular plant called the "Cantonese groin" was known to be used as a dildo. The plant was phallus-shaped, and when soaked in hot water it expanded and hardened into a perfect dildo. The development of modern rubber products in the late nineteenth century led of course to the current, and often ingenious, models of dildoes and buttplugs. A landmark federal decision in 1965 — involving a company that sold various sex devices and so-called "marital aids" through the mail — found no grounds for classifying dildoes as either obscene or illegal.

DILDO, EXECUTION FOR USE OF. On a journey through Italy in 1580, French author Michel de Montaigne recorded in his diary the recent hanging execution of a lesbian. She had been condemned for disguising herself as a man, marrying another woman, and using a dildo during intercourse. It was the use of the dildo more than anything that probably accounted for her execution; for a woman to use a dildo in what was seen as simulated heterosexual intercourse was regarded as a grave crime, often punishable by death throughout Europe.

DISCLAIMERS ABOUT HOMOSEXUALITY IN GAYTHEMED MOVIES. In a 1962 interview about his film *The Children's Hour* (based on Lillian Hellman's play), director William Wyler bristled at suggestions the film had anything to do with homosexuality and asserted, "*The Children's Hour* is not about lesbianism. It's about the power of lies to destroy people's lives." Other similar disclaimers through the years have included:

• "*Consenting Adult* is not so much about homosexuality: it's about unconditional love." (Actress Marlo Thomas, 1985)

• "*Personal Best* is not about lesbianism. To me the story is about innocence, purity, growing up." (Director Robert Towne, 1982)

• "*Making Love* is not simply about homosexuality. It is about how people can be split apart by forces beyond their control." (Publicity notes for the film, 1982)

• "*Windows* is not about homosexuality — it's about insanity." (Director Gordon Willis, 1979)

Rex Harrison and Richard Burton in *Staircase* (1969): Yet another movie *not* about homosexuality.

• "*Staircase* is not about homosexuality — it's about loneliness and human failure." (Actor Rex Harrison, 1971)

• "*The Boys in the Band* is not about homosexuality. It's about human problems." (Director William Friedkin, 1970)

• "*The Sergeant* is not about homosexuality. It's about loneliness." (Actor Rod Steiger, 1968)

• And actor Gene Barry, in 1985, discussing the musical version of *La Cage aux Folles*: "I have nothing against gays, but I don't think that is what our musical is really all about. It's the story of a loving family man who is trying to keep his family together."

A DISCOURSE ON THE WORSHIP OF PRIAPUS, controversial book, first published in 1786, by English author Richard Payne Knight. In it, Knight argued that phallic worship was an underlying motivation in many social, artistic, and architectural endeavors, and claimed that church spires, bell towers, chimneys, and even haystacks were all phallic symbols. Knight had braced himself for some controversy when the book was published; but the actual outpouring of rage and condemnation was so overwhelming, he quickly tried to buy up and suppress as many copies of it as possible.

DOUGLAS, LORD ALFRED (1870-1945), English poet, best remembered as the young lover of Oscar Wilde. By 1911 — eleven years after Wilde's death — Douglas had become a self-proclaimed convert to both Catholicism and heterosexuality. He eventually married (the marriage was a disaster and nearly ended in divorce), and fathered a child (the boy grew up with severe emotional problems and had to be institutionalized), and he consistently denounced his former life with Wilde. The denunciations reached a kind of peak when, testifying at a libel trial in 1918, Douglas publicly condemned Wilde as "the greatest force for evil that has appeared in Europe during the last 350 years."

The outspoken denunciations — and Douglas's assertions that he had completely turned his back on homosexuality — continued unabated until his death. In 1921, for example, the London *Evening News* prematurely announced his death and ran an obituary accusing him of "degeneracy." The obituary added that Douglas would be remembered only "by the scandals and the quarrels in which he involved himself." Douglas sued the paper for libel, and during the course of the three-day trial he renounced his earlier relationship with Wilde as "disgraceful," "idiotic," "horrible," and "wicked." "For many years I have conducted a regular campaign against that form of vice in every possible way," he added. Douglas brought forth numerous witnesses, including a Catholic bishop, to confirm that he now led a highly moral life and had wholeheartedly embraced Catholicism.

Despite the denunciations, however, there is considerable evidence that Douglas continued to have occasional homosexual relationships throughout his adult life. For example, in an interview in 1978, author Sam Steward recalled having had sex with Douglas in 1937, when Douglas was sixty-seven.

DOUGLAS, CHAD (b. 1954), gay porn star, sometimes referred to as "the nastiest man in porn" because of his tough, aggressive "top-man" only image. Douglas first got into the business after being spotted in a bar in Los Angeles by a photographer for *Advocate Men*. After he appeared in a layout in the magazine, he was approached by a gay porn producer about doing films. His first movie was *Below the Belt*, followed by, among others, *Splash Shot II*. Discussing his "hard-assed" image in films, Douglas told *Stallion* magazine in 1987, "In *all* the films, I *am* myself! My character does not change ... and whether people like that or not is their problem ... I know some people will eat dog food out of a dish while getting fucked and they think that's lovely and *avant garde* — but, that's not me."

DOUGLAS, JOHN SHOLTO (1844-1900), ninth marquess of Queensberry, father of Lord Alfred Douglas, and formulator of the once-standard marquess of Queensberry rules of boxing. He detested male homosexuals, as well as effeminate or artistic men of any sort, and often accused men he did not like — including his own father-in-law — of being gay. He became almost uncontrollably obsessed with the rela-tionship between his son and Oscar Wilde, and, with various prizefighter friends at his side, stalked the two throughout London and the English countryside, threatening to kill restaurant owners and hotel managers who served them. He frequently tried to disrupt performances of Wilde's plays — on the opening night of *The Importance of Being Earnest*, Wilde was obliged to hire twenty policemen to protect himself and the theater — and he later employed a gang of thugs to follow and intimidate Wilde everywhere he went. After nearly two years of this harassment, the marquess finally openly accused Wilde of being a "somdomite" [sic] — the infamous accusation that eventually led to Wilde's downfall and imprisonment.

DRAG, A BRIEF HISTORY OF.

600 B.C.: The Athenian statesman Solon finally defeated the Megarian army, after a long fruitless war. Solon's winning strategy: he disguised his troops as women and had them dance and play on a beach where the Megarian forces were about to land. Lulled into a false sense of security, the Megarians approached with their defenses down, and were defeated.

A.D. 41: The Roman emperor Caligula was assassinated. During his reign, he often wore women's clothing and sometimes went out in public dressed as Venus, the Goddess of Love. He was so infuriated by the profusion of hair all over his body that he made it a crime, punishable by death, for anyone to look down on him from above, lest they see the hair on his chest. It was also a crime to use the word "goat" in his presence.

218: A thirteen-year-old boy, Elagabalus, was proclaimed emperor of Rome. During his brief, four-year reign, he rejected traditional masculine dress and instead favored fine, flowing silks, heavy makeup, and jewel-encrusted slippers. Dressed in a wig and female attire, he sometimes practiced prostitution in the local taverns and brothels. In the most famous speech of his reign, he dressed as a woman, assembled together the prostitutes of Rome, and lectured them on the merits of the various positions for sexual intercourse. Like most of his predecessors, he was eventually assassi-

nated. His body was dumped in the sewers.

1574: Henry III became king of France. As king, he often appeared in public arrayed in extremely showy female attire, complete with extravagant jewelry. His taste in clothes, among other things, was so exorbitant that he nearly bankrupted the French treasury.

1632: The practice of using men to play women's roles on stage was so completely accepted at this time that when a French acting troupe, with real women actresses, performed in England, the women were jeered by the audience, pelted with apples, and driven from the stage.

1644: Francoise Timoleon de Choisy, later known as the Abbe de Choisy, was born. Because his mother originally wanted a daughter, he was raised as a girl: in fact, his mother put him in such constrictive corsets that his physique eventually developed a permanently feminine contour. After his mother's death, he settled in the provinces, where he continued to live as a woman; his neighbors all believed he was a young widow.

Later, he achieved fame after inheriting the Abbe de Saint Seine: he accepted his position as abbot and wore traditional, masculine garb during the day, but at night he quite openly reverted to dresses and wigs again. Throughout this lifelong charade, he always tried to affect a pale, effeminate appearance by having himself bled regularly and by sleeping with his arms locked unnaturally over his head. He died in 1724, at the age of eighty.

1701: Philippe, duke of Orleans, died in France. The younger brother of King Louis XIV, he was unabashed about both his homosexuality and his transvestism. One contemporary, the writer Saint-Simon, described him as "a little pot-bellied man, mounted on high heels. He always dressed as a woman and was covered with rings, bracelets, and precious stones everywhere. He wore a long wig, black and powdered, and ribbons wherever they could be placed." A distinguished and courageous soldier, Philippe also wore ribbons and jewelry into battle, but disdained hats because they mussed his hair. According to his soldiers, "He was more afraid of the sun, or the black smoke of gunpowder, than he was of musket bullets."

1839: Dressed in an exaggerated tutu and extravagant makeup, performer William Mitchell became famous in the U.S. for his burlesque ballet, "La Mosquito" — a drag parody of renowned ballerina Fanny Elssler, who was widely admired for her dance "La Tarantula."

1839: An extremely popular French erotic novel of the day, *Gynecocracy*, told the story of young, virile Julian Robinson, who — as a punishment for having seduced a female cousin — was forced to dress as a woman for the rest of his life and allow himself to be used sexually by other men, and by women. The book, written in three volumes, was highly sadomasochistic in tone: dubbed "Julia" by his tormentors, Julian was forced to undergo genital torture, bondage, anal rape, and the use of chastity devices, and finally concluded by the novel's end, "A man exists for something else than for procreation."

c. 1900: Drug-runner Paul La Baron, wanted by police for peddling narcotics, was found living as "Mrs. Esther Egan" in a San Francisco hotel. La Baron's deception was uncovered by another woman at the hotel who noticed that "Mrs. Egan"'s calves were too muscular.

1903: A fire broke out at Chicago's Iroquois Theater, and within eight minutes, more than six hundred people were killed. When the tragedy struck, vaudeville performer Eddie Foy was backstage getting ready for his burlesque performance as "Sister Anne." Hearing the pandemonium outside his dressing room, he rushed to the stage and, still dressed in his petticoats, helped save numerous women and children from the flames. Eyewitnesses later reported that Foy, his drag outfit covered in soot, was one of the last people to leave the burning theater alive.

1906: F. Scott Fitzgerald, in college, created a stir when he donned an elegant gown and attended a University of Minnesota dance on the arm of his close friend, Gus Schurmeier. Later, a photograph of Fitzgerald dressed in full drag for a college review prompted a local burlesque house to offer him a full-time job as a professional female impersonator.

1910: Noted sexologist Magnus Hirschfeld became the first writer to make a proper distinction between homosexuality and transvestism. He pointed out that many heterosexual men — married and with children — enjoy dressing in women's clothing. It was Hirschfeld, himself both a homosexual and a transvestite, who coined the word "transvestism."

1912: The *Titanic* slid to a watery grave in the north Atlantic. It was later claimed that some men escaped death on the sinking ship by disguising themselves as women and slipping into the lifeboats unnoticed.

1915: Charlie Chaplin, *sans* moustache, wrote, directed, and starred in *A Woman*, one of several films in which he appeared in drag. In the film, Chaplin spent much of his time on-screen as a woman, and had several scenes in which he flirted with an amorous, 250-pound man. "Chaplin's imitations of women are extremely convincing," wrote one critic, "because of his small stature and the delicacy and beauty of his features." In an earlier film, *The Masquerader* (which presaged Dustin Hoffman's 1982 hit, *Tootsie*), Chaplin starred as an out-of-work actor who, in

The inimitable Divine. (1946-1988): He got his start playing Jackie Kennedy.

desperation, disguises himself as a woman to win new roles.

1926: The apparent hanging-murder of a French government official, Raphael de la Chapelle, led French police to search for a mysterious Madame Cartier, who lived with Chapelle and who recently vanished. Mme. Cartier, a prime suspect in the murder, was remembered by neighbors for her wit, elegance, and beauty. Eventually, however, police investigators discovered that Mme. Cartier and de la Chapelle were one and the same person, and that dressed in drag as Mme. Cartier every night, Chapelle frequented Paris's gay nightclubs. Chapelle's murder remained unsolved, but there was growing suspicion that it was a suicide.

1955: Charles Pierce premiered his drag show at the Echo Club in Miami Beach. Because full drag was still against the law, he was forced to wear his female costumes over his trousers. Commenting, more than thirty years later, on the women he chose to impersonate throughout his career — Davis, Crawford, Bankhead, Hepburn, et al. — Pierce quipped, "These women are from a certain era, and they're imitable. Who are you going to imitate today — Molly Ringwald?"

1968: Divine (real name: Harris Glenn Milstead) made his film debut, portraying Jackie Kennedy, in *Eat Your Makeup*, a low-budget movie directed by his high-school friend, John Waters. Divine later said of himself, "I'm just another man in a dress."

Film star Albert Dekker: He also starred in *Strange Cargo, Seven Sinners,* and *The Pretender.*

1968: Film star Albert Dekker, best known for his title role in the 1940 horror film *Dr. Cyclops,* hanged himself in the bathroom of his Hollywood apartment. His body was found clothed in women's lingerie and was covered with obscenities he had scrawled all over himself with red lipstick.

1969: Appearing on Johnny Carson's *Tonight Show*, Truman Capote disparaged Jacqueline Susann, author of Valley of the Dolls, as looking just "like a truck driver in drag." The remark ignited howls of laughter from the studio audience — and sent Susann to her lawyer, Louis Nizer, to file a suit for libel. Although Susann eventually decided to let the matter drop, Capote continued on the offensive: he told audiences that she didn't sue him because he'd planned to bring a truck driver into court, put him in a dress, and let the jury see for themselves just exactly how much Susann did indeed look like a truck driver in drag.

1981: Former Iranian President Bani Sadr, dismissed from power by Khomeini's ruling Islamic party, fled Iran by disguising himself as a woman and slipping out of the country undetected. He later settled, in exile, in France.

1982: Three of the Academy Awards' best acting nomina-

John Lithgow as Roberta, the football player turned transsexual, in *The World According to Garp.*

tions were for men who performed at least part of their roles in drag: Dustin Hoffman in *Tootsie*, Robert Preston in *Victor/Victoria*, and John Lithgow in *The World According to Garp.*

1984: Asked in an interview how a nice boy from Brooklyn became a drag queen, actor and playwright Harvey Fierstein replied, "You get a nice dress, shoes to match, and a purse. If you pick the right gloves, you're a drag queen."

1988: To dramatize the arbitrariness of sex roles in modern American society, talk-show host Phil Donahue conducted an entire program while wearing a dress.

1988: In an obituary for Divine — who died March 7, 1988 — *Rolling Stone* magazine reported, "The pantheon of Hollywood's great divas could be painted in just a few vivid images: Greta Garbo wilting beatifically as Camille; Vivien Leigh flouncing defiantly around Tara; Gloria Swanson maniacally getting ready for her close-up; and, of course, Divine, the fat, fabulous drag queen eating a heaping lump of doggie-doo."

"THE DREADNOUGHT HOAX"
(1910), notorious English hoax perpetrated on the British Navy by Virginia Woolf, her brother Adrian, gay post-Impressionistic painter Duncan Grant, and three fellow conspirators. Under the direction of master hoaxer Horace de Vere Cole — a wealthy young dilettante infamous for his often lavish practical jokes — the group pretended to be a retinue of visiting Abyssinian royalty on an official state tour of Great Britain. For the occasion, Grant, Woolf, and two of the others wore convincing black face, and then donned beards, moustaches, turbans, jewelry, and other exotic Oriental garb. A forged telegram, claiming to be from the British Foreign Office, was then sent to the captain of the H.M.S. *Dreadnought*, flagship of the British Navy, anchored at Weymouth port, in southern England. The telegram informed the *Dreadnought* that the emperor of Abyssinia and three of his princes were on their way to inspect the ship and that the captain was to "kindly make all arrangements to receive them."

Not only did the group of impostors receive a tour of the *Dreadnought*, but they were accorded a full military reception, including red carpet, military band, and honor guard. Out of fear their accents would give them away (and out of Woolf's fear especially that she would be discovered to be a woman), the group limited themselves to muttering an occasional "chuck-a-choi, chuck-a-choi" or "bunga, bunga," and nodded their heads in approval at everything; they pretended to be especially excited by the ship's electric light bulbs and its heavy artillery. Woolf's brother Adrian acted as their official translator; his "Abyssinian" consisted of mispronounced Homer and Virgil mixed in with a few words of Swahili. The hoax, it turned out, was even more daring because, unbeknownst to Woolf and the others when they boarded the ship, the *Dreadnought*'s captain was a one-time acquaintance of one of the conspirators; but the captain apparently never saw through their disguises.

Unfortunately, at one point while the group was on deck, a steady light rain began to fall. Duncan Grant's moustache started to come loose, and all of the conspirators were afraid their stage makeup would soon begin to run. There was a brief moment of panic, but they were finally able to convince the captain to take them all below deck — on the pretext that Abyssinians were deathly afraid of rain — and Grant was able to fix his moustache without anyone noticing. The group returned to London on a train late in the day.

After the hoax was completed, Horace Cole went to the British press to reveal what he and the others had done. Soon there were outraged speeches denouncing the stunt, Scotland Yard considered taking action against the conspirators, and the Navy itself was furious. However, the British public was delighted with the whole affair, and the phrase "bunga, bunga" — first coined by the fake Abyssinian princes — soon became a legendary part of English slang.

The Navy, meanwhile, designed a mild and mostly ritual punishment for each of the conspirators. In the case of Duncan Grant, three young Naval officers kidnapped him from his home one morning while he was in the middle of breakfast and bundled him off to a field. There they administered a brief, ceremonial flogging to Grant's buttocks. He was then returned home.

Fred Dryer, star of NBC's *Hunter:* Always watching his rear.

DRYER, FRED (b. 1946), former professional football player with the New York Giants and Los Angeles Rams, turned actor in the NBC television series *Hunter*. In 1989, Dryer was asked by *Playboy* magazine what the NFL's lockerroom etiquette had been towards football players who were known to be gay. "I never played with anybody who was suspected of being or who I knew for a fact was homosexual," Dryer replied. "Some, like Dave Kopay, admitted it, but my attitude is, Hey, great, man. That's not my problem. I'm here to play football and let's push on. Whatever a guy wants to do, that's his own business. I may want to make sure that I turn the right way when I bend over to get my shoes, though."

DUSE, ELEONORE (1859-1924), Italian actress considered to be one of the greatest performers of her day, second only to Sarah Bernhardt. After a disastrous heterosexual affair with the poetic genius Gabriele D'Annunzio — who cheated her of her money, flaunted his infidelities in her face, and then wrote a scandalous book detailing their erotic relationship — Duse, then middle-aged, had a lesbian affair with a 23-year-old aspiring playwright. The playwright — known to history only as "Signorina R." — wrote at least one play for Duse and planned several others. According to friends, the two women's lovemaking was so loud that, on at least one occasion, their host was forced to abandon his own bedroom, adjoining theirs, and move to a different room to get a good night's sleep. The affair ended shortly after it had begun, when Signorina R. was institutionalized, reportedly for insanity.

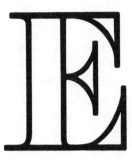

EDENITE, national club, founded in 1981, for gay men especially aroused by other men's chests. "Edenite," according to its founder, Duane Boulware, "is a club, support group, and a way for 'chest men' to meet other chesty men, share experiences, ideas, suggestions ... The club has bodybuilders into exhibitionism, men into jewelry for nipple piercings, chest S/M, nipple enlargement, nipple torture (hot wax, needles), and men into just sucking nipples or enjoying talk about male chests. There is a common bond of chest men, no matter what your chest interests are." The club publishes a lengthy listing of personal ads from all around the country. For more information write to P.O. Box 515, South Beloit, Illinois 61080.

EIKONES, popular weekly magazine in Greece, comparable to *Life* magazine in the U.S. In 1968, the Greek government confiscated copies of *Eikones* from newsstands — and arrested and imprisoned three of *Eikones's* journalists — after the magazine printed an article suggesting that many of ancient Greece's most famous statesmen and philosophers, including Alexander the Great and Socrates, were homosexual. The journalists were charged by the country's ruling military junta with "offending the memory of most of the spiritual and political leaders of ancient Greece." The three were acquitted and released several months later, but only after proving that the article was based on material supplied to them by the government's own

Minister of Education and Religion.

ELIZABETH CLUB, popular Tokyo club catering to heterosexual transvestite businessmen. At the club — which the operators stress, is *not* a gay club — Japanese businessmen can get together after work and change into women's clothes — a traditional kimono, a wedding gown, a geisha costume — and sit talking, gossiping, and relaxing with fellow "sisters."

ELLIS, EDITH LEES (1856-1916), lesbian wife of renowned sexologist Havelock Ellis. At the time of their marriage in 1891, Havelock was aware of Edith's lesbianism, but apparently thought that her love for him would preclude its expression. He was wrong: just three months after the wedding, she announced she was having a passionate affair with another woman, the first of numerous such involvements throughout their marriage. Despite some confusion and emotional anguish, the two remained married, and managed to maintain a mostly tender and understanding — but sexless — relationship for the next twenty-five years. "It is so wonderful," Edith once wrote, "to

have married a man who leaves a woman her soul. I'm utterly satisfied in you, Havelock. It passes all my comprehension, though, why you love me." "Think of me," she wrote him on another occasion, "and know that in your arms and on your breast is my one complete home."

Havelock's desire to write a book on "sexual inversion" — which became the first volume of his monumental series *Studies in the Psychology of Sex* — was in part a desire to understand and come to grips with Edith's lesbianism, as well as with the homosexuality of his close friend Edward Carpenter. (Edith also became a friend of Carpenter, and visited him so often at his home in Millthorpe that one of the local farmers asked him once, "When is that little lady coming again with that curly hair, like a lad's, and them blue eyes, what talked about pigs and cows? I shall never forget her.") Edith's "case history" eventually became one of dozens Havelock included in his book. (See also *SEXUAL INVERSION.*)

In later years, Edith began to suffer increasingly from emotional problems –- aggravated by diabetes — and she tried to commit suicide on three occasions. Her doctor concluded she was on the verge of insanity, and she was confined for a time to a nursing home. Not long after her release, she lapsed into a diabetic coma, and died shortly afterwards. Just before slipping into unconsciousness, she cried out the name of one of her female lovers, a painter named Lily, who had died some years earlier.

ERECTION, ANGLE OF. An erection stands almost completely flat against the belly in only about ten percent of all men. In about twenty percent, a full erection stands at about a forty-five-degree angle from the belly. In the overwhelming majority of men — close to seventy percent — a full erection stands at a nearly perpendicular or ninety-degree angle from the body.

ERNEST AUGUSTUS I, KING OF HANOVER — MURDER SCANDAL INVOLVING. Augustus — who was the son of King George III of England — held the title of duke of Cumberland before becoming king of Hanover. In 1810, while still duke, he was found in his bedroom one night with severe head injuries; on the bed was one of his valets, Sellis, lying dead amid blankets soaked in blood. The valet's throat was cut from ear to ear. The official explanation, released after a coroner's inquest, was that Sellis had cut his own throat in shame after trying to assassinate the duke. According to most reports, however, what actually happened was that Sellis innocently wandered into the bedroom while the duke was sodomizing another valet named Neale. Fearing exposure, the duke threatened Sellis, and then, after a brief struggle, murdered him.

Three years after the incident, an English journalist named Henry While was imprisoned for fifteen months by the Crown of England for having published the less savory version of that night's activities. Even twenty years later, the scandal was such a sensitive issue that another journalist, Joseph Phillips, was imprisoned for six months for "slander," after he publicly repeated the "unofficial" story of Sellis's death.

EUNUCHS, ABILITY TO ACHIEVE ERECTION AND EJACULATION. Contrary to widespread popular belief, a man who has had his testicles

– 117 –

removed retains the same sexual urges as before the operation, and can achieve both erection and ejaculation, if castration takes place *after* sexual maturation is complete (ie. puberty). The only significant difference is that the semen will be devoid of sperm. In ancient Rome, some women apparently preferred eunuchs as lovers because there was no risk of pregnancy and because castrated men were allegedly able to maintain an erection longer than the uncastrated. And, according to studies done of men who have had their testicles removed due to tuberculosis, some castrated men have actually reported an increase in their sex urges after the operation. Of course, throughout history, castration has often involved removal of both the testicles *and* the penis, thus effectively ending the ability to have sex.

EXON, JAMES (b. 1921), U.S.

J. James Exon: "Did you hear the one about the senator from Nebraska..."

senator from Nebraska, Democrat. Exon drew fire from the National Gay and Lesbian Task Force in 1987 when he told a truckers' convention in Omaha, "Why is it there are more lawyers in Washington, D.C. and more queers in San Francisco? The answer is obvious: San Francisco had first choice."

FALLEN ANGELS, national gay correspondence club for men into leather, bondage, discipline, sex toys, and other "kinks." According to its founder, "It is our hope that Fallen Angels would further unite the leather community and allow for people in less populated areas of the country to be able to join in that unity. Not everyone is able to partake of major cities like New York or San Francisco, and this club allows for fellow leathermen to communicate via the mail and to meet while traveling or through other special arrangements." The club publishes a quarterly membership roster, with information on each member's interests and fetishes. For more information send an SASE to P.O. Box 9221, Stockton, California 95208.

FASCINUM, Latin word for the penis, from which the modern English words "fascination" and "to fascinate" are derived. In Latin, the word had connotations of bewitchment and magic, since the penis was regarded as an object from which it was almost impossible to look away.

FELLATIO, DESCRIBED BY ANDRE GIDE. Although Gide was quite open about his homosexuality — he was, in fact, the first major international figure to publicly come out — he nonetheless once described homosexual fellatio as being like "a huge vampire feeding upon a corpse."

FETUSES, "CURING" OF HOMOSEXUALITY IN. In recent years, an East German scientist, Dr. Gunter Doerner, has championed the theory that homosexuals are born and not "made," and has used that theory to propose that homosexuality be cured in the prenatal stages of development, while the fetus is still in the womb.

In the early 1960s, Doerner and his wife were watching a performance of the Vienna Ballet on television. "There were some homosexual dancers with typical female behavior," Doerner recalled later. "Gestures that couldn't possibly be performed by heterosexual males. And there I had the idea that there must be a biological basis to homosexuality." After years of research, Doerner concluded that homosexual males are born as the result of a male sex hormone deficiency in the mother during a critical period of fetal brain development. He claimed that by taking a fluid sample from the womb, he could tell whether a fetus was at risk for being born homosexual. He further claimed that he might one day be able to correct the, in his words, "abnormal condition" by injecting the mother with the proper masculinizing hormones.

Confronting charges that this would be a form of "endo-crinological euthanasia of homosexuality," Doerner told an interviewer in 1982, "This is not manipulation. This is merely changing a biologically abnormal state to one that is normal." "They will see that I am right!" he added emphatically. Doerner — who is widely believed to have begun secret experiments on human test subjects in East Berlin — has for now proposed that a prenatal test for homosexuality be administered regularly to pregnant women, so that a decision can be made whether to abort the fetus, rather than give birth to a homosexual child. He claims this may be particularly beneficial in helping control the spread of AIDS in the world.

THE FOOT FRATERNITY, international gay organization, founded in 1979, for men especially aroused by other men's feet, boots, socks, and shoes. According to the organization's president, Doug Gaynes, "The Fraternity is for men who have an interest and take pleasure in feet and footwear, such as boots, shoes, sneakers, socks, and associated clothing such as Levi's, leather, uniforms, business suits, any type of sportsgear, sports clothing, hats, underwear, swimwear, and more. You need not be interested in feet or footwear; many members are just into certain types of clothing or gear. Many guys are into all three." The club publishes a quarterly roster which includes detailed physical descriptions of members, specific fetishes, and any additional likes and desires. It also sells photo sets and videos made specifically with the foot fetishist in mind. For more information, send an SASE to P.O. Box 24102, Cleveland, Ohio 44124.

FOOT GUYS, national gay organization, founded in 1987, "for men who share a common interest in feet, shoes, boots, sneakers, socks and/or the related clothing that guys wear with these items." The club publishes a quarterly listing of its members and their interests. Further information is available by writing P.O. Box 786, San Francisco, California 94101.

THE FOREVER WAR (1975), science-fiction novel by U.S. writer Joe Haldeman (b. 1943). In it, Haldeman predicted that by the year 2023, homosexuality would be encouraged on Earth as a means of controlling the planet's burgeoning population, and that by the year 2458, everyone still living on Earth would be homosexual.

FROST, ROBERT (1875-1963), U.S. poet, four-time winner of the Pulitzer Prize. In 1916, Frost — known for his puritanical values — tried to have a fellow professor at Amherst College, Stark Young, fired from the faculty because of Young's homosexuality. Young, an enormously popular English professor, had aroused Frost's wrath with his recent homoerotic attachments to certain male students. Frost went so far as to approach Amherst's president with a demand that Young be dismissed. However, his demand was rebuffed.

"GAY COURT." In 1982, the city council of Fremont, California felt obliged to change the name of Gay Court, a small cul-de-sac in the city, to Brookvale Court, after residents of the street and their children complained about being ridiculed and made fun of because of their address.

GAY IS NOT GOOD, 1980 book by U.S. writer Frank du Mas, published by Thomas Nelson Publishers in Nashville, Tennessee. In the book, du Mas recommended castration as an effective means of "containing anti-social homosexual behavior," and claimed that the only rights gay people have are "the rights of all sick people. They have 'patient rights' or 'client rights,' but that is all." Du Mas also claimed there was a conspiracy of homosexuals to keep heterosexuals out of certain professions — such as ballet, acting, and music — and that heterosexuals had a right, even a duty, to retaliate by keeping homosexuals out of certain other professions, such as teaching and police work. Among his other conclusions: Socrates was a "psychotic" and a child molester who deserved to be executed, and, in the future, "there is the possibility that homosexuals who seduce or induce young heterosexuals into their lifestyle could be sued for large amounts of money for damages done ... and theft of happiness."

GERE, RICHARD (b. 1949), U.S. actor. Never known for his fondness for interviews, Gere created a minor stir when, in

1979, he yanked down his pants in response to a female reporter from *The Ladies Home Journal* who asked, "How does it feel to be a sex symbol? Are you gay or *what?*"

"The answer, apparently," one columnist wrote later, "is that life as a semibankable sex symbol is an entirely flaccid experience." "It's nobody's business but mine who I'm fucking, who I'm not fucking," Gere said later, discussing the incident. "The rack sheets, the press blurbs, the gossip pages — it's all crap ... You can't possibly understand my deepest emotions."

GIELGUD, JOHN (b. 1904), English actor. In 1953, Gielgud was arrested on gay sex charges in London, and was fined the equivalent of twenty dollars after pleading guilty to "importuning." (Apparently hoping to go unrecognized in court, he listed his occupation as "clerk.") Despite his standing as one of the great actors of the twentieth century, he was later, because of the arrest, denied an entrance visa to perform in the United States.

At the time of the incident, entrapment of male homosexuals in London's public restrooms was so widespread that

Sir John Gielgud: He was once refused entry into the U.S. because of a previous morals conviction.

the English physicist Derek Jackson wrote to a friend in France, "Never go to a public lavatory in London. I always pee in the street. You may be fined a few pounds for committing a nuisance, but in a public lavatory you risk two years in prison because a policeman in plain clothes says you smiled at him."

GILBERT, MAURICE (dates unknown), enigmatic young man, apparently bisexual, who was one of Oscar Wilde's only loyal companions during Wilde's last years in exile in Paris. Little is known about him, except for what Wilde and his friends wrote. He came into Wilde's life sometime in Paris, and then vanished completely after Wilde's funeral in 1900.

A soldier in the infantry, Gilbert was, from all accounts, exceptionally good-looking. Wilde described him as "most sweet and kind ... a darling boy ... His mouth is the most beautiful mouth I know. It has the curves of Greek art and English flowers." Gilbert's father was English, his mother French, and he had a reputation as an avid young gambler. At the time of his friendship with Wilde, he was rather painfully involved in a *ménage à trois* with another young man and a girl. He also apparently had a brief sexual affair with Lord Alfred Douglas.

He and Wilde spent many hours together, playing cards, or dining, or touring the recently opened International Exposition in Paris. (Wilde later blamed himself for the financial failure of the Exposition: the English people would not stand him, he said, and when they saw him at the Exposition, they went away.) An exhibit of modern art at the Exposition bored Gilbert so much that Wilde finally took him to a kind of ring-toss game, where the younger man won a knife, which he then gave to Wilde as a present. Later, Wilde wanted to demonstrate his appreciation for Gilbert's companionship, and bought the young soldier a bicycle.

When Wilde's health took a dramatic turn for the worse, Gilbert often stayed by his bedside, though according to one of Wilde's friends, he "does not like being in the room." Gilbert hated the sight of Wilde's suffering and was deeply disturbed by the famous playwright's occasionally incoherent ravings as he slipped towards death. After Wilde died, it was Gilbert who took the last photograph of him, lying in state in the hotel room bed.

Although apparently of limited means, Gilbert was also one of the only people to send a floral wreath for Wilde's funeral. After that, he vanished into oblivion.

GIRAFFES, GAY. According to reports in the summer of 1985, officials at the Taipei Zoo in Taiwan became concerned when three male giraffes "turned gay," after the death of their female companion. "We

No, Chuck! The Coach says we're to get our exercise by hiking.

A cover (left) from a 1963 issue of *Go Guys,* one of the first gay magazines. Right: A cartoon from the same magazine.

are running out of explanations for the children visiting the zoo," the zoo's director complained. Zoo authorities later solved their dilemma by importing more female giraffes from Africa.

GO GUYS, early gay magazine, first published in the spring of 1963. In terms of content, *GO GUYS* was somewhere between the more traditional, less revealing physique magazines of the fifties and the slick, totally explicit gay magazines of today. Models were featured in multipage layouts almost identical to those in modern gay "slicks," except that full genital shots were still forbidden. Other pho-

tographic layouts, called "Fotoantics," highlighted two or three models in mildly erotic, comic strip-like stories — wrestling bouts, locker-room antics, vacations to the beach — usually full of double entendres: "With such an eventful trip behind them, Sven and David thought the rest of their vacation would be anti-climactic. But, as it turned out, they both found more than they had bargained for, and returned to the campus engaged to be married." There were also reasonably explicit gay cartoons, as well as fashion layouts, travel tips, and a smattering of gay history, such as features on famous artists — Michelangelo,

Goya, et al. — who were preoccupied by the male nude.

GRAFFITI, GAY — HISTORICAL.

Ancient graffiti — much of it gay — can be found on the Sphinx and the Great Pyramid, on the ruins of ancient Greece and Rome, and on medieval churches and castles. Rocks and canyons along the old Emigrant Trail — the route pioneers took to migrate from Missouri to California — are littered with inscriptions, usually carved or painted on with tar, from the nineteenth century. Through the years, some people, like author Norman Mailer, have championed graffiti as healthy, spontaneous, and meaningful. Others have condemned it. In his journals, for example, Henry David Thoreau disparaged "those who draw in privies." Most historical examples of gay graffiti have been lost to zealous janitors, energetic censors, and the inevitable ravages of time. But thanks to collectors, some examples have survived. Here are a few notable samples:

"Aristemos is beautiful, Polytime is a whore." (Ancient Athens)

"Pyrrhies, son of Akestor, is sex-crazed." (Ancient Thenos)

"Lysitheos says that he loves Mikion more than anyone in the city, for he is brave." (Ancient Athens)

"On this holy spot, sacred to Zeus, Krion has consummated his union with the son of Bathycles, and proclaiming it proudly to the world, dedicates to it this imperishable memorial." (Thebes, 7th century B.C.)

"And many Thebans with him and after him have united themselves with their boys on this same holy spot." (Chiseled just beneath the previous inscription)

"Beautiful is Arkhias." (On the Acropolis, Athens)

"Phoebus the perfume-maker fucks excellently." (Pompeii)

"O wall, so many men have come here to scrawl, I wonder that your burdened sides don't fall." (Pompeii)

"In this place fucking is done standing, farting and shitting is done sitting, and who doesn't want to join in is thrown out." (Men's room in Germany, 1909)

"May he who forbids lovemaking perish twice over!" (Pompeii)

"Perish the man who does not know how to make love!" (Pompeii)

"Here in this beautiful place Hans met his sweetheart." (Men's room in Germany, 1910)

"O, would I go in a woman's clothes — And had a cunt of pig leather, Then I would travel around the world And let myself be fucked for free." (Copenhagen, 1910)

"NOTICE: I will suck off all boys' (over 16) cocks next Sunday — July 25th at 12 PM. All wishing to be sucked off get a bone and wait. I will choose the best looking pricks. My friend will jack off the rest." (Chief Ranger Martindale Geyser Baths Swimming Pool, Old Faithful Camp, Yellowstone National Park, 1928)

"A Marine will suck you off and let you suck him, He'll fuck you in the ass and let you fuck him, But don't ever ask him to kiss you — Because *that's* queer!" (San Francisco, late 1950s)

"Get the Dick out of the White House and into your mouth." (Men's room, New Jersey, 1971)

"Lysias is beautiful." (On the Acropolis)

"Lesbianism is not an isolated subversive activity but a revolutionary identity." (New York City, 1969)

"To most of the world,
    Said Gertrude Stein,
It's me who is the star, the star,
But here at home,
    Sweet Alice B.,
And in my heart,
    you are you are."
(New York City, 1970)

"I want to fuck a man." (Pompeii)

"Judas had a bigger cock than Jesus." "Yes but Jesus has been screwing us for 2000 years." (New York City, 1970)

"Closets are for clothes." (New York City, 1969)

"Ronald Reagan's son is gay." "Nancy Reagan is a drag queen." "Al Haig loves to Dick Allen." (Washington, D.C., 1981)

"Flush twice to send a gift to Anita Bryant." "Don't bother — she's already got shit for brains." (San Francisco, 1977)

GRAVES OF FAMOUS GAY PEOPLE IN THE U.S. — WHERE LOCATED.

Horatio Alger (1832-1899), author.

His fame: Alger was best known for his "rags to riches" boys' novels, which were popular in the late nineteenth century. It was through these books — and the revelations he made in them about the abuse and mistreatment of children — that he was able to achieve actual social reforms that improved conditions for homeless youths, orphans, and runaways. Alger is also remembered for a sex scandal when, as pastor of the Unitarian Church in Brewster, Massachusetts, he was run out of town for his sexual involvement with some of the local youths.

Where buried: Glenwood Cemetery, South Natick, Massachusetts (ten miles southwest of Boston).

How he got there: Despite the fact that his more than one hundred novels sold in excess of 400,000,000 copies, Alger was, in his last years, a largely forgotten man whose books — with their simplistic writing and contrived plots — were now ignored by American readers. Penniless, he went, in 1896, to live with his sister in Natick, Massachusetts. He died there three years later.

Burial notes: Seven respected citizens — all former orphan boys whom Alger had befriended — acted as his pallbearers.

Susan B. Anthony (1820-1906), feminist and social reformer.

Susan B. Anthony: She died before seeing the full impact of her life's work.

Her fame: Anthony helped secure the first laws in New York giving women legal rights over children and property. A tireless leader in the movement to secure voting rights for women, she also organized the National Woman Suffrage Association. She is believed to have had a passionate involvement with abolitionist Anna E. Dickinson.

Where buried: Mt. Hope Cemetery, Rochester, New York.

How she got there: Anthony fell ill while traveling home from the National Suffrage Convention in Baltimore. She died of pneumonia three weeks later at her home in Rochester. Shortly before lapsing into a coma, she had told her sister, "To think that I have had more than sixty years of hard struggle for a little liberty, and then to die without it seems so cruel." The 19th Amendment, guaranteeing women the right to vote, was not passed until thirteen years after her death.

Burial notes: Despite a severe spring snow storm, almost ten thousand people waited outside the church during her funeral service in hopes of catching a last glimpse of her coffin. On the day of the funeral, flags in Rochester were flown at half-mast, and many private citizens draped their homes in black.

Last will and testament: Anthony bequeathed the sum of her total estate — roughly $10,000 — as a last gift to the suffrage movement.

Tallulah Bankhead (1903-1968), actress.

Her fame: Bankhead's flamboyant personality and extraordinary stage presence won her fame in England and the U.S. in plays (*The Little Foxes*), films (*Lifeboat, A Royal Scandal*), and on television and radio. Although she had numerous heterosexual affairs, she once described herself, accurately, as "ambisextrous."

Last words: In a delirium, "Codeine ... bourbon ... "

Where buried: Saint Paul's Churchyard, Chestertown, Maryland.

How she got there: Bankhead died of pneumonia, brought on by a case of influenza she'd contracted during a flu epidemic sweeping New York City in 1968. Although she died in New York, her body was taken for burial to Maryland, where she had soon intended to retire and where her sister lived.

Burial notes: Bankhead was buried in one of her favorite silk wrappers (dotted with the inevitable holes from cigarette burns). A rabbit's foot, which had once belonged to her father, was also placed inside the coffin.

Last will and testament: Bankhead's will was long, complicated, and full of specific bequests to each of her friends. For example, to George Cukor, she left "the portrait of me by Ambrose McEvoy." James Herlihy received $2,500; Estelle Winwood received $10,000 plus a diamond-and-sapphire pendant. Other friends received specific paintings or pieces of jewelry or cash bequests.

James Buchanan: We still aren't sure what went on between him and the senator from Alabama.

James Buchanan (1791-1868), U.S. president.

His fame: There is still debate over whether Buchanan, the nation's 15th president and the only U.S. president to have been a bachelor, was homosexual. Some sources have suggested he was lovers with Alabama senator William Rufus de Vane King — a claim bolstered by recently discovered letters between the two men.

Last words: "Oh Lord Almighty, as Thou wilt."

Where buried: Woodward Hill Cemetery, Lancaster, Pennsylvania.

How he got there: Buchanan became seriously ill with a bad cold in May 1868, and died, at his estate in Wheatland Pennsylvania, two weeks later.

Epitaph: "Here lie the remains of JAMES BUCHANAN, fifteenth president of the United States. Born in Franklin County, Pennsylvania, April 23, 1791; died at his residence at Wheatland, Lancaster County, Pennsylvania on June 1, 1868." Buchanan had written out the epitaph himself, a few days before his death, leaving only the final date blank.

Willa Cather (1876-1947), author.

Her fame: One of the most distinctive voices in American literature, Cather wrote such acclaimed novels as *My Antonia, Death Comes For the Archbishop,* and *O Pioneers.* She won the Pulitzer Prize in 1923.

Where buried: Old Burying Ground, Jaffrey Center, New Hampshire.

How she got there: Cather died of a massive cerebral hemorrhage at her apartment in New York City. In accordance with instructions she had once given friends, her body was taken for burial to Jaffrey Center, New Hampshire, a picturesque and rural community where she often summered and where she wrote much of *My Antonia* and *Death Comes For the Archbishop*. The body of her long-time companion, Edith Lewis, was also buried there, in 1972, at the foot of Cather's grave.

Epitaph: "That is happiness, to be dissolved into something complete and great." (Taken from a line in *My Antonia*).

Last will and testament: In accordance with instructions in Cather's will, many of her private letters and personal papers were destroyed after her death. She also expressed the ardent desire that none of her works should ever be made into movies or television programs. All of her material possessions, plus one-third of her money, went to Edith Lewis. The rest of the estate went to Cather's nieces and nephews.

Montgomery Clift (1920-1966), actor.

His fame: Known for his portrayals of introspective, often troubled heroes, Clift gained fame for his insightful performances in From Here to Eternity, A Place in the Sun, The Misfits, and other films. He re-

Montgomery Clift: An introspective personality off-screen and on.

ceived four Academy Award nominations during his career.

Where buried: Brooklyn Quaker Cemetery, Prospect Park, New York.

How he got there: After a disfiguring car accident in 1957, Clift began to rely more heavily on alcohol and drugs to ease his physical discomfort and emotional distress. At one point, he had a fourteen-foot high medicine cabinet installed in his bathroom just to house the dozens of drugs, both legal and illegal, he was taking. In 1966, Clift — then forty-five — suffered a fatal heart attack in the middle of the night, at his brownstone duplex in Manhattan. A lifelong Quaker, he was buried, in accordance with his wishes, at a Friends cemetery in Brooklyn.

Burial notes: The simple granite marker over Clift's grave was designed by John Benson, who had also designed John F. Kennedy's gravestone at Arlington. The grave site is marked by two hundred crocuses, planted there by Clift's close friend Nancy Walker.

James Dean (1931-1955), actor.

His fame: Dean had major roles in only three films during his brief career — *East of Eden*, *Rebel Without a Cause*, and *Giant* — but it was enough to make him one of Hollywood's most idolized and legendary young stars. Speculation about his sexuality still abounds. He once bragged to friends, "I've had my cock sucked by five of the big names in Hollywood," and when asked once if he were gay, he replied, enigmatically, "Well, I'm certainly not going through life with one hand tied behind my back."

Last words: "That guy up there's gotta stop; he'll see us" — just before his car smashed into another car making a left turn on Route 466 near Cholame, California. Dean's neck was broken instantly. A passenger, friend Rolf Wutherich, survived the accident.

Where buried: Park Cemetery, Fairmount, Indiana (about seventy miles northeast of Indianapolis).

How he got there: Dean's body was taken back to Fairmount — where he had grown up — so that he could be buried beside his mother, who had died in 1940.

Burial notes: Over three thousand people descended on the small town of Fairmount for Dean's funeral. A simple pink-gray granite stone was placed over the grave. Through the years, the letters and numbers on the stone were chiseled out by souvenir hunters; for a time, one could even buy rings purportedly set with a small chunk from the headstone. Later, a memorial bronze bust of Dean was sawed off and stolen from the pillar where it had been erected at the cemetery's entrance. Arbor vitae — tough evergreens with heavy roots — were eventually planted on either side of the grave, in part to discourage anyone from actually trying to dig up the body itself.

Post-mortem: The crumpled aluminum shell of the car Dean had been killed in was eventually put on display by a California couple who charged twenty-five cents to view it, fifty cents to actually sit behind the wheel. Fragments of the car's body were later sold as souvenirs.

Paul Goodman (1911-1972), author.

His fame: Goodman — poet, novelist, and social commentator — is best remembered for his book *Growing Up Absurd*, published in 1960.

Where buried: Stratford Center Cemetery, Stratford, New Hampshire.

How he got there: Goodman died of a heart attack — his third — at his farm in North Stratford, New Hampshire.

J. Edgar Hoover (1895-1972), FBI director.

His fame: Hoover was director of the FBI from 1924 to 1972, and in that position became one of the most powerful — and feared — political figures in America.

Where buried: Congressional Cemetery, Washington, D.C.

How he got there: Hoover suffered a fatal heart attack in the early morning hours of May 2, 1972. His housekeeper found his body crouched by the side of his bed. On May 3, Hoover became the first civilian ever to lie in state, in a flag-draped coffin, in the rotunda of the Capitol Building.

Last will and testament: Hoover left the bulk of his $551,000 estate to his close companion of more than forty years, Clyde Tolson. Tolson also received the flag that had draped Hoover's coffin. Later, Tolson himself was buried in Congressional Cemetery, in a plot close to Hoover's.

J.W. King (1955-1986), porn star.

His fame: King was one of the most popular stars in the history of gay porn films, having appeared in such hits as *Nighthawks in Leather*, *Pacific Coast Highway*, and *Face to Face*. He was also, according to one co-worker, "just simply one of the nicest guys ever to work in the industry."

Where buried: Laurel Land Cemetery, Dallas, Texas.

How he got there: King died of AIDS at Hollywood Community Hospital on December 5, 1986, barely a month after his lover had also died from the disease.

His body was sent back for burial to Dallas, where his family lives and where he was born.

Burial notes: King was buried under his real name, James Waldrop.

Charles Laughton: He once said he had a face "like an elephant's behind."

Charles Laughton (1899-1962), actor.

His fame: Laughton was widely regarded as one of the most versatile and effective character actors in the history of the movies. Among his best known films were *Witness for the Prosecution, Mutiny on the Bounty,* and *The Private Life of Henry VIII.* He also directed the 1955 classic *The Night of the Hunter.*

His thirty-three-year marriage to actress Elsa Lanchester survived many vicissitudes, including the revelation in 1931 that he was gay.

Where buried: Forest Lawn Memorial Park, Glendale, California.

How he got there: Laughton was on tour when he slipped and fell in a hotel bathtub in Flint, Michigan. He was flown to New York City for treatment, where doctors discovered he was also suffering from bone cancer. Laughton died of cancer at his home in Hollywood several months later.

Burial notes: Laughton's graveside eulogy was read by his friend Christopher Isherwood.

D.H. Lawrence (1885-1930), author.

His fame: Although best known for his novels extolling the virtues of heterosexual passion — *Lady Chatterley's Lover, Women in Love, The Fox,* et al. — Lawrence was, according to one biographer, "about eighty-five percent hetero and fifteen percent homo."

Where buried: San Cristobal Ranch, about ten miles north of Taos, off of Highway 3 in northern New Mexico.

How he got there: Lawrence died of tuberculosis in southern France in 1930, and was originally buried there, in a simple grave. Several years later, however, his wife, Frieda, decided to move to Taos, New Mexico — where she and Lawrence had once spent some time — and she decided to take Lawrence's remains with her. She had the body exhumed and cremated; but she ran into considerable trouble getting the ashes into the United States. Lawrence, whose reputation here was still that of a "tubercular, smut-flinging degenerate," was *persona non grata* even in death. It was only through the intervention of some highly placed friends that his ashes were finally allowed into the country.

In New Mexico, Frieda stayed with an old acquaintance, Mabel Dodge Luhan. Luhan was a formidable woman: a flamboyant salon hostess and patroness of the arts who had tried, unsuccessfully, to seduce Lawrence on several different occasions. A fierce rivalry over the dead author's remains broke out between the two women. Mabel insisted that Lawrence's ashes be scattered across the New Mexico countryside, and

claimed that Lawrence had once confided that wish to her. Frieda, on the other hand, was already building a memorial chapel for her husband and planned to bury his ashes inside.

At one point, Mabel actually plotted to steal the ashes and scatter them secretly; she was thwarted when Frieda — informed of the plot — hired a 24-hour guard to protect them. Mabel finally told Frieda it didn't matter what she did, because once Frieda herself was dead, Mabel intended to exhume Lawrence's ashes and scatter them properly. It was then that Frieda hit on an ingenious solution: she had the ashes mixed with concrete to create a one-ton cement block to be used as the altar in Lawrence's memorial chapel. Mabel finally let the issue drop, and Lawrence's remains can be seen today as a very distinct part of his memorial chapel.

Leonard Matlovich (1943-1988), gay-rights activist and former Air Force sergeant.

His fame: Matlovich became famous, and appeared on the cover of *Time* magazine in 1975, when he set himself up as a test case to challenge the U.S. military's policy of automatically discharging homosexuals from the armed forces.

Where buried: Congressional Cemetery, Washington, D.C.

How he got there: After Matlovich died of AIDS in 1988, his body was taken to Washington for burial in the plot he had chosen for himself four years earlier. He is buried near J. Edgar Hoover's long-time companion, Clyde Tolson.

Burial notes: Despite his long legal battle with the U.S. military, Matlovich was buried with full military honors. The flag that draped his coffin was presented to his mother. Matlovich's gravestone — which he originally intended as a memorial to all gay and lesbian veterans — consists of an imposing black granite marker engraved with the epitaph, "A Gay Vietnam Vet. When I was in the military they gave me a medal for killing two men — and a discharge for loving one." Poignantly, Matlovich's father had once suggested that the words "Mission Accomplished" also be added somewhere on the marker. "I knew," Matlovich said shortly before his death, "there were thousands of gay veterans like me who would be proud to be remembered not only for their sacrifice but also

Leonard Matlovich: When the Air Force inducted him in 1963, they never guessed how much they would later regret it.

for their sense of self-worth as gay people. I wanted it to be their monument as well as my own."

Sal Mineo (1939-1976), actor.

His fame: Mineo achieved his greatest fame in the films *Rebel Without a Cause, Exodus,* and *The Gene Krupa Story,* and was twice nominated for an Academy Award during his career. He also did considerable theater work, as both an actor and a director.

Where buried: Gate of Heaven Cemetery, Hawthorne, New York.

How he got there: On the night of February 12, 1976, Mineo was stabbed outside the garage of his West Hollywood apartment; he had just returned home from play rehearsals. Neighbors later testified they heard him scream, "My God! Help me! No! No!" He died almost immediately of wounds through the heart; he was killed with a hunting knife.

His body was taken back to New York City, where his mother lived, and was buried next to the grave of his father. For two years, police tried to track down Mineo's killer, but they were hindered by an apparent lack of motive in the case. When they finally found the killer — 21-year-old Lionel Ray Williams, who had bragged to friends he had killed Mineo — it became apparent there *was* no motive. Described by the presiding judge as "a sadistic killer" and "a midnight marauder," Williams had apparently murdered the actor just for the fun of it. Williams was found guilty of the slaying and sentenced to life imprisonment, with the judge's recommendation that there be no parole.

Post-Mortem: Typical of the many obituaries that were run for Mineo, the New York Post, in speaking of Mineo's private life,

Sal Mineo: He was laid to rest next to his father in a cemetery in Hawthorne, New York.

commented only that, "He dated many girls, but always said he did not want the relationship to get too serious."

Ramon Novarro (1899-1968), actor.

His fame: Novarro — a darkly handsome star of the silent era — was the first of Hollywood's popular Latin lovers. His most famous part was in the title role of Cecil B. De Mille's monumental production Ben-Hur in 1926. Novarro was known throughout Hollywood as an extremely gracious and generous man, who also happened to be gay.

Ramon Novarro: He epitomized the handsome Latin lover to moviegoers of the twenties.

Where buried: Calvary Cemetery, Los Angeles, California.

How he got there: On Halloween night, 1968, Novarro was robbed and then brutally beaten by two hustler brothers, Tom and Paul Ferguson, who ransacked the actor's home looking for valuables. After first brutalizing Novarro, the Ferguson brothers shoved a large dildo down the former star's throat; Novarro choked to death on his own blood. Tracking down the killers proved unexpectedly easy: one of them made a long-distance phone call on Novarro's telephone, to a girlfriend in Chicago, to brag about the slaying.

Cole Porter (1892-1964), composer and lyricist.

His fame: Porter wrote such immortal songs as *Night and Day, You're the Top,* and *Begin the Beguine.* In his private life, he was known as abrasive, haughty, and demanding, with a penchant for hustlers.

Where buried: Mount Hope Cemetery, Peru, Indiana.

How he got there: Porter died of pneumonia in a Santa Monica, California hospital in 1964. His body was taken back for burial to Peru, Indiana, his birthplace.

Burial notes: Porter was buried next to his father. A small, simple stone marks the grave.

Tyrone Power (1913-1958), actor.

His fame: Power was one of Hollywood's most popular stars in the 1940s and 1950s. Three of his best-known performances were in *Captain from Castille, The Eddie Duchin Story,* and *Witness for the Prosecution.*

Where buried: Hollywood Memorial Park Cemetery, Los Angeles, California.

How he got there: Power died of a massive heart attack, after a heated argument with actor George Sanders on the set of

Solomon and Sheba, which was filming on location in Spain. His body was flown back to Hollywood for burial.

Burial notes: Power's funeral was used as the occasion for an outing by hundreds of curious onlookers, who had picnic lunches, played hoola-hoop, and laughed and carried on while the mourners were gathered around the graveside. The grave is marked by a large white marble bench engraved with Power's name and ornamented with the masks of comedy and tragedy.

Eleanor Roosevelt (1884-1962), U.S. first lady.

Her fame: Mrs. Roosevelt served as first lady from 1933 to 1945. After the death of President Roosevelt, she traveled around the world as a lecturer, columnist, and goodwill ambassador, seeking international peace. Shortly before her death, she was voted The Most Admired Woman in America. Recently discovered letters between her and journalist Lorena Hickok indicate that the two women may have had a lesbian relationship.

Where buried: At the Roosevelt family estate at Hyde Park, New York, now a national historic site.

How she got there: Mrs. Roosevelt died of a rare form of tuberculosis of the bone marrow. She was laid to rest next to her husband.

Burial notes: Mrs. Roosevelt asked that she be buried in a plain wood coffin covered in pine boughs, so that her body would more quickly decay into the soil and nourish the nearby trees which she had loved. Also at her instruction, no embalming was done; but because she had a terror of being buried alive, she asked that her veins be opened before interment.

Friedrich Wilhelm Von Steuben (1730-1794), Revolutionary War hero.

His fame: A former aide to Frederick the Great, Steuben came to the U.S. to help train the Continental Army for combat against the British. He was later made inspector general. According to many sources, he had originally been forced to leave Prussia because he had taken "indecent liberties" with various young men.

Where buried: Steuben Memorial, Remsen, New York (about fifteen miles north of Utica).

How he got there: Steuben, who died nearly bankrupt, was initially buried in an unmarked grave on his 16,000-acre farm north of Utica. When the building of a new road threatened to desecrate the gravesite, his body was moved to a new location on the farm and was suitably marked with a gravestone.

Epitaph: "Indispensable to the achievement of American independence."

Clifton Webb (1891-1966), actor.

His fame: Webb was best known for his sophisticated and often acidic performances in such films as *Laura, Sitting Pretty,* and *The Razor's Edge.* Within Hollywood circles, he was also known for his extraordinarily close attachment to his mother, Mabelle, with whom he lived for most of his life. Their attachment to one another was so pronounced that *The New York Times,* in its obituary for Webb, devoted a sizable section to describing the mother-son relationship.

Where buried: Hollywood Memorial Park Cemetery, Los Angeles, California.

How he got there: Webb died of a heart attack in Los Angeles in 1966. Friends said that his health had gone into a sharp decline ever since the death of his mother, four years earlier.

Walt Whitman (1819-1892), poet.

His fame: Perhaps the greatest poet in U.S. history, Whitman penned the immortal *Leaves of Grass,* a milestone in American literature.

Where buried: Harleigh Cemetery, Camden, New Jersey.

How he got there: The great poet suffered from steadily declining health for the last several years of his life. He died, on the evening of March 26, 1892, from pulmonary emphysema.

Burial notes: Whitman designed his own tomb — a huge, rough-hewn, granite mausoleum — and supervised its construction while he was still alive; in fact, he often liked to take friends on carriage rides to the tomb, to show them how work was progressing. The vault contained eight burial spaces, and after Whitman's death, the bodies of his mother and father, and other family members, were interred alongside his. A bold inscription, "WALT WHITMAN," stands above the mausoleum's entrance.

Last will and testament: Whitman left the bulk of his estate in trust for his mentally retarded brother, Eddy. To his former lover Peter Doyle, Whitman left his prized silver watch, "with my love."

Post-mortem: During an autopsy on Whitman's body, his brain was removed and sent for study and research at the American Anthropometric Society. Unfortunately, while carrying the brain in its glass case one morning, a lab worker dropped it on the floor. Both the case and Whitman's brain were instantly demolished.

Thornton Wilder (1897-1975), author.

His fame: Wilder was best known for his plays *Our Town* and *The Matchmaker* (later made into the musical *Hello Dolly!*), and for his novella *The Bridge of San Luis Rey.*

Where buried: Mt. Carmel Cemetery, Hamden, Connecticut.

How he got there: Wilder suffered from hypertension, emphysema, and prostate cancer in his last days. He died of congestive heart failure, at his home in Connecticut.

Monty Woolley (1888-1963), actor.

His fame: A former Yale professor, Woolley abandoned teaching in 1936 to pursue an acting career. His best-known role was in the stage and screen versions of *The Man Who Came to Dinner.*

Where buried: Greenridge Cemetery, Saratoga Springs, New York.

How he got there: Woolley died of heart and kidney ailments in a hospital in Albany, New York. At the time of his death, he was living at his family's Victorian mansion in Saratoga Springs.

GUNS N' ROSES, popular hard-rock band. In a 1989 interview in *Rolling Stone* magazine, the band's lead singer Axle Rose described himself as "proheterosexual," and acknowledged that he'll sometimes drive down Santa Monica Boulevard and verbally harass gays. "I've had some very bad experiences with homosexuals," he said. When asked by the magazine if he were "anti-homosexual," Axle replied, "I'm not against them doing what they want to do as long as it's not hurting anybody else and they're not forcing it upon me. I don't need them in my face or, pardon the pun, up my ass about it." He acknowledged that his attitude towards homosexuals might be "hypocritical" because, "I'd rather see two women together than just about anything else."

In 1988, the Guns n' Roses hard-rock band was dropped from a New York City AIDS benefit, because of one of their songs, "One in Million," which claimed that "faggots ... come to our country ... and spread some fuckin' disease."

H I

HAHN, JESSICA (b. 1958). Hahn helped bring down the now-notorious PTL television ministry after she publicly acknowledged having had a sexual affair with PTL tele-evangelist James Bakker. Not long after the scandal broke, with her new-found celebrity giving her entree to circles she probably never would have been allowed in otherwise, she met and became friends for a time with the flamboyant pianist Liberace. "He was a perfect gentleman," she said later. "He never made you feel like he was a star and you were something less." She even spent considerable time at his West Coast home. Nonetheless, after it was announced Liberace had died of AIDS, Hahn felt compelled to immediately undergo an AIDS-antibody test — because she had once eaten a few bites of food from Liberace's plate. Her test results were negative.

HALL, RADCLYFFE — ON HOUSEKEEPING. According to British writer Beverley Nichols, who knew Hall, "It was her boast that she knew nothing about housekeeping. She must have regarded this as a sign of virility, because she so often referred to it. 'Couldn't boil an egg,' she would proclaim gruffly, jerking out her knees with extra gusto. 'Couldn't light a fire, couldn't dust a chimney piece.'"

HAMPTON, JACK (b. 1932), Texas state district judge who ignited a nationwide controversy in 1988 when he gave a lighter-than-usual sentence to an eighteen-year-old murderer, Richard Lee Bednarski, because Bednarski's two victims were gay.

Bednarski was convicted of shooting to death two gay men in the Oak Lawn section of Dallas. On the night of May 15, 1988, he and nine of his friends — all college students — had gone out cruising in their car and were jeering and shouting obscenities at passers-by. They were, they admitted later, looking to harass gays in particular. Bednarski had a loaded pistol in his pocket.

They finally found two gay men, 34-year-old Tommy Trimble and 27-year-old Lloyd Griffin. After Trimble and Griffin made sexual overtures to Bednarski and his friends, Bednarski got out of the car, and pulled out his pistol. He ordered the two men to strip, and tried to rob them at gunpoint. When Trimble and Griffin refused to cooperate, Bednarski started shooting. The two gay men were killed instantly.

Bednarski was convicted of murder, but instead of sentencing him to the maximum of life in prison, State District Judge Jack Hampton gave him a lighter-than-usual sentence, thirty years in prison. "I don't care much for queers cruising the streets," Hampton later explained. "These two guys that got killed wouldn't have been killed if they hadn't been cruising the streets picking up teenage boys." Hampton admitted he would have given a harsher sentence to Bednarski if the victims had been, for example, "a couple of housewives out shopping."

Hampton's remarks provoked a storm of controversy, and there were immediate calls, from members of both the straight and gay communities, for his resignation. Asked, however, if he had any reservations about the sentence or the controversy surrounding it, Hampton replied, "Just spell my name right. If it makes anybody mad, they'll forget about it by 1990 [the next election year]."

HAUK, A. ANDREW (b. 1913), U.S. district judge in Los Angeles. Sentencing a Mexican citizen who had illegally entered the U.S. to visit his child, Hauk casually commented, "And he isn't even a fag, like all these faggots from Cuba we're letting in." His remarks drew sharp criticism from the gay community and from other Los Angeles judges, but Hauk remained firm: "The

Steve Reeves: The film *Hercules* (1959) launched him to international stardom.

judge's appropriate obligation," he responded, in a public statement that some regarded as a near-perfect political *non sequitur*, "is to apply and enforce the law as it is, not as altered or amended by the attempts of activists to legalize passing fads or fancies, which result in perversions and deviations in the law."

HEARTTHROBS, YESTERDAY'S. A gallery of entertainment figures gay men idolized and fantasized about in the 1950s and 1960s.

Steve Reeves (b. 1926).

Reeves was one of the youngest men ever to win the "Mr. America" title, in 1944, and he went on to later become "Mr. USA," "Mr. World," and "Mr. Universe" as well. The strikingly handsome, perfectly proportioned bodybuilder tried to get into films as early as 1948, but was told that because of his size he would dwarf other actors. Finally, after being considered — and rejected — for the lead in Cecil B. DeMille's *Samson and Delilah*, he was given a bit part in the

1954 MGM musical *Athena*, starring Jane Powell and Debbie Reynolds. *Athena* was his first and only Hollywood film venture.

In 1957, Reeves was discovered by Italian film director Pietro Francisci, who cast him in the Italian costume epic *Hercules*. *Hercules*, the prototype for all the so-called "cloak-and-sandal" epics to come, was an enormous hit in both Europe and the United States, and it made Reeves an international star. By 1960, Reeves was ranked as the number-one box-office draw in twenty-five countries around the world.

Reeves was paid only ten thousand dollars apiece for his first two *Hercules* films. After that he demanded — and received — $150,000 each for his performances in such epics as *The Last Days of Pompeii, Duel of the Titans*, and *Son of Spartacus*. His last film, an Italian "spaghetti" western titled *A Long Ride From Hell*, was released in 1968. "I found acting very stressful," Reeves told writer Richard Lamparski in 1986. "I never liked it ... I ended up with an ulcer." After completing *A Long Ride From Hell*, Reeves retired to his ranch outside Hollywood, where he lives with his wife, and grows avocados and lemons.

Ron Ely (b. 1938) (Real name: Ronald Pierce).

For many gay men growing up in front of their television sets in the 1960s, tall, muscular Ron Ely provided more unclothed male flesh than they had ever seen on the small screen before. Wandering through the jungle each week in his revealing brown loincloth, Ely was television's first Tarzan, and the fourteenth actor in Hollywood history to portray the Lord of the Apes. His NBC television series, *Tarzan*, debuted in September 1966, and lasted three seasons, before going off the air in 1969.

Ely did virtually all of his own stunts for the series, and suffered two dozen major injuries in the process, including two broken shoulders and various lion bites. However, the famous Tarzan yell used in the program was actually a recording made twenty years earlier by another famous Tarzan, Johnny Weissmuller.

Ely also starred in two films — *Tarzan's Deadly Silence* and *Tarzan's Jungle Rebellion* — which were spin-offs from the series. Now in his early fifties, he hosts a television game show, "Face the Music," on the USA television network.

Tony Dow (b. 1945).

Beaver Cleaver's older brother, Wally, wasn't much to look at when the series *Leave It to Beaver* first started in 1957; but by the series' end in 1963, Wally had matured into a good-looking, clean-cut young jock, and the actor who played him — Tony Dow — had developed a large and loyal following. As gay writer Larry Duplechan explained, in a tribute to Dow in *In Touch* magazine, "How I dreamed of the chest that lay beneath Wally Cleaver's baggy shirts. Many an episode ended with a scene of the boys preparing for bed, usually with the Beav already in jammies and Wally taking forever, I mean *for ever*, to unbutton his shirt as the brothers engaged in a few minutes of inane juvenile repartee. Somehow, Wally never seemed to get past the second button before the laugh track crescendoed, the theme music entered, the credits rolled, and my hopes were dashed yet again. I never glimpsed so much as a nipple."

Tony Dow: Answering fan mail kept him busy.

Leave It to Beaver lasted through 234 episodes, a respectable run of six years. However, despite its place as one of the best-known T.V. shows from the period, it actually never made it any higher than number twenty-six in the Nielsen ratings during its original run. Years of syndication have helped boost its popularity.

After the show's cancellation in 1963, Dow guest-starred on numerous other T.V. shows, but he inevitably suffered from typecasting. "Even if I play a murderer," he told *People* magazine in 1983,

Vince Edwards: "The Barefoot Boy" bared other things, too — always to good effect.

"there will always be people who say, 'Gee, you were exactly like Wally.'" In 1983, the original cast of *Leave It to Beaver* — minus Hugh Beaumont, who had died in 1982 — re-assembled for a made-for-TV movie, *Still the Beaver*, about life for the Cleaver clan twenty years later. In the update, Wally — now a bit paunchy, and sporting a perm — had become a successful attorney who suffered from impotence, and Beaver, now in his thirties, was dealing with a failing marriage. The movie was so successful it eventually became a new ongoing series.

Vince Edwards (b. 1928) (Real name: Vincent Edward Zoine).

Nicknamed "the barefoot boy" because of his disdain for shoes or socks, Edwards grew up in Brooklyn, where he quickly established a reputation for rebelliousness. The dark and powerfully built young actor (he was a champion swimmer at Ohio State University) made his acting debut when he was nineteen, and appeared in over a dozen films, mostly gritty, low-budget melodramas, before landing his most famous role as T.V.'s intense and brooding neurosurgeon, Ben Casey, in 1961.

Comparing the domineering Ben Casey to his blond rival, Dr. Kildare, on NBC, one critic mused: "Dr. Kildare seems like the hygienic chairman of the junior prom. Ben Casey belongs in a black leather jacket on the back of a motorcycle." Edwards achieved instant and lasting fame in the role of Ben Casey, but his rise as an American sex symbol was so intense, he complained to one magazine, "I never get a moment to myself," and he confessed irritation at the more than eighty people a day, mostly women, who stopped him on the street for medical advice. *Ben Casey* lasted on the air six seasons before it was cancelled by ABC in 1966.

Edwards has since appeared in numerous made-for-T.V. movies and mini-series, and was most recently seen in a series of television commercials for a national chain of weight-loss clinics.

Edd Byrnes (b. 1933) (Real name: Edward Breitenberger).

Edd Byrnes's Hollywood career rose and fell precipitously on a single role: Kookie, the wired-up, jive-talking parking-lot attendant on the hit T.V. series *77 Sunset Strip*. From the show's premiere in 1958 to Byrnes's departure in 1963, Kookie was America's national television hero, the Fonz of his day. "Kookie wows the kids!" exclaimed *Look* magazine in 1959, and added, "It's been wowsville for the young actor from Yorkville all the way!" Kookie's habit of compulsively combing his hair spawned a catchy number-one hit single, "Kookie, Kookie, Lend Me Your Comb" (recorded by Byrnes and Connie Stevens in 1960), which became the anthem for vain teenage boys across the land. Later, Kookie combs, Kookie wallets, and Kookie belts were marketed by the tens of thousands. "My ambitions are so great that I can't discuss them," Byrnes, a former gymnast, told an interviewer in 1959. "I just stand in awe of them."

Initially, Kookie played only a small part in the T.V. series. But his wisecracking attitude, quirky but likable mannerisms, and distinctive slang made the character a hit with audiences, and helped push the show into the Nielsen Top Ten. "Kookie talk," as it was called, became the rage: "squaresville" for a dull party, "piling up the Z's" for sleeping, "antsville" for a big crowd, "the ginchiest" for the best.

Tab Hunter: The fantasy that could have been...

In 1963, as the show's ratings started to sag miserably, Byrnes was given the ax, as was most of the original cast, and the entire series was revamped. Though Kookie remains a memorable icon of the period, Byrnes all but disappeared for two-and-a-half decades into show-business obscurity. However, he announced in 1989 that he was trying to secure the rights to *77 Sunset Strip*, to produce a new T.V. series based on it.

Tab Hunter (b. 1931) (Real name: Arthur Gelien).

Perhaps more than any young actor of his time, Hunter was idolized and fantasized about by thousands of gay men. Later revelations that Hunter was himself gay left those fans ambivalent and slightly pained: it was like finding out, twenty years later, that the boy you'd been madly in love with in high school had been available after all. The reaction was often a wistful, "If only I had known ... "

Hunter ran away from home when he was fifteen and lied about his age to join the Coast Guard in 1947. After his discharge, he made his way to Hollywood, where he was discovered by agent Henry Willson, the flamboyant and controversial homosexual who also discovered and renamed Rock

Hudson, Guy Madison, and Rory Calhoun. (See also WILL-SON, HENRY.) Hunter made his film debut, with no previous acting experience, when he was eighteen. Five years — and six films — later, he was one of Hollywood's most idolized young heartthrobs.

The fan magazines were full of him: "TAB — AND THEY CALL HIM DREAMBOAT!" "I'LL WEAR TAB HUNTER'S BRACE-LET FOREVER!" There were even occasional articles by Tab himself: "MY HAWAIIAN DIARY!" and "I'M IN LOVE WITH A WONDERFUL MOM!" He was boyish, athletic, eager, and — at over six feet tall — enormously good-looking: the kind of wholesome, clean-cut young star who would have a wonderful mom and be in love with her.

Before Hunter's re-emer-gence as a kind of cult hero in the 1980s, it was difficult even to recall a single Tab Hunter performance. All one remem-bered were the healthy good looks, the beach-boy body, the winning smile. He made thir-teen movies during the 1950s. Battle Cry and the musical Damn Yankees are the only ones anyone really remembers now. Most of the others — Gun Belt, Island of Desire, Lafayette Escadrille, et al. — are the stuff of trivia games and film ency-clopaedias.

During the 1960s, Hunter's career started to nosedive, hastened no doubt by an ill-fated T.V. series, The Tab Hunter Show, in 1961. He even-tually decided to buy out his contract at Warner Brothers — "I just wanted my freedom," he said later — and went to Europe where he appeared in numerous "spaghetti" west-erns and low-budget war films.

Then in the late 1970s, when Hunter was fast approaching fifty, an unusual thing happened: he re-emerged from the swamp of teen idol oblivion and became a charac-ter actor whose style often gently parodied his own pre-vious image. It started when he became a series regular on the satirical T.V. soap opera Mary Hartman, Mary Hartman in 1977. In 1981, he starred in John Waters's comedy Poly-ester, as a Baltimore drive-in owner pursued by a love-starved housewife (Divine). The critics were amused — and generous in their praise — and gay audiences in particular seemed happy that Tab Hunter was back on the screen. Roles in Grease 2 (as an oversexed biology professor singing about

Brandon de Wilde in *Hud:* A star at age eight; dead at thirty.

reproduction) and *Lust in the Dust* (with Divine again) followed, but both films were box-office failures.

Hunter still isn't much of an actor, but then he doesn't really pretend to be. He remains a cult hero, a symbol of a bygone era and its imagery. Still extraordinarily handsome as he approaches sixty, he spends much of his time now breeding and raising horses. "I'm happiest when I'm shoveling shit," he told an interviewer.

Brandon de Wilde (1942-1972).

Shortly after Brandon de Wilde's violent death in a car accident at the age of thirty, his close friend and former co-star Julie Harris wrote in *The New York Times*, "He was the most beautiful, loving, golden child … a real artist." More pointedly, in a recent tribute to de Wilde, one gay magazine editor observed, "That mouth alone is obscenely beautiful."

De Wilde was already a star by the time he was eight years old, when he appeared on Broadway in a stage adaptation of Carson McCullers's *The Member of the Wedding.* He received the kind of rave reviews and audience adulation that older, more experienced actors yearn for. He repeated the role in the 1952 film version of the play, and the following year he was nominated for an Academy Award for his performance as the towheaded rancher's son in the classic western *Shane*. De Wilde's final line in the film — "Shane. Come back, Shane" — quickly became one of the most legendary parting lines in film history.

For more than a decade after that, up until his early twenties, de Wilde was cast as a series of sensitive, naive, usually thoughtful young men — always with a touch of hero-worship in them — in such films as *Hud*, *All Fall Down*, and *In Harm's Way*. To many, he personified the eternal American teenage boy — troubled, aching, and headed for disillusionment — and while his characters often at first admired the icons of American manhood (womanizing, hard drinking, emotional indifference) they later discarded them as hollow and phoney. Aside from his extraordinarily charismatic looks, it was this, perhaps more than anything, that gave him his tremendous appeal to gay men. (Rumors that de Wilde was himself gay have never been confirmed. He was married for a time to actress Susan Maw.)

De Wilde was never able to sustain the success of his youth into adulthood. Producers felt that the soulful, adolescent Brandon de Wilde was too firmly entrenched in audience's minds for him to be successful as anything else. Yet, astonishingly for a Hollywood child star, he never turned bitter or self-destructive as he grew up and out of the spotlight. Virtually everyone who ever worked with him remembered him as unpretentious, funny, and surprisingly unobsessed with the Hollywood dream machine.

By 1972, he was doing mostly stage work. On the afternoon of his death, he was driving to appear in a production of *Butterflies Are Free* at a local amusement park theater in Denver. A violent thunderstorm passed over the highway, and de Wilde was apparently blinded for a moment: he was killed instantly when his van slammed into the back of a truck parked by the side of the road.

Robert Conrad (b. 1935) (Real name: Conrad Robert Falk).

It was Robert Conrad's appearance every Friday night, from 1965 to 1969, on the CBS series *The Wild, Wild West* that made him a memorable Hollywood heartthrob for thousands of gay adolescents growing up in the sixties. Even though Conrad had had other roles — in the films *Palm Springs Weekend* and *Young Dillinger*, and in the T.V. series *Hawaiian Eye* — he is best remembered today as James T. West, special undercover agent for President Ulysses S. Grant. Whether shirtless, tied up, and waiting to be tortured at the hands of the villainous dwarf, Dr. Loveless, or just strutting across the prairie in his skin-tight black pants, Conrad — a former nightclub singer — helped boost the ratings of CBS's Friday night line-up for four consecutive years.

Robert Conrad calling... Best remembered as special agent James West.

After *The Wild, Wild West* was canceled in 1969, Conrad — known in real life as a fierce political conservative — went on to star in half a dozen other T.V. series, including *Assignment Vienna*, *Baa Baa Black Sheep*, *The D.A.*, *The Duke*, and *High Mountain Rangers* (co-starring his sons, Christian and Shane). He also appeared in the NBC miniseries *Centennial*, and showed up on various specials, including *Battle of the Network Stars*.

He is currently at work on another T.V. series for CBS.

Troy Donahue (b. 1936) (Real name: Merle Johnson, Jr.).

If certain studio executives had had their way, there might never have been a Troy Donahue. Instead, they originally wanted to call him Paris Donahue, "Paris" after the legendary lover of Helen of Troy. "But I guess they thought they couldn't, because there was already a Paris, France and a Paris, Illinois," Donahue recalled, years later. So the executives settled for "Troy."

Donahue first established himself as a star in 1959, op-

Troy Donahue: He was almost Paris Donahue.

posite Sandra Dee, in the popular wide-screen soap-opera *A Summer Place*. His success rested almost entirely on his youthful, blond-haired good looks and smooth, surfer's body. His Hollywood career — bolstered by such hit films as *Susan Slade* and *Rome Adventure* — peaked around 1962. After that, it quickly started to slide.

In 1963, Donahue began a twenty-year addiction to booze and drugs. "The unknown scared me most when I started to fade in the late sixties," he said later. By his own admission, breakfast every morning consisted of three aspirins, codeine, a pint of vodka, and four lines of cocaine. Audiences were shocked when he re-appeared, in 1971, as a drug-crazed, Charles Manson-like killer in the low budget, sex-ploitation shocker *Sweet Saviour*. Even when he got an important part — as Talia Shire's boyfriend in *The Godfather Part II* in 1974 — much of his salary went for drugs.

Finally, in 1982, he entered a drug treatment program, and successfully overcame his drug and alcohol dependencies. He was last seen on American movie screens as an oversexed washing-machine salesman — with a penchant for bondage — in the 1984 comedy *Grandview U.S.A.*

Mark Frechette (1948-1972).

In 1970, Mark Frechette was snatched from obscurity and given the starring role in film director Michelangelo Antonioni's controversial and highly publicized movie *Zabriskie Point*. Frechette was from a poor family, and at the time of his discovery he was living in a commune in Boston's Fort Hill ghetto. The commune, according to Frechette, was "devoted to the teachings of Christ, Thoreau, and Emerson," and Frechette was their

Mark Frechette: His life had more to say about the sixties than *Zabriskie Point* ever could.

resident carpenter. He was also active in draft-resistance work. "He has the elegance of an aristocrat, though from a poor family," Antonioni later remarked. "There is something mystical about him." An Antonioni talent scout first spotted Mark having a fist fight at a Boston bus stop.

Zabriskie Point was to have been Antonioni's volcanic vision of America: an explosive look at the Vietnam War protest years, a study of the clash between alienated, idealistic youth and materialistic American values. In it, Mark played the central role of a restless, unfulfilled college student who blindly entangles himself in a student uprising and then later becomes an urban terrorist.

"My only worry about the film," MGM president James Aubrey announced before its release, "is that the kids will rip up the seats right out of the theater." He needn't have worried: not only were America's theater seats safe, but "the kids" largely ignored the film, and the critics, almost without exception, panned it. The fact is that *Zabriskie Point*, which was to have been Mark Frechette's catapult to stardom, was a mess — chaotic, incoherent, and one-dimensional — and Frechette himself, though strikingly good-looking and sexy, was no actor. "Frechette has a movie star face," wrote one critic. "He looks like a cross between Warren Beatty and Peter Fonda — but he's a nothing on the screen."

Despite its failure with audiences, the film managed to generate a sizable controversy. Both the Justice Department and the FBI allegedly tried to interfere with its release, and various right-wing political groups made threats against Antonioni and MGM. Frechette claimed that his phone was being tapped, his mail was being opened, and that he was being followed by the FBI. The storm soon passed, however, and Frechette eventually returned to his commune in Boston, taking *Zabriskie Point*'s female co-star, Daria Halprin, with him.

Nothing was heard of him again, until three years later, when he was arrested on armed-robbery charges, after an abortive bank hold-up in Boston; his accomplice was shot to death at the scene by police. When the case came to trial in 1974, Frechette pleaded guilty and was sentenced to fifteen years in prison. He died behind bars. He was apparently trying to benchpress 160 pounds in the prison's weight room, when he lost his grip on the weight bar, and it dropped on his throat. His neck was instantly broken.

Aldo Ray (b. 1926) (Real name: Aldo DaRe).

Aldo Ray deserves credit. When his Hollywood career started to slump in the sixties and the market dried up for his wide-screen portrayals of big-hearted redneck goons, he took

Aldo Ray: A man and his pole...

his best assets in hand and jumped into the burgeoning porno-movie busines. He was a natural: his uncut endowment was huge. The husky, bull-necked actor — popular in such legitimate films as *Miss Sadie Thompson* (1953), *Battle Cry* (1955), and *The Naked and the Dead* (1958) — kept his celluloid career moving right along.

A former Navy frogman and small-town sheriff, Ray was discovered in 1951 and first appeared as a football player in the sports melodrama *Saturday's Hero*. For ten years after that, he played, almost without exception, a succession of strutting, pushy, loud-mouthed rednecks, usually from the military or sometimes from the world of sports.

With his thick-necked, muscular physique, foghorn voice, and insinuating smile, he brought a certain unabashed sexuality to his roles. It was lustiness with a reckless, slightly sadistic edge; his characters often seemed to exemplify the military saying, "If you can't eat it or fuck it, then piss on it." He was the kind of fifties sex symbol overlooked in large part by fan magazines, gossip columnists, and the average American housewife; but gay men caught on quickly. Beefy and aggressive, Aldo Ray turned on an entire generation, and then some.

By 1961, his career had gone off the tracks. Although he continued to work, most of the films he was in — *The Green Berets, Sanctuary for Evil*, et al. — were badly received. By then in his forties, but still virile and sexy, he made a successful leap into straight porno films.

Joe Dallesandro (b. 1948).

"If you watch carefully," Dallesandro once quipped, "you'll see that my best performing comes when I have my clothes off." But when Joe Dallesandro had his clothes off, no one was watching his acting.

Joe Dallesandro: "A fucking god."

They were watching *him*: the big muscles, the perfect ass, the prominent nipples, the cool, impassive good looks. "The man is a fucking god," one gay magazine noted, in a tribute to him. By contrast, a prominent film critic once remarked of Dallesandro's acting, "He isn't just impotent; he's barely alive."

Dallesandro was born in Pensacola, Florida, where his father was stationed in the Navy. The family later moved, and Joe grew up on Long Island, first with his real parents, then with a foster family. In his teens he went to California looking for a job. He posed nude in a now-famous session for the

Athletic Model Guild, supposedly made spare cash working as a hustler (though he later denied he had ever "really" hustled), and eventually fell in with Andy Warhol's bizarre entourage of freaky would-be actresses, male transvestites, and chi-chi drug addicts. "I started working here [at Andy Warhol's Factory] one day doing odd jobs," Dallesandro said in a 1970 interview. "Finally, one day they said, 'You're gonna be in a movie,' and I said, 'Oh, yeah.' And that's how I became an actor."

Warhol cast the astonishing good-looking teenager (Joe was nineteen at the time) in the 1967 film *The Loves of Ondine*. The next year, Dallesandro starred in Warhol's quasi-pornographic *Lonesome Cowboys*, followed by *Trash, Flesh*, and *Heat*. The ads were often more interesting than the films themselves: for example, the ad for *Flesh* featured a nude photo of Dallessandro, cropped just above the pubic hair, with the titillating caption, "Can a boy be *too* attractive?"

In most of his movies, Dallesandro played an impassive hustler type, a beautiful boy drifting through life and content to be manipulated by others. The films were cheaply made and semi-improvisational: Warhol's style was often to let the camera run while his performers loitered around in front of it. There was rarely a script. The films' lethargic, meandering style caught on with counterculture audiences in the late sixties and early seventies, and Joe, who was billed as "Warhol's male superstar," became a cultural anti-hero and male sex symbol. Lou Reed's *Walk on the Wild Side*, with its lyrics, "Little Joe never gave it away, everyone had to pay and pay," was a tribute of sorts to Dallesandro and other members of Warhol's inner circle; though Joe later decried that image of himself — as a kind of pop-art Casey Donovan — as "bullshit." Nor did he think of himself as a sex symbol: "Are you kidding?" he once told an interviewer. "If you lived at my house you wouldn't feel like much of a sex symbol. My second wife is pregnant. We even wear pajamas to bed."

In 1974, Dallesandro starred in his first non-Warhol movie, a cheap Mexican horror film called *Seeds of Evil*, in which he played a mysterious gardener who can turn himself into a tree. Later that year he went to Europe and starred in *Andy Warhol's Frankenstein*, followed by *Andy Warhol's Dracula*, both of which were trounced by the critics. They fared little better with audiences. Dallesandro was also in a dozen other films, including Louis Malle's surreal cult classic *Black Moon*, and Francis Ford Coppola's *Cotton Club*.

Dallesandro returned to Hollywood in the early 1980s hoping to establish a mainstream acting career for himself. In an interview in 1983 he said he wanted to do "something to be proud of. Something where I can say I've made a statement. Not something that I made just because somebody asked me to do it."

HEPBURN, JOHN AND THOMAS WHITE (died together on the scaffold in 1811). Hepburn was a young British ensign and White a drummer in the Guardsmen. In 1811, the two men were found guilty of having committed sodomy together and were hanged in front of a large crowd, including several noblemen, outside Newgate Prison in London. Hepburn claimed to the last he was innocent, and, with a noose around his neck, begged for his life. White, who according to all reports was exceedingly handsome, was known as a frequent customer at the White Swan, a then-infamous London club for homosexuals.

HOBSON, CHRISTOPHER (b. 1941), gay son of U.S. novelist Laura Z. Hobson; Laura Hobson was best known for her books *Gentleman's Agreement* and *Consenting Adult*, the latter about a mother and father's reaction to the revelation that their son is gay.

Christopher told his mother he was gay in a letter to her when he was seventeen. Twelve years later, he wrote her another letter announcing he had come out publicly and joined the gay liberation movement. "As I read his words," Laura wrote many years later, in her autobiography, "I had to keep brushing at my eyes so that I could see. The courage, I thought, the young courage, just as I had over that other letter when he was only seventeen. Now he was a man of twenty-nine, and he too had made the decision to reject the world's ancient judgements."

However, Laura's decision, the following year, to write a novel about homosexuality — *Consenting Adult* — caused a serious rift between mother and son, a rift that resulted in them not speaking to one another for nearly three years. "I could sympathize with her aims," Christopher later explained, "but I felt she should not write the book at all. I was disturbed by the amount of detail the manuscript drew from my own life — as I suppose many authors' relatives have been. More fundamentally, I felt, rightly or wrongly, that to focus as the book did on the parents' reactions and conflicts inevitably gave some ground to the idea that homosexuality itself was a problem, that it was undesirable, even if accepted in the end." Christopher's objections — and his mother's responses to them — snowballed into a fierce and serious quarrel between them.

The estrangement ended in 1978, when Laura was operated on for uterine cancer. "Then," Christopher noted, "we did agree to disagree — we had no other choice ... And this time we were determined to hurt each other no more — not in those deep, fundamental ways that tear families apart, and too often find no healing before death."

THE HOLLYWOOD REPORTER — SEXIEST SCREEN ACTORS OF TODAY, ACCORDING TO. For its 54th anniversary issue,

The Hollywood Reporter polled directors, producers, agents, and journalists for a list of the nine sexiest actors working in Hollywood today. At the top of the list was Mel Gibson. Following him were: Prince, Tom Selleck, Rob Lowe, Sam Shepard, Richard Gere, Steven Bauer, Matt Dillon, and Tom Cruise.

HOLMES JOHN (1944-1988), U.S. porn star — also known as "Johnny Wadd" — renowned for his extraordinarily large endowment; his penis, he liked to say, "was bigger than a pay phone, smaller than a Cadillac." He once boasted of having had more than 14,000 sex partners — including three governors and one U.S. senator — during his lifetime, and at the peak of his career he made more than three thousand dollars a day, from film appearances and from servicing well-to-do men and women across the country and in Europe. "A happy gardener is one with dirty fingernails," he once said, "and a happy cook is a fat cook. I never get tired of what I do because I'm a sex fiend. I'm very lusty."

Holmes's film career began to wane in the early 1980s, largely because of a heavy cocaine habit; the cocaine affected his ability to get an erection, and he eventually stopped working in porn altogether and turned instead to dealing drugs. Then, in the summer of 1985, he was diagnosed with AIDS. According to his wife, Laurie, "John said he felt like he was chosen to get AIDS because of who he was, how he lived. He felt like he was an example." Holmes died from the disease in March 1988, at the age of forty-three.

THE HORN BOOK (c. 1890), nineteenth-century sex manual. Its full title was *The Horn Book, or Modern Studies in the Science of Stroking*.

A chapter on male homosexuality, titled "Sodomy, or Man With Man," began with the author reassuring his readers that, "I can only speak from hearsay of the joys of two or more men together, without women, as I have never given way to this diversion." That disclaimer out of the way, he then explained the basics of mutual masturbation, fellatio, and anal intercourse between men. Acknowledging that homosexuals' brains have been largely "weakened by vile debauchery," he described how "they often prefer to suck a prick when it has just left an arse-hole still reeking with whatever is lurking therein, and one of the pleasures of bottom-fucking is when the cock is found to have changed colour on leaving the tight hole, having become brown or yellow ... There are many buggers who only care to get up a man just when he feels inclined to go to stool. They say in such a case that their cock finds a softer nook to wallow in and that the real pleasure of the true sodomitical arse-hole piercer is to plunge his instrument in a hot pudding obstructing the anus, bursting to force its way out. So before beginning their bottom-fuck they make sure by means of an investigating finger that the 'egg' is there; that the rectum is full and the bird about to lay. In a word, these depraved fellows give themselves up together to everything that the most filthy and crapulous imagination can devise and the more horribly dirty it is, the more pleasure they experience."

The author ended the chapter by giving a sampling of late nineteenth century gay slang:

Bottle and Glass: Buttocks
North Pole: Anus
Tommy Dodd: Sodomite
Hampton Wick: Penis
Dicky Dirt: Shirt
Round the House's: Pants

Tommy Rollocks: Testicles
Jack-in-the-Box: Syphilis
Horse and Trap: Gonorrhea

HORRY COUNTY, SOUTH CAROLINA. In 1989, officials in Horry County, South Carolina banned all books on homosexuality from school libraries, after a statewide AIDS bill (passed in 1988) forbade students from being taught that homosexuality is an alternative lifestyle. The new law also prohibited teachers from discussing gay and lesbian relationships, except in the context of sexually transmitted diseases.

HUDSON, ROCK — ATTEMPTED RESURRECTION BY SHIRLEY BOONE AND OTHERS. As Rock Hudson lay dying of AIDS in his Beverly Hills home in late 1985, members of a Pentecostal church in Van Nuys, California were allowed into his bedroom to try to cure him of the disease through faith-healing, fasting, and speaking in tongues. Included in the group — which also tried to "spiritually release" Hudson from his homosexuality — were entertainer Pat Boone and his wife, Shirley. "I had a feeling that if Rock were to recover miraculously," Pat Boone said

Pat Boone: Physician Heal Thyself.

later, "he would then have not only a wonderful story to tell about God's goodness but he would have hope to offer other AIDS victims and other homosexuals. That's what I hoped to see happen. I prayed that he would be healed and that God's love and power would be demonstrated through the situation."

The night before Hudson died, the Pentecostal group was so certain they had made progress in reversing his condition, they ordered some "happy clothes" be laid out for him in the morning. "Get some bright clothes for him," one of the group said. "He's tired tonight, but he's going to feel better in the morning, so get him some happy clothes to put on!" The next morning, one of Hudson's nurses — also a born-again Christian — forced the half-coherent actor out of bed and into his "happy clothes." According to one eyewitness, Hudson looked as if he were in agonizing pain, and once the clothes were on "he was lying there like a doll, not moving." The actor started to drool all over himself. Two hours later, he was dead.

Even after Hudson died, Shirley Boone returned to his bedroom and attempted to bring him back to life through prayer. In fact, she later claimed she could feel Hudson's feet getting warm again. However, her ministrations were interupted when messengers from the mortuary arrived to remove the actor's body. "It was difficult for any of us to believe that there had been a final reversal in what we'd seen the night before," Pat Boone said afterward. "He had already gone, but they prayed at the bedside for some time. It's like the three women who went to the tomb of Jesus. They, of course, had different results."

"THE HULK," Marvel Comics character created in 1962 by Stan Lee and Jack Kirby. In one 1980 comic book, the Hulk (a.k.a. Bruce Banner) travels through New York City, where he is molested by homosexuals in the showers of the YMCA. "Hey! W-hat do you guys want?" Banner asks, standing in the showers naked. "Umm!" says a black gay man, touching Banner's chest. "You're *soft!* And all pearly white — and you've got the cutest little cheeks! Think he'll whine, Dewey?" Dewey — a long-haired blond in a tanktop — replies, "Yeah, Luellen — an' I *like* it when they whine!" Banner escapes the "fate worse than death" by turning into the Hulk. The homophobic strip drew fire from the National Gay and Lesbian Task Force and other gay groups.

HUNT, LESTER (d. 1955), U.S. senator from Wyoming. In 1955, with the U.S. Senate almost evenly divided between Democrats and Republicans, Hunt — a popular Democratic politician — was approached by Republican Party strategists who wanted his senate seat and who informed him that if he ran for re-election in November, they would see to it that news of his son's homosexuality was spread from coast to coast in the national newspapers. Hunt's son had recently been arrested in Washington, D.C. for soliciting an undercover policeman for homosexual acts. Hunt eventually acquiesced to the Republican blackmail and withdrew from the race. Eleven days later, he shot himself to death with a rifle.

HUNT, NANCY (b. 1927), U.S. journalist and transsexual. As a combat reporter in Vietnam for the Chicago *Tribune*, Hunt gained a reputation for being courageous, gutsy, and, in the words of one colleague, "supermasculine." Inwardly, however, he was miserable. One night when he was forty-four, he finally confessed to his wife, Ellen, that he'd always wanted to be a woman. "That shouldn't be hard to arrange," she told him. Shortly afterwards, she began helping him dress up in woman's clothing, bought him wigs, and helped him learn the art of applying makeup. Hunt's co-workers at the *Tribune* were startled to see their formerly plain-dressed, moustached colleague arriving for work in increasingly effeminate dress, with his moustache shaved off and just "the tiniest bit of makeup" on his face.

"The men simply could not believe their eyes," Hunt recalled. "I was the combat correspondent, the old police reporter ... I finally retired from the men's room when I saw one of the men glaring at me as I washed my hands. He was outraged at my presence in his sanctuary ... My mad careen toward womanhood was like being on a greased shuttle. I don't know if I could have stopped."

Finally, in February 1976, Hunt underwent "gender reassignment" surgery at the University of Virginia. "Tomorrow they are going to cut off your sex organs!" a psychiatrist screamed at him the night before the operation. Shortly afterward, Hunt re-emerged as a woman.

Ellen, who had stayed by him through the whole process and who accompanied him to the hospital for surgery, filed for divorce three months later. "She feels now like she was an accomplice to murder," Hunt explained. At work, Hunt was transferred "off the street, out of public view" to a more innocuous job at the copy desk.

Yet for Nancy Hunt, it's all been worth it. "All the years as

John Hurt as a gay undercover detective in *Partners* (1982)

a man," she told *People* magazine in 1979, "I would look in the mirror and hate myself. Now I'm an avowed sexual freak. Yet I look in that mirror, and after a lifetime of self-loathing I can say, 'Hey, I like me.'"

HURT, JOHN (b. 1940), English actor. Hurt played a gay man helping police solve a murder in the 1982 comedy *Partners*. Asked if the movie drew any complaints from gay men while it was filming in Los Angeles, Hurt said, "They didn't like it that I was wearing a lilac-colored track suit in it. They say homosexuals do not necessarily do that. And the person who's saying this is sitting there in a *pink* track suit. It's a crazy world we live in."

INDEX LIBRORUM PROHIBITORUM, the Catholic Index of Forbidden Books, a list of books forbidden to members of the Roman Catholic Church by the Vatican. The Index was started in 1559 by Pope Paul IV, and soon became one of the most powerful forces for censorship in world history. Through the centuries, several gay writers and gay-themed works were added to the Index — including, in 1955, the complete *opus* of French writer Andre Gide — although the Index was primarily concerned with blasphemy, anticlericalism, and heresy. The Vatican continued compiling the Index for more than four centuries, before essentially abandoning it in 1966.

IRAN-*CONTRA* SCANDAL — GAY INVOLVEMENT IN. One of the first men to plead guilty to charges of fraud in the Iran-*contra* scandal was Carl "Spitz" Channell, a gay Washington conservative. Channell, a political protégé to the late Terry Dolan, became Oliver North's favorite fund-raiser for aid to the Nicaraguan *contras*. He was convicted of illegally setting up a tax-free foundation to funnel aid to the Nicaraguan rebels, and also helped auction off presidential photo opportunities with Ronald Reagan to would-be donors to the *contra* cause.

Like Terry Dolan — who later died of AIDS — Channell also helped various right-wing, "pro-family" groups, including the virulently anti-gay organization of a Texas businessman, Berl Hurlbut; the organization was dedicated to "opposing the homosexual expansion" in America. Hurlbut has said of the group, to which Channell made a sizable contribution, "If AIDS had not come along to more or less do it for us, we would have been readily in the middle of a vigorous opposition to what the homosexuals were doing to the moral structure of the country."

In 1989, Channell was given a two-year suspended sentence and a fifty-dollar fine for his part in the Iran-*contra* scandal.

The presiding judge said he was loath to send him to prison, "because Channell so obviously cares about what happens to this country."

ISAIAH OF RHODES AND ALEXANDER OF DIOSPOLIS, bishops during the reign of the Roman emperor Justinian (A.D. 475-565). The two were found guilty of sodomy, deposed, and then brutally punished. Under Justinian law, punishment for homosexual acts included having one's penis cut off, the hands amputated, and being tortured by the insertion of sharp reeds into the urethra, anus, and various other sensitive parts of the body. After undergoing torture, the two bishops were dragged through the streets of Constantinople. Justinian had made homosexual acts punishable by death in part after coming to believe that continued tolerance for homosexuality was responsible for recent devastating earthquakes and famines.

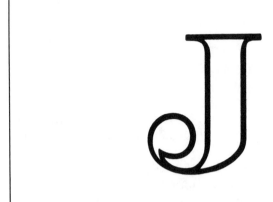

"JADED QUEEN" — ORIGIN OF EXPRESSION. The term "jaded" — meaning worn-out, weary, or blasé — goes back to the sixteenth century; "jade" was originally a term for a "vicious, worthless, ill-tempered horse," a horse that no longer had any energy or one that was no longer able to function properly.

JAIL, GAY MEN WHO SPENT TIME IN.

Jon King (b. 1957), U.S. porn star. He spent five months in a minimum-security prison for juveniles when he was nineteen, after he was convicted of theft. "It wasn't the hell-hole of prison blocks that people imagine," he said later, but added, "It also wasn't an orgiastic all-boy harem."

Truman Capote (1924-1984), U.S. writer. Capote was thrown into jail for eighteen hours on a contempt of court citation, after he refused to testify at the trial of a murderer he had once interviewed. Just before his incarceration, he light-heartedly told the press, "I've been in thirty or forty jails and prisons, but this is the first time I'll ever be in one as a prisoner." The brief experience devastated him: he came out of jail looking, according to one friend, "as if he had been raped, rolled, and beaten up." He was immediately taken to a hospital. In 1983, he was once again jailed for a brief period, this time for drunk driving.

Dave Connors (1945-1985), U.S. porn star. Shortly after his discharge from the Marines,

Connors spent time in jail for dealing drugs.

Rev. Troy Perry (b. 1940), U.S. minister and activist, founder of the Metropolitan Community Church. In 1970, Perry was arrested by police for "blocking the sidewalk" while he was watching a gay pride parade in Hollywood. He spent the night in jail. It was in jail that he witnessed the brutal beating of a male-to-female transsexual by a group of heterosexual prisoners. The next morning, Perry arranged for the transsexual's release, as well as his own, and thereafter pushed for laws ending the mixing of transsexual prisoners with heterosexual males in jails and prisons.

Lord Alfred Douglas (1870-1945), British poet and lover to Oscar Wilde. Douglas spent five months in prison in 1924, after he was convicted of criminally libelling Winston Churchill in a political pamphlet.

Gennady Trifonov (b. 1945), Soviet writer, the only openly gay writer in the Soviet Union. Trifonov was arrested in 1976 and sentenced to four years in a labor camp for having written and circulated explicitly homo-erotic poetry. At one point during his imprisonment, he was placed in a cell with violent criminals who were instructed by the guards to go ahead and "teach the fairy a lesson"; Trifonov was then brutally beaten by the other inmates. He was released in 1980.

Hart Crane (1899-1932), U.S. poet. Crane spent time in jails in Paris, New York City, and Mexico for, among other things, public drunkenness, failing to pay his bills, assaulting police officers, and trying to pick up sailors.

Oscar Wilde (1854-1900), Irish playwright and wit. "Prison life," wrote Oscar Wilde, "makes one see people and things as they really are. That is why it turns one to stone." Wilde spent two years at hard labor in an English prison for having committed homosexual acts. His experience left him a bankrupt and in many ways broken man, and his only literary work after he was released was *The Ballad of Reading Gaol*, a plea for more humane prison conditions in England.

Joe Orton (1933-1967), British playwright. In 1962, he and his lover, Kenneth Halliwell, were incarcerated for six months, in separate prisons, for stealing and defacing library books; they wrote pornographic jacket blurbs for the books and then pasted them on the inside covers, or pasted comical pictures on the fronts of otherwise serious works. "I didn't suffer or anything the way Oscar Wilde suffered from being in prison," Orton once told an interviewer. In fact, Orton credited his liberation as a writer to his incarceration: being in prison, he said, had helped give his writing maturity and detachment.

Casey Klinger (b. 1958), U.S. gay magazine publisher. Klinger spent almost two years in federal prison on mail-fraud charges, involving the illegal use of credit cards belonging to subscribers of a magazine he had started. He later described his incarceration as similar to "being in a cage with a bunch of dirty monkeys. The illegal aliens would shit in the shower and constantly attempt to conquer me sexually." Klinger described his months in prison as "long, horrid months ... months of fighting off illegal aliens and dope dealers."

Bill Tilden (1893-1953), U.S. tennis champion. Tilden spent eight months at a California honor farm after being found guilty of indecent acts with a

minor. Shortly after his release, he was arrested again, on the same charge, and was sent to a road camp. Despite his standing as one of the great athletes of the century, he lived out his last remaining years, following his release, in disgrace and near oblivion.

Taylor Mead (b. 1940), U.S. poet and actor. Mead has spent time in jails in New York (for solicitation), South Carolina (for criminal trespassing), Las Vegas (for vagrancy), and New Orleans (also for vagrancy).

Paul Verlaine (1844-1896), French poet. In 1873, Verlaine was sentenced to two years in prison for attempted manslaughter, after he tried to kill his younger lover, Arthur Rimbaud, with a pistol (Rimbaud escaped with only a gunshot wound to his hand). Verlaine later said that his only consolation in prison was religion.

Jean Genet (1910-1986), French writer. His first taste of imprisonment came when he was ten years old; he was convicted of theft and sent to the Mettray Reformatory. Throughout his life, Genet was convicted and imprisoned at least ten more times on various theft charges. After the tenth conviction, he was sentenced by the courts to mandatory life imprisonment. He was later pardoned and released through the efforts of such prominent literary figures as Jean Cocteau and Jean-Paul Sartre.

JOCKEY BRIEFS, popular brand of men's brief-style underwear, and a significant fetish object for many gay men. The standard white underwear brief was first developed by the Jockey International Company in 1934; it was inspired by a photograph one of the company's marketing executives had seen of a man on the French Riviera wearing swimming trunks cut in a brief-style. Before then, men's underwear had consisted mostly of either long-johns or boxer shorts. The actual designer of the Jockey brief was A.R. Kniebler. His original design had no fly opening in the front; the opening was added in 1936, and the version sold today is the same as it was fifty-three years ago. In volume of sales, Fruit of the Loom currently outsells Jockey; but for many gay men with a fetish for briefs, Jockey remains the preferred brand.

JOCKSTRAP, or athletic supporter. The modern jockstrap was invented by a Finnish athlete, Parvo Nakacheker, between 1895 and 1900. According to one source, Nakacheker "devoted much time to the study of pure anatomy and the special demands of such an item."

JORGENSEN, CHRISTINE (1926-1989), U.S. transsexual and nightclub entertainer. Formerly George Jorgensen. The one-time army private made international headlines in 1953 after becoming the world's first well-publicized, successful transsexual. "I received, according to editors and publishers, more newspaper print than any other human being in the history of newspapers," Jorgensen once said. "That included Roosevelt, Churchill, Stalin, and Hitler." Jorgensen was twenty-six at the time she completed her sex-change therapy.

All of his life, Jorgensen had felt he should have been born a girl. Shortly after his discharge from the U.S. Army in 1947, he began taking estrogen without a prescription, and in 1950, he flew to Copenhagen to consult with a medical expert, Dr. Christian Hamburger. Hamburger told him, "You are the victim of a problem that usually starts in early childhood, an irresistible feeling that you wish to be regarded by society and by yourself, as belonging to the opposite sex. Nothing is able to change this feeling ... I think the trouble is very deeply rooted in the cells of your body. Outwardly, you have many of the sex characteristics of a man. But your body chemistry and all of your body cells, including your brain cells, may be female." Shortly afterward, Jorgensen underwent the necessary operations — and the more than two thousand hormone injections — to change genders.

Jorgensen's return to the United States in 1953 unleashed a storm of publicity and controversy. At the time of her return, the *New York Daily News* reported, "Christine Jorgensen, the lad who became a lady, arrived home from Denmark yesterday, lit a cigarette like a girl, husked 'Hello,' and tossed off a Bloody Mary like a guy, then opened her fur coat. Jane Russell has nothing to worry about." "Through the years," Jorgensen said three decades later, "I've encountered every attitude and response known. Some people thought me a courageous pioneer, others regarded me as dis-

gusting and immoral; some of the clergy considered that I had committed an ungodly act..."

Not long after her return, she embarked on a successful career as a writer, lecturer, talk-show guest, and nightclub entertainer. In 1982, she was able to tell an interviewer, "I am the woman I always wanted to be. I'm happy and I love life. And it is a fairly normal life, too." She later added, "My neighbors don't pay any more attention to me than to any other 54-year-old lady wandering around the supermarket looking for a bargain."

JURADO, CONCHITA (1864-1961), male impersonator, regarded as one of the great impostors of the century. She was born in Mexico City.

A soft-spoken, retiring woman with an extraordinary gift for mimicry, Jurado fooled literally thousands of people — generals, businessmen, fortune-hunting women, detectives — with her impersonation of a bombastic, adventurous, skirt-chasing Mexican millionaire whom she called Don Carlos Balmori. It began as an occasional (and reasonably innocent) entertainment for close friends and relatives when she was in her late teens.

By the time she was sixty, the masquerade was being played out on a grand scale and had evolved into an extravagant hoax that duped an entire city.

Disguised as Balmori, the eccentric and profligate tycoon, Jurado made national headlines with her lavish business deals, amorous adventures, and political maneuverings. People were invited to attend Balmori's parties at which they were led to believe they might receive large sums of money from the whimsical multimillionaire. The point was to see how far people would go, to what extent they would humiliate themselves, to win the tycoon's favor and some of his cash. The climax of each gathering was always the same: Jurado would rip off her moustache, let down her hair, and announce to the victims of the hoax, "Nothing is exactly as it seems to be. Nothing is real. The truth is always hidden."

Far from being insulted, most people seemed strangely delighted by having been duped, and Jurado's victims were all sworn to silence, to keep the secret of Don Carlos Balmori's real identity until their deaths. Past victims became automatic members of "Los Balmori," an exclusive society which planned forthcoming parties and chose new victims for the hoax. Meanwhile, the newspapers kept reporting the activities of Balmori — complete with photographs of "him" on big-game hunts, or with an intended bride — as if he were a real person.

Jurado gave her last performance as Don Carlos Balmori in 1931, when she was sixty-six years old and dying of cancer. After her death, the entire hoax was revealed to the public. The reaction was one of widespread amusement and astonishment, and Jurado — who had wanted to prove that every man, and woman, has their price — immediately became a legend in Mexico City. Today, her tomb is a popular tourist spot, and is covered with painted tiles, each one depicting a memorable episode from her famous impersonation.

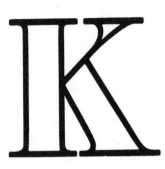

KAEL, PAULINE (b. 1919), *New Yorker* film critic, considered by many to be the most important film critic of her time, certainly one of the most influential, but often accused of being homophobic as well. A sampling from some of her reviews most frequently cited as homophobic:

The Damned (1969): "It seems to be not so much a political movie as a homosexual fantasy ... It's really a story about a good boy who loves his wicked mother, and how she emasculates him and makes him decadent — the basic mother-son romance of homo-erotic literature, dressed up in Nazi drag."

Rich and Famous (1981): "*Rich and Famous* isn't camp, exactly; it's more like a homosexual fantasy. Jacqueline

Biset's affairs, with their masochistic overtones, are creepy, because they don't seem like what a woman would get into. And Candice Bergen is used almost as if she were a big, goosey female impersonator."

Victor/Victoria (1982): "When homosexuals were despised, there was a compensatory myth that they had better taste than anybody else. Their enthusiasm for *Victor/Victoria* should help debunk that myth."

Kael has also been criticized for her occasional use of the word "faggot" — as in her early review of *The Boys in the Band* — when referring to gay men.

On the other hand, she was one of the earliest critics to take exception to Hollywood's "knee-jerk" use of homosexuals as convenient villains (as in her review of *The Laughing Policeman*: "Once again the mad mass murderer is some implausible sort of fancy homosexual"). She was also — despite whatever homophobic undertones may have existed in the review — one of the few critics to condemn *The Damned* because it seemed to equate homosexuality with Nazism: "It's easy to say that the decadence in this movie is a metaphor for Nazism, but it's a dubious metaphor, and I think people take it not as a metaphor but as an *explanation*; I think they really want to believe that German perversions and moral decay were what caused the Second World War." She has also, on occasion, attacked the shallowness with which gay men have been portrayed on the screen (as in her review of *Funny Lady*, in which she called Roddy McDowall's role as a homosexual performer "wasted" and "unenviable," because the script called for him to be the cheap target of everyone else's abuse while never allowing him the opportunity to wittily rebuff or answer them).

Confronted directly with questions about her alleged homophobia, Kael told *Mandate* magazine in 1983, "I don't believe that the overt or honest expression of a homosexual theme has ever offended me in any way; it's only the covert that I've kidded — and never, I hope, as a hanging judge."

KALISAYA BAR, turn-of-the-century gay bar in Paris, located in the Boulevard des Italiens. The bar was frequented by Oscar Wilde during his last years. Wilde gathered there with his friends — most of them young, would-be poets — at five o'clock every afternoon. "One beautiful boy of bad character," wrote Wilde, "of the name of Georges, goes there too, but he is so like Antinous, and so smart, that he is allowed to talk to poets ... He is like a very handsome Roman boy, dark, and bronze-like, with splendidly chiseled nose and mouth... " Wilde later learned that Georges, a male prostitute, had gone to Nice to improve his fortunes. "It is beautiful, and encouraging," Wilde remarked, "to find people who can combine romance with business — blend them indeed, and make them one."

KENNEDY, ANTHONY (b. 1936), U.S. Supreme Court justice. In 1980, as a federal appeals court judge, Kennedy questioned the U.S. military's policy of automatically discharging homosexuals. The case, *Beller vs. Middendorf*, concerned three sailors who were discharged from the Navy when it became known they were gay. Kennedy upheld the constitutional right of the Navy to exclude gays, but challenged the wisdom of such a policy. "The Navy's blanket rule requiring discharge of all who have engaged in homosexual conduct," he wrote, "is perhaps broader than necessary to accomplish some of its goals ... Upholding the challenged regulations as constitutional is distinct from a statement that they are wise."

Kennedy's appointment to the U.S. Supreme Court, in February 1988, came after a first nominee, Robert Bork, was rejected by the U.S. Senate, and after a second nominee, Douglas Ginsburg, withdrew when it was learned he had smoked marijuana. Initially, Kennedy was to have been the Reagan Administration's next choice after Bork; but hard-line conservatives made it clear they would oppose Kennedy, in part because he was perceived as being "soft" on homosexuals. After the Bork and Ginsburg disasters, however, there was no outspoken objection to Kennedy's nomination, and he was confirmed by a Senate vote of 97-0.

KHOMEINI, AYATOLLAH (1900-1989), spiritual leader of Iran. After an Islamic revolution toppled the Shah's government in 1979, Khomeini returned to power in Iran after several years of exile in France. Under his leadership, hundreds of alleged homosexuals were summarily executed. Former supporters of the Shah were also routinely charged with sodomy and then shot by firing squads. Khomeini's vehemence about homosexuality extended even to bestial relations between men and animals. "Sexual relations with an animal are reserved for men alone," he once wrote. "A man may have sexual relations with animals only if the animal is female. Sexual relations with a male animal are a mortal sin."

KINSEY, DR. ALFRED (1894-1956), U.S. zoologist whose examination of human sexual behavior in the U.S. led to the groundbreaking — and controversial — studies *Sexual Behavior in the Human Male* (1948) and *Sexual Behavior in the Human Female* (1953), otherwise known as "The Kinsey Reports."

The researcher who forever changed the way Americans view themselves and their sexuality — and who paved the way for the "sexual revolution" — was in fact a conservative and deeply religious man who had once recommended prayer and religious devotion as a cure for the "sin" of masturbation. Kinsey — who received his doctorate in entymology — first became interested in human sexuality when he was chosen to teach a course in sex education at Indiana University in 1937; he was chosen to teach the class *because* he was so conservative and had such deeply held religious beliefs. However, in trying to prepare the course, he soon discovered there was a scarcity of information on the subject, and he was unable to answer his students' questions about masturbation, pre-marital sex, homosexuality, and other topics, since very little scientific research had ever been done in those fields. Frustrated and intrigued, he began his own investigation into human sexual behavior: a study that eventually involved over 18,500 personal interviews with men and women, and that initially consumed more than a decade of his life.

Among other things, Kinsey found that thirteen percent of American males were predominantly homosexual for at least a three-year period in their lives; more than one-third had experienced at least one homosexual experience to the point of orgasm. Additionally, five percent reported they were bisexual, with homosexual and heterosexual experiences about equally balanced in their lives. He also found that twenty-eight percent of the women he interviewed had had at least one or more lesbian experiences by the time they were forty-five; the better educated a woman was, the more likely it was she had had some kind of lesbian experience to the point of orgasm.

"The homosexual," Kinsey concluded, "has been a significant part of human sexual activity ever since the dawn of history, primarily because it is an expression of capacities that are basic in the human animal. There are those who will contend that the immorality of homosexual behavior calls for its suppression ... Some have demanded that homosexuals be completely eliminated from society by a concentrated attack upon it ... The evidence indicates that at least one-third of the population would have to be isolated from the rest of the community ... "

When Kinsey first published his findings in 1948, there was a general outcry from moral and religious leaders across the country. His work remains controversial today, as evidenced by the remark of one religious critic who commented recently, "The world would have been a cleaner place if Kinsey had stuck to his rats." Though published by a small medical publishing house, Kinsey's first book, *Sexual Behavior in the Human Male*, became a national bestseller and was translated into more than a dozen languages. The royalties might have made Kinsey a wealthy man; however, he funneled all of the money back into the Institute of Sex Research, which he had founded in 1947 as an ongoing center for the investigation of human sexuality.

KOMSOMOLSKAYA PRAVDA, Soviet youth newspaper. In 1987, the newspaper ran a series of letters from Soviet citizens on the subject of AIDS. It was seen as a significant step in the ongoing process of *glasnost*, since up until then Soviet authorities had tried to maintain that AIDS was strictly a problem of the "morally corrupt" West. Among some of the letters:

A soldier called for "a campaign of terror" against prostitutes to help halt the spread of AIDS. The campaign, he suggested, should be in memory of all the young comrades who had died in the war in Afghanistan.

Twenty-six foreign exchange students from Africa signed a letter protesting the increased racial prejudice they had experienced in Moscow as a result of the hysteria surrounding AIDS. One student complained that he and a friend were walking in a park when a little boy ran up to them. The boy's anxious mother quickly grabbed her son and yelled at him, "Stay away from them! You can catch AIDS!"

A fifteen-year-old girl suggested that the AIDS epidemic was simply a "cheap trick" by the government to intimidate young people from enjoying themselves sexually.

A doctor urged that all Soviet citizens traveling abroad be tested for AIDS before being re-admitted to the country. Likewise, all foreigners entering the country should be tested. "Those with the AIDS virus," she said, "should be sent back to their motherlands."

Another letter claimed that AIDS was a blessing in disguise, since it would eliminate all drug addicts, homosexuals, and prostitutes from Soviet society.

And, finally, several readers complained about the lack of condoms and sex education in the Soviet Union. (Only one factory in the Soviet Union manufactures condoms.) One reader suggested that the government publish "an illustrated weekly sex magazine" to educate the public not only about AIDS but about sex in general. He noted, "It will sell like hot cakes."

KRAMER, TIM (b. 1957), onetime gay porno star, popular in the early 1980s. "Basically the queens are always the ones who are on the bottom," he once said of his co-stars. "Basically, they're just a piece of meat and all I do is use them. People don't care who they are, people just care who I am, doing it to them. I don't feel bottoms are as powerful or as big a star as a top. I don't know how Leo Ford or some of these other queens ever got to be such big stars. They're always on the bottom. You can hardly see them."

KUANG-HSU (1875-1908), second-to-the-last emperor of China. His powerful aunt, the Dowager Empress Tzu Hsi, chose him to be emperor of China when he was four years old, and adopted him as her own son so that she could rule in his name until he became an adult. As he grew into a young man, he developed a trait that caused considerable comment: his terrible stutter. Another trait, his apparent homosexuality, was attributed to the fact he'd grown up surrounded almost entirely by women and eunuchs.

When Kuang-hsu was eighteen, his aunt finally went into semi-retirement, and handed him the reins of government. She was soon dismayed, however, by his growing interest in Western culture and technology, and she took back control of the government when he tried to initiate the so-called "100 Days of Reform," which called for a complete liberalization of China. In trying to initiate the reforms, Kuang-hsu openly condemned what he called the heretofore "bigoted conservatism and unpractical customs" of his country. A-ghast at such notions, Tzu Hsi banished him to exile and restored herself to the throne. She died on November 15, 1908, but not before choosing her successor — two-year-old Pu Yi, who later became the subject of the film *The Last Emperor* — and not before having Kuang-hsu poisoned to death, presumably so that he would not be a political threat to Pu Yi. According to biographer Arnold C. Brackman, Pu Yi also grew up with strong homosexual tendencies.

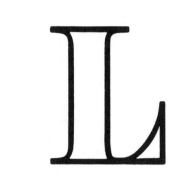

**LA CAGE AUX FOLLES —
NEWSWEEK REVIEW OF
(1983).** A glowing review in
Newsweek of the musical *La
Cage aux Folles* provoked a
handful of angry letters from
unhappy readers. "Your review
of *La Cage aux Folles*," wrote
one man from Oklahoma, "had
its prohomosexual slip showing. You stated that 'only Jerry
Falwell would refuse to admit
the emotional validity of the
prideful anthem "I Am What I
Am"' ... Falwell is not so lonely
as some would think, and only
those who are determined to
pretend that 'gay is good' would
refuse to admit the emotional
validity of our position."

Another disgruntled reader,
a woman from Florida, wrote,
"No matter how creative, colorful or well choreographed, it is
alarming that 'La Cage' could

be so acclaimed — bringing
audiences 'laughing and cheering into the wide-open '80s.'
Wide open to what? To quote
Saint Matthew, ' ... the gate is
wide, and the way is broad that
leads to destruction, and many
are those who enter by it.'"

**LAST WORDS OF FAMOUS
GAY MEN.**

English critic and biographer
Lytton Strachey (died in
Hungerford, England — 1932):
"If this is dying, then I don't
think much of it."

English novelist **W. Somerset
Maugham** (died in Nice, France
— 1965): There are two versions of Maugham's last words.
In one, he allegedly remarked
just before dying, "Dying is a
very dull, dreary affair. And my
advice to you is to have nothing

whatever to do with it." In the other, he grasped the hand of his lover, Alan Searle, and whispered, "I want to shake your hand and thank you for all that you've done for me."

Russian author **Nikolai Gogol** (died in Moscow — 1852): Hallucinating on his deathbed, "The ladder! Quick, pass me the ladder!"

English writer **Lord Alfred Douglas** (died in Crawley, Sussex — 1945): Douglas's last articulate request was for a friend to place a wager on a horse for him, "Mixed bark doubles, Nicholson's mounts."

Italian film director **Luchino Visconti** (died in Milan — 1976): After listening to Brahms's Second Symphony several times, "Enough now ..."

English poet **Gerald Manley Hopkins** (died in Dublin — 1889): "I'm so happy! I'm so happy! I'm so happy!"

French author **Marcel Proust** (died in Paris — 1922): "Mother..."

Russian dancer **Vaslav Nijinsky** (died in London — 1950): "Mamasha!"

English poet **A.E. Housman** (died in Cambridge — 1936): After his doctor told him a dirty joke, "Yes, that's a good one, and tomorrow I shall be telling it again on the Golden Floor."

U.S. poet **Hart Crane** (died in the middle of the Caribbean Ocean — 1932): As he jumped overboard from a ship, "Goodbye, everybody!"

Italian sculptor and artist **Michelangelo** (died in Rome — 1564): On his deathbed, making his last confession, "I regret that I have not done enough for the salvation of my soul, and that I die just as I am beginning to learn the alphabet of my profession."

French author **André Gide** (died in Paris — 1951): "It is good. It is very good."

Greek philosopher **Socrates** (died in Athens — 399 B.C.): "Crito, I owe a cock to Asclepius; will you repay him?"

Nazi leader **Ernst Röhm** (died in a Munich prison — 1934): Given a gun by his prison guards and ordered to shoot himself, "Let Adolf do his own dirty work!" The guards then shot him to death.

Irish patriot hanged by the British for treason **Sir Roger**

Casement (died in London — 1916): "It is better that I die thus on the scaffold."

Roman emperor **Nero** (died in Rome — A.D. 68): After stabbing himself through the throat to commit suicide, he lay bleeding to death. A centurion cntered the room and feigned concern for the despised emperor. Nero murmured sarcastically, "Too late. How *loyal* you are!"

English short-story writer **Hector Hugh Monro**, better known as "SAKI" (died on the battlefield in France during World War I): Monro and his fellow soldiers had just come out of the trenches and were lying on their stomachs in mud waiting to be engaged by the Germans. It was still night. A soldier next to Munro suddenly lit up a cigarette. "Put that bloody cigarette out!" Monro snapped at him. At that same instant, a German sniper saw the flicker of light and fired. The bullet hit Monro in the head, killing him instantly.

LEAVES OF GRASS, collection of poems by poet Walt Whitman. First published in 1855, it was re-issued in several revised and augmented editions up until 1892.

Social reformer Wendell Phillips: He was looking for fig leaves.

Long before *Leaves of Grass* achieved its reputation as an enduring American classic, it went through a long period of controversy when public opinion was sharply divided over its merits. Oliver Wendell Holmes denounced the book as "among the most cynical instances of indecent exposure I recollect, outside what is sold as obscene literature," and social activist Wendell Phillips quipped, "Here be all sorts of leaves except fig leaves." One reviewer called Whitman "the dirtiest beast of his age." On the other hand, Ralph Waldo Emerson defended the work in a letter to *The New York Times*; he called *Leaves of Grass* "the most extraordinary piece of wit and wisdom that America has yet contributed." (Emerson did, however, plead with Whitman to delete some of the book's racier passages; Whitman refused.) The controversy raged on for several decades; in 1881, twenty-six years after the book was first published, it was banned in Boston.

In 1865, Walt Whitman himself felt repercussions from the controversy: he was fired from his job at the U.S. Department of the Interior after Interior Secretary James Harlan, a devout Methodist, learned that Whitman was the author of *Leaves of Grass*. Harlan — who reviled the book as outrageous, offensive, and un-Christian — said of Whitman, "I will not have the author of that book in this Department. No, if the President of the United States should order his reinstatement, I would resign sooner than I would put him back." Whitman almost immediately found new employment — thanks to the influence of friends — in the nearby Attorney General's office, where he remained for many years.

Whitman later told a friend, "Don't ever assail Harlan as if he was a scoundrel. He was only a fool: there was only a dim light in his noddle: he had to steer by that light: what else could he do?"

LEVI'S FETISH — MOST EXTREME EXAMPLE OF. Although there have been reports of men asking to be buried in their favorite pair of Levi's, or in a coffin lined with other men's Levi's, the most extreme example of a Levi's fetishist was probably Bret Heidrich, a thirty-year-old construction worker from Reno, Nevada. Heidrich had numerous dressers in his home containing hundreds of pairs of Levi's that he had bought, traded, stolen, or in his words, "begged off tricks." Some of the pairs in his collection allegedly belonged to such stars as James Dean and Jim Morrison. Heidrich advertised worldwide for his fetish, and gained a reputation for refusing to have sex with anyone who wasn't wearing a pair of 501 Levi's; he also refused to completely remove his own Levi's whenever he had sex. Shortly after his thirtieth birthday, in 1982, he committed suicide by shooting himself while sitting in his truck near Lake Tahoe. Surrounding him on the front seat were reportedly numerous pairs of favorite Levi's from his collection.

LIMERICKS, GAY.

Two jocks, stripped quite bare
    in the lockers,
Were discussing the joys of
    girls' knockers.
        Their cocks started to
        soar.
        They were soon on the
        floor,
Having sex extempore — what
    a shocker!

⊓

There was a young plumber
    named Lee,
Who was plumbing a lad by
    the sea.
        Said the lad, "Stop your
        plumbing.
        There's somebody com-
        ing!"
Said the plumber, still plumb-
    ing, "It's me!"

⊓

Said a playwright and poet
    named Wilde,
Whose life and good name
    were reviled,
        "What on earth was the
        harm?
        No one twisted their
        arm—
And not one of the boys is
    with child!"

There once was a boy from
    Nantucket
Whose dick was so long he
    could suck it.
        He said with a laugh,
        As it hung to his calf,
"If my ear were my ass I could
    fuck it!"

⊓

There once was a slave, name
    of Jack,
Who liked to be tied to the
    rack.
        As they started to pull,
        His erection got full,
And he came with a back-
    breaking, Crack!

⊓

There was a young man of
    Bombay,
Who modeled boys' butts out
    of clay,
        But the heat of his prick
        Turned the clay into
        brick,
Which wore all his foreskin
    away.

⊓

A zoology student named
    Newt
Trained a snake to retrieve
    and salute
        And to give a massage
        And indulge in frottage
And then serve as a cockring,
    to boot.

These words spoke the King of
  Siam,
"For women, I don't give a
  damn.
    But a plump-bottomed
      boy
    Is my pride and my joy.
You may call me a bugger —
  I am!"

          ❏

A dentist whose name was
  Kildare,
Was fucking a hunk in the
  chair.
    On the forty-fifth stroke,
    The dental chair broke;
The poor doc shot his load in
  mid-air.

          ❏

A young Scottish soldier
  named Rex
Likes love with his very own
  sex.
    But that thing in his kilt
    Keeps causing him
      guilt—
He suffers from a kilt complex.

          ❏

There was a young man of
  Tibet
  — And this is the strangest
  one yet —
    His prick was so long,
    So pointed, so strong,
He could bugger six Greeks *en*
  brochette.

There was a young tutor most
  wise
Who loved to feel cocks, just
  for size.
    At every school dance,
    He'd unzip the boys'
    pants.
They nicknamed him, "The
  Lord of the Flies."

          ❏

That naughty old Sappho of
  Greece
Said, "What I prefer to a piece
    Is to have my pudenda
    Rubbed hard by the
      enda
The little pink nose of my
  niece."

          ❏

An inventive young lad in
  Corona
Remarked as he bought a
  bologna,
    "It's as big as a whale!
    Just right for my tail.
I think I will call the thing 'Jo-
  nah'!"

          ❏

There was a young fellow of
  King's
Who was weary of women and
  things.
    Said he, "My desire
    Is a boy from the choir,
With an ass that's like Jello
  on springs!"

In Pottsdam the padre is poor.
His penis is puny, what's
    more.
    When the Pope went to
    blow him,
    There was nothing to
    show him.
Said the Pope, "I've seen nuns
who have more!"
                    ❒

A randy young gay from north
    Wimley
Was reproached for not acting
    quite primly.
    Said he, "Lord above,
    I known sex isn't love,
But it's such an attractive fac-
    simile."
                    ❒

There was a young man from
    the docks,
With a yen for used, smelly,
    old jocks.
    He'd get all the men
    To remove them, and
    then
He'd beg them to throw in
    their socks.
                    ❒

There are ten different ways
    to tie
Any unwilling but hot-looking
    guy:
    All you need is some string
    And a painful cockring,
And soon he'll be sucking you
dry.

There was a young sailor
    named Gates,
Who got along well with his
    mates,
    'Til he fell on a cutlass,
    Which rendered him
    buttless,
Thus practically useless on
dates.
                    ❒

There was a young man of
    Belize
Whose life was a study in
    sleaze.
    Though himself, he was
    runty
    Of men he had plenty
And scabs where he should
    have had knees.
                    ❒

A diamond collector named
    Euell
Loved boys who were hung
    like a mule.
    His eyepiece in place,
    He'd examine their mace
And shout, "Mmm, that's
    what I call a jewel!"
                    ❒

There was a young fellow at sea
Who complained that it hurt
    him to pee.
    "Aha!" said a mate,
    "*That* accounts for the
    state
Of the captain, the boatswain,
    and me."

LIONS, GAY. In their 1984 book, *Cry of the Kalahari*, Mark and Delia Owens reported the case of two male lions, both young adults living in the wild, who were inseparable. In the Owenses' experience, strong bonding between young male lions was not unusual, but in the case

First cockroaches, now lions: Where will it end?

of "Pappy" and "Brother," as they were called, the bonding seemed unusually intense. When the two naturalists tried to tranquilize Pappy with a dart gun (for routine ear-tagging and measurements), Brother suddenly came forward, pulled the imbedded tranquilizer dart from Pappy's fur with his teeth, chewed it to pieces, and then spat it out. He then "rubbed his head against Pappy's, cooing softly," and tried to pull Pappy, who was quickly falling under the influence of the tranquilizer, back to his feet. Mark and Delia were eventually able to take their measurements, with Brother watching their every move; afterward, they put Pappy under a shaded tree to recover from the tranquilizer. Their last view of the two lions was of Brother lying close to Pappy and rubbing his head and muzzle against Pappy's body.

According to many wildlife experts, ardent homosexuality among adult male lions is relatively common.

LUDLAM, CHARLES (1943-1987), U.S. actor, writer, and entertainer, founder of the Ridiculous Theatrical Company in New York City. The Company got its name after theater critic Brendan Gill came to see one of Ludlam's plays and remarked, "This isn't farce. This isn't absurd. This is absolutely ridiculous!"

Ludlam's plays — *The Mystery of Irma Vep, The Ventriloquist's Wife, Der Ring Gott Farblonjet*, et al. — were, by turns, send-ups of gothic novels, Wagner, popular culture, old movies, and anything else that caught Ludlam's eye, just so long as he thought it would work onstage and get a laugh. Colleagues called him "The Thief of Bad Gags." He once told a friend that his primary literary influence had been Proust; on another occasion he confided that his major influence was actually the *Conan the Barbarian* series. Ludlam himself performed in all of his plays, often in drag. "I don't want to be laughed with," he frequently said. "I want to be laughed *at*."

Ludlam died of AIDS at a hospital in New York City. The day before he died, a physician, trying to ascertain whether dementia had set in, interrogated him as to what year it was, what day of the week, who were the president and vice-president of the United States. Unable to speak, Ludlam took a pen and quickly wrote in response on a pad of paper, "I'm sorry. I have not yet read the *Times* this morning." The next day, at the age of forty-four, he was dead.

LULLY, JEAN BAPTISTE (1632-1687), French composer best known for his operas and ballets, among them *Alceste, Cadmus et Hermione,* and *Amadis.* Lully was one of sev-

eral French noblemen who allegedly belonged to a secret seventeenth-century homosexual society called "The Sacred Fraternity of Glorious Pederasts." Members supposedly held homosexual orgies and delighted in performing fellatio on distinguished guests. They were said to wear an identifying medallion around their necks, embossed with the Fraternity's insignia: an emblem of a man stomping on a woman.

Paul Lynde: In real life, high-strung and amusingly bitchy, with a passion for antiques.

LYNDE, PAUL (1926-1982), U.S. television performer best known for his appearances on the popular T.V. game show

The Hollywood Squares. Lynde originally wanted to be a serious actor, and he studied drama at Northwestern University; but because of his distinctive voice and outrageous mannerisms, "I had to do dramatic readings in my professor's office after class because the kids would start to laugh as soon as I stood up and took a breath."

Lynde first broke into movies in 1954. He had memorable roles in the films *Bye, Bye Birdie*, *Send Me No Flowers*, and *The Glass Bottom Boat*, and on various T.V. series including *Bewitched* and *The Paul Lynde Show*; but he was best known for his wisecracking, often vitriolic humor on *The Hollywood Squares*. Asked on one show, "Why do motorcyclists wear leather?" he replied, "Because chiffon wrinkles so easily." On another occasion he was asked what the I.Q. of the average American was. "Judging from the fact *Laverne and Shirley* is the number one show in the country," he shot back, "I'd say about seventy-five."

In real life Lynde was, according to friends, boisterous and high-strung, with a fondness for antiques and beautiful young hustlers. He died of a heart attack in 1982. After his death, one writer characterized him as "the prissy kvetch that was TV's archetypal homosexual."

MADONNA — RUMORS ABOUT LESBIANISM OF. A 1989 benefit performance by Madonna and comedian Sandra Bernhard to help save the Amazon rain forests was overshadowed by increasing public rumors that the two were having an affair. "What is going on between Madonna and Sandra Bernhard?" asked *People* magazine, in its coverage of the benefit. "Madonna and I have a heart-and-soul friendship," Bernhard said later. "Beyond that, it's nobody's business. The way we act together is a political statement. It's to say to the world, 'Get past the judgments. Accept people for what they are.' The rain forest is dying. What do you care more about, the rain forest or our sexuality?"

MAHARIS, GEORGE (b. 1928), U.S. actor. A product of the famous Actors Studio in New York, Maharis first shot to stardom in the early 1960s in the popular T.V. series *Route 66.* Critics described him as "volatile," "cunning," "passionate," and "explosively sexy" — "and he can act," noted one writer, "a boorish detail usually dismissed by the packagers of soap operas."

Route 66 — about two idealistic adventurers criss-crossing the country in a souped-up Corvette, in search of truth, jobs, and girls — lasted only four seasons, from 1960 to 1964, but it catapulted both Maharis and his co-star, Martin Milner, to fame. During the series' heyday, Maharis received hundreds of fan letters a

George Maharis in *The Satan Bug* (1965): He had real-life brushes with the law, as well.

week — including numerous marriage proposals — mostly from women who wanted to mother him. "That boy, with those eyes," wrote one housewife, "couldn't be bad. I know." Among producers and directors, however, Maharis was regarded more warily: as enormously talented but also difficult, inflexible, and arrogant.

In 1963, Maharis was suspended from *Route 66*, ostensibly because of repeated absences from the set due to a bad case of hepatitis. He was replaced by Glenn Corbet. After he left the series, his career faltered. He went on to appear in over half-a-dozen indifferently received films — *Quick Before It Melts, The Satan Bug, A Covenant With Death*, et al. — and also starred in a second television series, *The Most Deadly Game*, in 1970; the series lasted only four months.

His career was doubtless complicated by several well-publicized brushes with the law. He was first arrested in 1967, in the restroom of a Hollywood restaurant, and was charged with "lewd conduct" after he allegedly solicited an undercover vice officer. "We categorically deny the charges," Maharis's lawyer told the press. "Maharis will be completely vindicated. To comment further at this time would lend dignity to the charges which we feel are totally unjustified."

Another arrest followed in 1974, for "performing an act of oral copulation" with a 33-year-old male hairdresser in a gas station washroom in West Los Angeles. Maharis was booked on charges of "sex perversion" and "lewd conduct." He pleaded not guilty. Later, the charge was reduced to "trespassing," and Maharis entered a new plea of no contest. He was fined $500 and given three years probation.

In 1979, Maharis became the heir to a large inheritance bequeathed to him by a close friend, a 69-year-old sculptor and art instructor from Greenwich Village. Estimates of the legacy varied from $500,000 to $2 million. Whatever the amount, it was more than enough to retire on, and by the 1980s, Maharis had all but vanished from the public eye.

MAILER, NORMAN (b. 1923), U.S. author. Addressing the issue of anti-homosexual prejudice, Mailer wrote, in his essay "The Homosexual as Villain": "If the homosexual is ever to achieve real social equality and acceptance, he too will have to work the hard row of shedding his own prejudices. Driven into defiance, it is natural if regrettable, that many homosexuals go to the direction of assuming that there is something intrinsically superior in homosexuality, and carried far enough it is a viewpoint which is as stultifying, as ridiculous, and as anti-human as the heterosexual's prejudice."

MANual, popular physique magazine, started in 1959. MANual was especially popular because, unlike most other physique magazines of the day,

MANual magazine, May 1962: Breaking a taboo.

it often showed some male pubic hair in its photographs.

MAURICE — DIFFICULTIES IN MAKING FILM OF. The making of the 1987 film, based on E.M. Forster's novel, was fraught with difficulties despite the fact director James Ivory and producer Ismail Merchant had had their greatest commercial and critical triumph the year before with *A Room With a View*.

To begin with, Forster's literary executors didn't want Merchant and Ivory to make a film of *Maurice*; although the estate never created any seri-

Maurice (1987): The actor originally slotted for the title role had a last-minute change of heart.

films, bowed out of the project, refusing to write the screenplay because she thought *Maurice* was "a flawed book." And finally, the handsome blond actor Julian Sands, who had played the male lead in *Room With a View* and who had agreed to play the title role in *Maurice*, suddenly withdrew from the project for "personal reasons." On top of all this, there were, of course, the inevitable admonitions from various quarters that it was inappropriate to make "a salute to homosexual passion" in the midst of the AIDS epidemic.

ous legal obstacles, they did try to steer the two filmmakers to a different one of Forster's literary properties. After finally securing the rights, Merchant found it more difficult than usual to find investors for the film, even though *A Room With a View* had grossed more than $50 million, paid its investors back four hundred percent, and won three Academy Awards. Then, Ruth Prawer Jhabvala, screenwriter on most of Merchant and Ivory's feature

Still, investors were finally found, Ivory decided to write the screenplay himself (with the help of a thirty-year-old Cambridge graduate, Kit Hesketh-Harvey), and the film was made with actor James Wilby in the title role. It opened in 1987 to generally strong reviews and good box office.

MENNINGER, KARL (b. 1893), U.S. psychiatrist and founder of the Menninger Clinic in Topeka, Kansas. Although Menninger favored the decriminalization of homosexual acts between consenting adults, he staunchly maintained that homosexuality was nonetheless an illness. "From the standpoint of the psychiatrist," he wrote in 1963, "homosexuality ... constitutes evidence of immature sexuality and either arrested psychological development or regression. Whatever it be called by the public, there is no question in the minds of psychiatrists regarding the abnormality of such behavior."

MERRILL, GEORGE, lover of Victorian social activist Edward Carpenter (1844-1929). The two men were, in almost every way, complete opposites. Carpenter was a committed social activist, drawn to the issues of feminism and pacifism; Merrill was a child of the slums, one of nine children, with almost no formal education. Merrill was twenty-six, Carpenter a youthful-looking forty-seven. Carpenter had originally studied to become a priest; Merrill had worked at numerous odd jobs throughout his youth, including handing out towels at a public bathhouse, waiting tables at a pub (where he also apparently did a bit of hustling), and selling encyclopaedias door-to-door. They first met after exchanging "a look of recognition" while traveling together in the same railway car in London. Not long afterward, in 1898, Merrill moved into Carpenter's country home at Millthorpe. He remained for the next three decades.

Tall and physically attractive with a completely frank and masculine manner, Merrill kept house, gardened, cared for the chickens, and cooked, while Carpenter devoted himself to his work. Their house became a haven for gay intellectuals and social activists of the day. One visitor was Mohandas Gandhi, who came to discuss vegetarianism and the doctrine of nonviolence with Carpenter. Another was novelist E.M. Forster, who recalled that he conceived the entire plot and structure of *Maurice* one afternoon, after Merrill gave him a friendly pat on the buttocks. ("The sensation was unusual," Forster said later, "and I still remember it. It seemed to go straight through the small of my back into my ideas ... ") The character of Alec, the gameskeeper, in *Maurice* was loosely based on Merrill.

Merrill occasionally found

himself at the center of minor scandals, usually involving his lust for some of the local good-looking boys and hired hands. Yet it was a tribute to both him and Carpenter — and to their rural neighbors — that the scandals never amounted to much. "It was on such occasions," Carpenter recalled, "that the real affection of the country people showed itself, and they breathed slaughter against our assailants. George in fact was accepted and one may say beloved by both my manual worker friends and my more aristocratic friends."

Merrill once described his life with Carpenter as "heaven." Heaven continued for some thirty years, until Merrill died, in his late fifties, in 1928. Carpenter, approaching eighty, couldn't bear to stay on alone in the old house. He moved to a bungalow in Guildford where he died only a year later.

MICHAEL, GEORGE (b. 1963), English pop star. Asked about the persistent rumors he is gay, Michael told *Rolling Stone* magazine in 1988, "I've always thought that people speculated so much because I was so quiet about my private life, and secondly, because I've always had a very ambiguous sounding voice — I'm not exactly Bruce Springsteen to listen to, you know ... I've never been concerned with who was doing what with who in bed, you know? I've always thought that people ought to get on with what they're doing in their own beds."

MICHIGAN, LIQUOR LAWS OF. In 1948, Michigan passed a law making it illegal for bars to serve liquor to homosexuals. The law remained on the books for the next thirty-three years, until it was finally repealed in 1981.

MONA LISA (1506), painting by Leonardo da Vinci, probably the most famous painting in history. For over four centuries, the exact identity of the model has remained a mystery, the subject of much debate and controversy, and millions have speculated as to the meaning of the Mona Lisa's tantalizing, enigmatic smile.

In 1986, after careful study involving the use of computer analysis, historian Lillian Schwartz shocked the art world when she concluded that the mysterious face in the painting was in fact Leonardo da Vinci's own, and that — whether as a prank or an exercise or an accident of the unconscious — the painting represented Leonardo in the guise of a woman. Schwartz reached the conclusion after using a computer to juxtapose Leonardo's self-portraits on the image of the Mona Lisa: all of the major features aligned almost perfectly.

MONKEYS, GAY. Monkeys have been observed engaging in oral sex, mutual masturbation, auto-fellatio, masturbation with inanimate objects, and homosexual behavior. One 1976 study described two rhesus monkeys, both males, who lived together for nineteen months and engaged in "reciprocal mounting with anal penetration." Although the two males would engage in heterosexual behavior when paired individually with females, they would still engage in homosexual behavior if put in a cage with just one female. Lesbian sexual behavior has also been observed in adult female monkeys; in particular, a 1942 study found that such behavior "resembled in many respects a male-female consort relationship." By contrast, Jane Goodall has said she has never observed any signs of homosexuality among the chimpanzees she has studied in Africa.

MORGAN, JULIA (1872-1957), U.S. architect, best known for her design and construction of Hearst's Castle at San Simeon, California.

"Miss Morgan, we are tired of camping out in the open at the ranch at San Simeon and I would like to build a little something..." With those words, William Randolph Hearst, the multimillionaire publishing magnate, began an obsessive building project that consumed the next thirty years of his life, as well as the life of his architect, Julia Morgan. The project was Hearst's Castle, a sprawling palace containing over 100,000 square feet of living space and over 150 extravagantly appointed rooms, set on a huge site overlooking the Pacific Ocean, about two hundred and fifty miles north of Los Angeles. Hearst's Castle has been labeled an architectural masterpiece, an architectural disaster, the fulfillment of an enchanted dream, and a fatuous monument to the failure of one's man life. Its architect, Julia Morgan, designed dozens of other noteworthy buildings in her lifetime, but it is the Castle for which she is best remembered today.

A small, driven, fiercely energetic woman, Morgan was

the first female engineering student at the University of California at Berkeley, the first female graduate of the École des Beaux-Arts in Paris, and the first woman to receive an architect's license in the state of California. Quiet and masculine in bearing — she favored wearing trim, dark suits tailored for men — she shunned publicity and tried to remain as anonymous as possible throughout most of her life. She almost never allowed photographs to be taken of her, and she avoided socializing, even to the point of refusing to join several of the professional organizations standard to architects. Her personal life remains a compelling mystery. In virtually everything written about her, there is little mention of a private life, and reference books maintain — as they do in the case of numerous gay men and lesbians — that she was too involved in her work to have any outside interests, as if devotion to the cause of architecture had somehow elevated her to a plane of serene asexuality.

Morgan's first commissions came after the disastrous 1906 earthquake in San Francisco. She was hired to help rebuild the city, and soon gained a reputation as both a gifted archi-

A guest 'bungalow' at Hearst's Castle, designed by Julia Morgan.

tect and a meticulous engineer. One of her associates later remarked, "Not only was she one of the most talented of West Coast architects; she was also far more accomplished in the area of building technology than any of the men I have known."

As her practice grew, Morgan made a point of hiring as many women as possible for drafting work and as her assistant architects. Later, after she had begun work on Hearst's Castle, she used Hearst's patronage as a springboard for financially aiding various women's colleges, and she also helped set up tuition trust funds for many of her employees' children. Her generosity was such that, when she received payment from a client, she often took only what she needed for her own expenses and then distributed the rest among her employees.

Among her most famous architectural achievements were the Chapel of the Chimes in Oakland, the rebuilding of San Francisco's Fairmount Hotel after the 1906 earthquake, the Oakland YWCA, the Berkeley Women's City Club, and parts of the campuses at both U.C. Berkeley and Mills College. She also designed numerous private residences, including one in Berkeley for a lesbian couple, Dr. M.L. Williams and Dr. E.L. Mitchell. In 1919, Hearst approached her to build the lavish residence at San Simeon.

For the next three decades, Morgan worked at designing, shaping, reshaping, building, and rebuilding Hearst's Castle. During those years she had other commissions from other clients, but her work for Hearst was the focus of her career. With an army of carpenters, plasterers, pavers, and painters at her side, she built Hearst a monolithic central residence — looking more like a cathedral than a home — surrounded by several guest houses, each with approximately 6,000 square feet of living space. The residence also included tennis courts, a private zoo, and several luxurious swimming pools.

Hearst died in 1951, leaving many additional plans for the Castle unfinished. Morgan, by then approaching eighty, decided it was time to close down her practice. She spent her last years as a recluse; during the last four years of her life, with her physical energy suddenly waning and her memory failing, she rarely went outside of her house. She died of a stroke in San Francisco in 1957. Almost all of her papers were burned immediately after her death. The Castle is now a California State Historic Landmark and one of the most popular tourist attractions in the state.

MOTHERS, FASCINATING OF FAMOUS GAY MEN.

Edwina Dakin Williams, mother of playwright Tennessee Williams.

"I can stand my mother for only fifteen minutes at a time," Tennessee Williams once told a friend. "Then I have to flee." On various other occasions, Williams described his mother as "a moderately controlled hysteric" and "a little Prussian officer in drag." The object of all this vitriol was a beautiful, iron-willed, puritanical woman who made Williams's life hell with her piety, her social pretensions, and her incessant nagging.

When Tennessee was a boy, Edwina tried to infantalize him. She convinced herself, with no medical evidence, that he had a life-threatening illness, and she kept him isolated from other children: the boys were all too "rough," and the girls were all "common." Later, as he grew up, she was so gravely disappointed that he wanted to be a writer, she gave him articles about Edgar Allan Poe dying in the gutter, hoping to dissuade him.

Tennessee's sister, Rose, was mentally ill, suffering one breakdown after another. But Mrs. Williams refused to acknowledge the severity of the problem, and was convinced it could all be taken care of with a little prayer and hymn-singing. (Rose wound up being institutionalized.) Tennessee later described how his mother "panicked" when Rose began using four-letter words. "Do anything!" Edwina told the doctors. "Don't let her talk like that!" As a result, Rose was lobotomized, a procedure to which Edwina gave her approval, and for which Tennessee never forgave her.

Even after Williams achieved international fame as a playwright, his mother's meddling and possessiveness continued unabated. Finally, in an argument one night, all of his pent-up rage came pouring out, and he screamed at her, "Why do women bring children into the world and then destroy them?!"

The character of Amanda Wingfield in *The Glass Menagerie* was closely modeled after her; family friends said it was an "extremely generous" characterization. Although Edwina went to see the play — and was apparently shocked to see so many of her own words and eccentricities duplicated on a public stage — she pretended to friends there was no possible similarity between her and Amanda. Tennessee eventually gave her half the rights to the play, providing her with a steady source of income in her old age.

Edwina died in 1980, at the age of ninety-five. "I cannot feel anything about my mother," Tennessee said shortly before her death. "I dream about her, but I can't feel anything." Ambivalent to the end, he had her coffin covered in a blanket of two thousand imported English violets, her favorite flower.

For further reading: Memoirs *by Tennessee Williams (Doubleday, 1975) and* The Kindness of Strangers: The Life of Tennessee Williams *by Donald Spoto (Little Brown, 1985)*

Lady Speranza Francesca Wilde, mother of playwright Oscar Wilde.

Described by one disapproving contemporary as "the silliest woman who ever lived," Lady Speranza Francesca Wilde stood almost six feet tall and claimed to have been an eagle in a previous life. Her love of high drama compelled her to change her given name, Jane Frances, to the more impressive-sounding Speranza Francesca. A moderately talented poet and an occasionally superb epigrammist, she once wrote, "I should like to rage through life; this orthodox creeping is too tame for me."

Speranza was active in the women's rights movement of her day, and became a national figure in Ireland for her impassioned patriotic editorials denouncing English rule; she was hailed by fellow patriots as "one of Ireland's noblest daughters."

Lady Wilde: "One of Ireland's noblest daughters" — or "the silliest woman who ever lived"?

She also aspired to become a major Irish poet — an ambition reportedly conceived when she came upon an ostentatious funeral procession for Dublin poet Thomas Davis — and throughout her life, she published numerous volumes of her work: poetry, political and cultural essays, translations, and Irish folk tales — all now forgotten.

She gave birth to her first son, William Wilde, in 1852. Two years later, Oscar Fingal O'Flahertie Wills Wilde was born. At first, Willie was her favorite, but she later changed affections and told a friend, "Willie is all right, but as for Oscar, he will turn out something wonderful!" Her admiration for Oscar never diminished. When his novel *The Picture of Dorian Gray* was published in 1891, she wrote to tell him, "It is the most wonderful piece of writing in all the fiction of the day ... I nearly fainted at the last scene."

Viewed by contemporaries as frivolous and bombastic, Speranza lived in London at the height of Oscar's fame and held artistic salons where she greeted guests — such as William Butler Yeats and George Bernard Shaw — bedecked in showy jewelry, an oversized black wig, and mammoth headdresses usually made from the feathers of ostriches and other exotic birds. Like her son, she tried to cultivate an image of sophisticated decadence. Asked once to receive a "respectable" young woman in her home, Speranza tartly replied, "You must never employ that description in this house. It is only tradespeople who are respectable. We are above respectability." On another occasion, in her sixties, she told a visitor, "When you are as old as I, young man, you will know there is only one thing worth living for, and that is sin." She and Oscar once agreed to found a "society for the suppression of virtue," apparently in reaction to the Society for the Suppression of Vice previously founded in the U.S.

When Oscar was arrested in 1895 and charged with having committed "indecent acts," his mother was one of those who persuaded him to stay in England and face trial rather than flee to Paris, as he might have done. She saw it partly as a matter of honor. "If you stay, even if you go to prison," she told him, "you will always be my son. It will make no difference to my affection. But if you go, I will never speak to you again." He stayed — and was sentenced to two years hard labor.

It was in the darkness of his cell one night that he supposedly had a vision of her: she suddenly appeared to him, dressed as if for a long trip; but when he asked her to take off her hat and stay for a while, she merely shook her head and vanished. The next day, he learned she was dead. "Her death," he wrote, "was so terrible to me, that I, once a lord of language, have no words in which to express my anguish..." It was later reported that, on her deathbed, Speranza had asked to see Oscar one last time. Reminded that he was in Reading Gaol, she exclaimed, "May the prison help him!" She then turned her face to the wall, and died.

For further reading: Oscar Wilde *by* H. *Montomgery Hyde, (Farrar, Straus and Giroux, 1975) and* Oscar Wilde *by Richard Ellmann (Knopf, 1988)*

Carla Elba Visconti, mother of film director Luchino Visconti.

Called "the richest and most beautiful girl in Milan," Carla Visconti was from an enormously wealthy, aristocratic family. For years, she set the pace of style in Milan, and people would actually come out of their houses just to catch a glimpse of her as she walked by. Luchino, like the rest of Milan, was fascinated by her. In later years, he called her "the goddess" and "the being I loved the most."

When he was still a little boy, he made a pact with her: no matter where she was, no matter how sick she had become, if she knew she was dying she would wait for him to arrive so he could give her one last kiss. In reality, that's exactly what happened: in 1939, at the age of fifty-nine, she became desperately ill. She sent word to Luchino she was dying. He arrived just in time to give her a final kiss and to hear her whisper his name. Her death left him devastated.

For further reading: Luchino Visconti: A Biography *by Gaia Servadio (Franklin Watts, 1983)*

Frances Zuchowski Liberace, mother of entertainer Liberace.

Liberace's budding career as a pianist might have come to an abrupt end in his mid-teens if it hadn't been for his mother. When he was fifteen, he developed a hangnail that became so badly infected it led to blood poisoning; the family doctor recommended that the grotesquely swollen finger — perhaps the entire forearm — be amputated. Liberace's mother refused even to consider it; her son showed the promise of becoming a brilliant pianist. Instead, she took him home and administered an old Polish cure, which included briefly plunging her son's entire arm into boiling water. The cure worked, the infection subsided, and Liberace resumed his musical training.

"There are so many little things about my mother that I hold precious," Liberace once said. "I feel terrible sometimes that my appreciation and admiration of her as a lovable and very special person has been ridiculed." The ridicule began early in Liberace's career, when critics reviled not only his flamboyant showmanship (and "populist" piano playing), but his often effusive public adoration for his mother as well. She often traveled with him on tour, and during his concerts she sat in the front row wearing her customary mink coat and orchid corsage. He introduced her to audiences worldwide, and she became a standard part of his stage routine.

"Momism," the critics called it, always giving the word a slightly sinister quality, as if it were somehow equatable with "fascism" or "communism." The attacks on Liberace's "Momism" peaked with two widely publicized incidents in the 1950s. In one episode, in 1956, a critic for the London *Daily Mirror* reviewed Liberace's recent European tour and called the pianist "a fruit-flavored, mincing, ice-covered heap of mother love." "Without doubt," the critic added, "he is the biggest sentimental vomit of all time." The review also strongly intimated that Liberace was homosexual. The attack left Liberace's mother prostrate with anxiety, and she was placed under a doctor's care. Liberace himself sued both the critic and the newspaper for libel. He won.

In another incident, in 1957, Liberace's mother was attacked in her garage one night by two strange men in hoods, who apparently only wanted the satisfaction of beating her up. They knocked her down, broke one rib, kicked her in the back, and one said to the other, "Kick her again. Then we'll have something to laugh about later." She lost consciousness while they continued to beat her. There were no signs of burglary, and police never solved the case. They concluded it was "a sadistic act of revenge."

Although she died in 1980, Liberace always believed her spirit was still with him. For example, when some sheets of music once fell off a music stand, he told friends, "Mom's here." And even in death she remained a part of his popular stage show. "She is up there," Liberace liked to tell his audiences, while the orchestra played a softly sentimental theme, "in the best seat in the house."

For further reading: Liberace: The True Story *by Bob Thomas (St. Martin's Press, 1987)*

Grace Hart Crane, mother of poet Hart Crane.

Shortly after poet Hart Crane committed suicide in 1932, by jumping over the railing of a ship in the middle of the Caribbean, his mother, Grace, went to consult a medium. She longed for a reconciliation with her dead son, and she and the medium worked for months to contact him. Ultimately, they believed they succeeded, and soon Hart was allegedly dictating the drafts of new poems from beyond the grave. Grace collected these and tried to have them published as "posthumous" works; editors refused, and must have shaken their heads in painful disbelief at the woman who was so single-mindedly obsessed with her dead child.

It was an ironic turn of events. For the last four years of his life, Hart had wanted nothing to do with his mother, to the point that once, when he heard she would be visiting a town an hour from where he was staying, he immediately fled, afraid he might run into her. Theirs had been a troubled love-hate relationship.

Grace Hart was a great beauty — statuesque, regal, and glamorous — when, at an early age, she hastily entered into an ill-conceived marriage with Clarence Crane, a sales-man. That marriage has been described by one biographer as "a source of mutual agony." Her only consolation was her little boy, Hart. She adored him. She was, however, a sharp-tongued, unpredictable mother: affectionate and doting, but also clutching and difficult to please. One moment she told him that life was meaningless without him, that she needed him more than she needed her own parents or her husband; the next, she would tease and ridicule him mercilessly. She made life hell for the sensitive boy — her manipulative accusations and reprimands often drove Hart to feelings of madness — and on those occasions when she became most harsh and disapproving, he lapsed into illness.

Hart was eighteen when his parents finally divorced. He sided with his mother during the dispute, a decision he later regretted because it cut him off from ever fully knowing or appreciating his father. Then, at twenty-eight, he told her he was a homosexual. She seemed neither to approve nor disapprove, but later acknowledged to a friend that the revelation came as "a profound shock." Shortly afterward, Hart had a complete break with her, after she threatened to deny him a family inheritance unless he stayed with her. He walked out of her life, and they never saw each other again. Four years later, as the result of alcoholism and ongoing emotional turmoil, he committed suicide.

In her later years, Grace had little money and often worked as a scrubwoman or cook to make ends meet. Her spare time was devoted to trying to establish her son's reputation as a major American poet: she collected his correspondence for publication, assisted his biographers, and searched for good editors for his poems.

In 1947, fifteen years after Hart's suicide, she lay ill in a hospital in Teaneck, New Jersey. A friend in the room mentioned Hart's name, and Grace muttered in response, "Poor boy." Those were her last words.

For further reading: Voyager: A Life of Hart Crane *by John Unterecker (Farrar, Straus and Giroux, 1969)*

Lillie Mae Faulk, mother of writer Truman Capote.

"It was," said one family friend, "the kind of relationship that would make teams of psychiatrists happy for years." Lillie Mae Faulk was a small but strikingly pretty and ambitious Southern belle who drank heavily and committed suicide at the age of forty-seven. Her son, Truman, was precocious, effeminate, and homosexual — and Lillie Mae despised him. She hated him almost from the beginning, initially as a reminder of her failed first marriage (to Joe Capote), and later because of his effeminacy and sexual habits. "That boy is so strange," she once told the family cook, "he doesn't look or act like a normal boy. He's just like his father sometimes — little Miss Mouse Fart." Lillie Mae had desperately wanted to have an abortion while she was pregnant with Truman, but relatives talked her out of it. When she became pregnant on two other occasions, she went through with the abortions, because, she told friends, she couldn't stand the thought of having any more children as repulsive as little Truman.

Even at an early age, Truman was an androgynous child, and before he reached puberty, Lillie Mae dragged him to two different psychiatrists, hoping to have him "fixed" and turned into a presentable, "normal" little boy. When he was twelve, she shipped him off to a military school "to make a man of him." The experience was a failure as far as his mother was concerned and a nightmare for Truman, who had a terror of abandonment.

When Truman was a teenager, Lillie Mae started drinking heavily. She told friends it was because of her fears that Truman was a homosexual. "You're a pansy!" she once screamed at him. "You're a fairy! You're going to wind up in jail!" During one of her drunken binges, she tore up all of his manuscripts to get back at him for being an embarrassment to her. In another drunken rage, she threw open the windows of her apartment and tossed all of Truman's letters into the middle of Park Avenue. She became so obsessed with his sexuality that once, when a Broadway producer, Miss Cheryl Crawford, called and left word for Truman to call her back, Lillie Mae snapped into the phone, "You know, whatever you boys do is perfectly all right with me. But I do think it's going a little far when you start calling yourself *Miss!*"

Truman finally acknowledged his homosexuality to her when she tried to take him to a doctor for male hormone injections. He refused to go, and told her he was gay. Shortly afterward, he got an apartment of his own, after he caught her obsessively reading his love letters one night.

In later years, Lillie Mae turned to Alcoholics Anonymous and attempted a reconciliation with her son. But it was too late: the damage had been done. She eventually turned to drinking again, as a result of her second husband's financial setbacks and extramarital affairs. In January of 1954, she committed suicide with a lethal dose of Seconals. Her death devastated Truman, though he acknowledged to one interviewer that she had been "the single worst person in my life."

For further reading: Capote: A Biography *by Gerald Clarke (Simon and Schuster, 1988) and* Conversations With Capote *by Lawrence Grobel (New American Library, 1985)*

Ethel Sara Turing, mother of scientist Alan Turing.

When Alan Turing was arrested on charges of "gross indecency" in 1952, he paid his aging mother a personal visit to tell her about the arrest, and to tell her he was gay. She was seventy at the time; he was thirty-nine. Except for the fact they had a brief argument, nothing of what passed between them that day has come down to us, but the outcome was still the same: Mrs. Turing never allowed the arrest, or her son's sexuality, to come between them. In fact, their relationship actually grew closer and more mutually supportive after his trial and conviction.

She had, indirectly, always worried that something like this would happen to her son. Even though she understood and encouraged his profound love of science as a boy, she was worried he would one day grow up to be an eccentric or an intellectual crank. A strongly conventional woman, she was often exasperated at his peculiar habits and his absorption in math and science to the exclusion of his other studies. She wanted him to be "well-rounded," and his seeming obliviousness to many of the more practical aspects of life — such as clothes and haircuts and manners — frustrated and sometimes even infuriated her. In later years, even after he had achieved international recognition for his work in mathematics and the then-fledgling field of computer science, she regarded him as "brilliant but unsound" and often worried over his ingenuous indifference to convention.

In 1954, two years after his conviction on the charges of "gross indecency," Turing committed suicide, in part as a result of court-ordered drug treatments he'd undergone to "cure" his homosexuality. (The treatments, which consisted of female hormone injections, left him depressed and with female breasts.) According to an inquest, Turing had purposefully dipped an apple in cyanide and then taken a bite of it. His death was devastating to his mother, especially because of the renewed and growing relationship between them. But she adamantly refused to believe it was suicide: she knew that her son sometimes worked with poisonous chemicals, and she remembered frequently admonishing him, "Wash your hands, Alan, and get your nails clean. And don't put your fingers in your mouth!" She was convinced the death had been an accident.

After his death, she became increasingly dissatisfied with the posthumous assessments of his scientific work, and at the age of seventy-five, with no real training in science or mathematics, she undertook the formidable task of writing his biography herself — not a memoir, but a straightforward, detached biography that sought, among other things, to analyze the importance of his scientific contributions. She labored over it for months, seeking outside assistance to help her with some of the more complex aspects of her son's theoretical work. It was published in 1959, and remained for many years one of the standard reference works on the life and achievements of Alan Turing.

Mrs. Turing outlived her son by twenty-two years. She died in 1976, at the age of ninety-five.

For further reading: Alan Turing: The Enigma *by Andrew Hodges (Simon and Schuster, 1983)*

Elsie Orton, mother of playwright Joe Orton.

"I look back on my life," Elsie Orton wrote her son Joe in 1963, "and wonder where I have slipped up." It was an astonishing moment of candor for a woman who had spent so much of her life steadfastly refusing to acknowledge the drabness, monotony, and lower-middle-class poverty of her existence. Orton's father was a minicipal gardener who never earned more than fourteen pounds a week in the heavily industrial city of Leicester, ninety miles north of London. Elsie was a machinist, stitching underwear and blouses, in a local factory.

Elsie had always wanted a monied and leisurely life; she envied the wealthy, and was obsessed with keeping up appearances. She was self-concious and full of pretensions: she often lied to people about the cheap glass dish from Woolworth's she kept locked away in the living room sideboard — she claimed it was a "Jacobean heirloom" — and she liked to brag that the shoddy beaver coat she wore was an expensive anniversary present from her husband (actually, she'd bought it for herself). Her appetite for money was relentless; there was never enough to satisfy her expectations. Once, when her husband gave her some spending money, she threw it back in his face and shouted, "I want more than this!" Another time, when one of her daughters gave her some money, Elsie angrily wondered aloud if she was expected to "shit miracles" with it. Her only respite came at the local pub, where she entertained friends with her singing and bemoaned the show-business career she might have had if only she hadn't been so poor as a child. Later, after Joe's success in London, she was frequently in debt, with creditors literally banging at her door. Joe often bailed her out.

Of the four children, Joe was her favorite (she pawned her wedding ring to send him to a private school), but he fled the household, with few regrets, when he was eighteen. It had been an affectionless household: not one of the children could ever remember seeing their parents kiss, and Elsie, who despised sex, banished her husband to a separate bedroom after the birth of their fourth child. (A complete prude, she was later shocked when she saw her son's play *Entertaining Mr. Sloane*: she thought it was "awful in parts.")

She died in the winter of 1966, and when Joe returned home for the funeral, the only memento he took back to London was a pair of her false teeth, to be used as a prop in the production of his play *Loot*. He rarely talked with friends or interviewers about his parents or his upbringing, except to say, "I'm from the gutter. And don't you ever forget it, because I won't."

For further reading: Prick Up Your Ears: The Biography of Joe Orton *by John Lahr (Knopf, 1978) and* The Orton Diaries *edited by John Lahr (Harper and Row, 1986)*

Agrippina, mother of the Roman emperor Nero.

It was perhaps the ultimate mother-son horror story. After his mother had spent a lifetime tirelessly murdering and scheming to get him on the throne of Rome, Nero, at the age of twenty-two, decided he'd had enough of her meddling, and plotted to have her assassinated.

First he tried to poison her, on three separate occasions; but each time, Agrippina — an expert in poisons herself — took the antidotes in advance. Then he rigged the panels of her bedroom ceiling to fall and crush her while she slept; but one co-conspirator warned her of the plot, and the panels came crashing down on an empty bed. He then had a collapsible boat built to drown her; but when the boat sank, Agrippina — an exceedingly strong woman — swam easily to shore. Finally, in exasperation, Nero ordered his guards to simply go to her villa and stab her to death. This finally did the trick, though according to historians, it took an unusual number of sword thrusts to finally bring the lady down.

Nero announced to the people of Rome that his mother had committed suicide. But even then, he was not completely rid of her: he bitterly complained for the rest of his life that her ghost — restless, angry, and vengeful — often haunted him and pursued him through the corridors of his villa.

MOTION PICTURE PRODUCTION CODE (1934). During the 1920s, film directors were becoming more and more daring in what they showed on-screen. To stem what was seen as a rising tide of immorality — and to head off censorship forces from outside the industry — the studios adopted the Motion Picture Production Code, which set forth moral and ethical standards for the content of films.

The Code was first written in 1930, but wasn't actually put into effect until 1934. For more than two decades its reigning principle was, "No picture shall be produced which will lower the standards of those who see it. Hence the sympathy of the audience should never be thrown to the side of crime, wrongdoing, evil or sin." Films

that refused to follow the Code were denied an official seal of approval, and often went un-exhibited.

Among the Code's specific admonitions were, "Sex perversion or any inference to it is forbidden," and "The sanctity of the institution of marriage and the home shall be upheld. Pictures shall not infer that low forms of sex relationships are the accepted or common thing." Thus, the Code effectively banned the portrayal of homosexuals or gay themes on the screen for the next twenty-seven years.

In the 1960s, the Code gave way to the current rating system for motion pictures.

"THE EDDIE MURPHY'S DISEASE FOUNDATION," ad hoc group formed by six professionals in Los Angeles — not all of them gay — to protest the homophobia and continuing AIDS "jokes" of entertainer Eddie Murphy. The Foundation took out ads in several major magazines, including *Rolling Stone* and *Billboard*, to protest Murphy's homophobic comedy special *Eddie Murphy: Delirious*, first broadcast on Home Box Office in October 1983.

"Poor Eddie Murphy," the ads read. "He has one of the

most debilitating diseases a creative mind can have — and chances are he doesn't even know it. Yet, Eddie Murphy is such an eloquent spokesman for the disease, we've decided to name it after him ... Yes, Eddie Murphy, like millions of his friends, suffers from homophobia, an irrational and uncontrollable fear of homosexuality ... All scientific evidence indicates that you cannot contract AIDS through casual contact with AIDS victims. Unfortunately, casual contact with Eddie Murphy has been linked to the spread of Eddie Murphy's Disease ... Would you like to see Eddie Murphy's Disease contained within the Moral Majority? You can. Here are some suggestions."

The ads recommended writing protest letters to Home Box Office and other corporations promoting Murphy's career, including Columbia Records and Paramount Studios. It also invited readers to write to the Foundation's Los Angeles address for a free bumper sticker, "Eddie Murphy's Disease Can Be Cured!"

"His tirade is no different from any uneducated bigot's," one of the Foundation organizers told *The Advocate* in 1984. "It's not just the casual use of the word 'faggot' we object to ... It's a human rights issue and a health issue. Not only are his remarks on AIDS inaccurate, they are dangerous."

Murphy first commented on the Foundation six months later, in an interview in *Rolling Stone.* "The way I feel about it is, what they did helped my album," Murphy insisted, "because the majority of the country is heterosexual, and they read that homosexuals don't like Eddie Murphy and they think, 'Hey, all right!' They're wasting their money. They blew it all out of proportion, and if they want to, I don't give a fuck. Kiss my ass."

Shortly afterward, Murphy told another interviewer, "I want my work to have meaning. If you think of the sixties, you think of the Beatles. The fifties, you think of Elvis. I hope, when you think of the eighties, you think of Eddie Murphy."

MUSCLES À GO-GO, physique magazine, more explicitly gay than most, first published in February 1966. *Muscles à Go-Go* featured model layouts under such titles as "He's Butch!" and "Oh Mary, They're Hairy!" The Athletic Model Guild, Bruce of Kensington Road, and other major physique photog-

Muscles à Go-Go in 1966: A change from the physique magazines of the fifties.

raphers were all regular contributors.

THE MYRMIDONS (5th century B.C.), lost masterpiece by the Greek playwright Aeschylus. The play — which has only survived in fragments quoted by later writers — dealt with the love relationship between Achilles and Patroclus during the Trojan War, the death of Patroclus at the hands of Hector, and Achilles' resulting grief and revenge. Thought by some scholars to have been the most impassioned piece of homoerotic literature produced by the ancient world, the play was enormously popular in its time, and Achilles' feverish speech lamenting the death of Patroclus was much celebrated among the ancient Greeks.

NATIONAL VIEWERS' AND LISTENERS' ASSOCIATION, British anti-pornography group headquartered in London. In 1981, the Association's president, Mary Whitehurst, filed suit against the play *The Romans in Britain*, because it featured an act of simulated sodomy in one scene. Critics argued that the play was a serious effort and that the simulated sodomy scene was entirely justified in its context.

Whitehurst acknowledged having neither seen nor read the play — "That would have done no good at all," she said — but took action on the basis of other people's descriptions to her. "The Lord wanted me to do this," she told the press. Unable to file suit under any other section of British law, Whitehurst claimed the play violated the Sexual Offenses Act, which prohibits people from having intercourse in public places. "If this act took place on the street," said Whitehurst's lawyer, "it would clearly be an offense. I see no difference if it takes place on the stage of the National."

After four days of testimony, the suit was dismissed by a British court. However, the presiding judge — in a statement that jolted the British theater community — ruled that the Sexual Offenses Act *could* legitimately be applied in the future to works of drama presented on the stage, if such works included the explicit recreation of certain sex acts. Said the London *Times* in a scathing editorial, "This judicial refusal to distinguish between the simulated and the real is alarming."

One noted drama critic asserted that the case "threatens the theatre as no other has for years."

THE NEW YORK TIMES, USE OF THE WORD "GAY." In July 1987, the *Times* reversed its previous policy and circulated a memo advising its editorial staff that the use of the word "gay" was now permissible as a synonym for homosexual, providing it was used only as an adjective and not as a noun. By comparison, use of the title "Ms." was not allowed in the newspaper until 1986, and the term "black" for "Negro" did not appear until about 1969.

Jack Nicholson: Was his character secretly in love with Art Garfunkel's, in *Carnal Knowledge?*

THE NEW YORKER — REJECTION OF GAY ADVERTISING. In 1979, *The New Yorker* rejected a small print advertisement from the literary gay magazine *Christopher Street*, on the grounds it could not accept "gay advertising."

NICHOLSON, JACK (b. 1937), U.S. actor. Reacting to critics who suggested that his on-screen relationship with Art Garfunkel in the 1971 film *Carnal Knowledge* was one of "latent homosexuality," Nicholson told *Playboy* magazine, "When the term latent homosexuality is used by a lay person, it's as valid, medically speaking, as was the use of leeches or any other remedy of the Dark Ages. I suppose any time you're doing a piece of work with two male leads, there will be some connotation of latent homosexuality. But you could probably project that implication onto Romulus and Remus or Abbott and Costello."

NIPPLES, MEN'S — LAWS AGAINST EXHIBITING IN PUBLIC. In 1981, Arizona state legislator James Cooper — a Republican and a Mormon — introduced a bill that would have made it a crime in Arizona for men to go out in public with bare chests. "My wife doesn't like to see a man without a shirt on," Cooper said, "and many people feel the same way. Even if they used something the size of a dollar to cover the nipples, it would go a long way to help." The bill was defeated on a voice vote.

That same year, a similar law was actually passed in Palm Beach, Florida. The Palm Beach City Council approved an ordinance making it illegal for men to go around bare-chested in public, except within one hundred and fifty feet of a beach. Proponents of the measure claimed that the sight of bare-chested men playing tennis or jogging around town was giving the city a bad image.

NIPPLES, PERCENTAGE OF MEN'S WHICH BECOME ERECT DURING SEX. About sixty percent of all men get erect nipples during sex.

NUDE, PERCENTAGE OF AMERICAN MEN WHO SLEEP IN. According to one 1985 study, about nineteen percent of American men like to sleep in the nude. The highest percentage of men sleeping in the nude was found in the Western states; the lowest was found in the South. The study also revealed that the three most popular forms of bedtime wear for men were: pajamas (thirty-seven percent); underwear (thirty-three percent); and long-johns (two percent).

The orchid: Anybody care for an orchidectomy? Look it up, first.

ORCHIDS, flowering plants of the family *Orchidaceae*. The name *orchid* comes from a Greek word meaning "testicles." The ancient Greeks saw a strong resemblance between testicles and the bulbs of certain orchid plants, and believed that orchids grew wherever a man's semen — or the semen of an animal — fell to the ground.

In some nineteenth-century erotica, the term "orchid-eater" was used as a euphemism for a gay man, especially for one who delighted in fellatio. In Norman Douglas's 1917 novel *South Wind*, the pejorative "carnivorous orchid" was applied to a young man, with a similar meaning.

Today, the technical medical term for castration is *orchidectomy*.

ORGASMS, MALE — NUMBER PER SECOND IN THE UNITED STATES. Sexologists estimate that at any given second in the United States, approximately eight hundred men are experiencing orgasm.

ORGASMS, MULTIPLE — IN MEN. Although men do not have multiple orgasms in the same sense that women do, some men — less than five percent over the age of thirty-five — have an ability to achieve several ejaculations within a relatively short time-span. This ability is pronounced during a man's teens: an estimated twenty percent of all adolescents can achieve multiple ejaculations with a markedly brief recovery period after each one. One researcher recorded the case of a boy in his mid-teens who was able to have as many as eleven orgasms within four hours.

ORGASMS, NUMBER PER MAN IN A LIFETIME. The average American male will have approximately 6,500 orgasms during his lifetime.

PACINO, AL (b. 1940), U.S. actor. Pacino has said that his first reaction when he saw himself in the movie *Cruising* was, "Where do I go now? What do I do? I thought I had reached the bottom..." In the film's defense, he added, "I don't believe Billy Friedkin shot the entire script. He went and stripped scenes. He took the meat out of them."

PARKER, AL (b. 1952), gay porn star who, after Casey Donovan, has probably been the most famous and popular in the history of the business. Al Parker is not his real name; the name was assigned to him by Colt Studios when he first began modeling. ("I hated it," he once said.) His actual first name is Drew.

Parker got his start modeling — for fifty dollars a session — for Colt Studios in his early twenties, and soon became one of the hottest properties in gay erotica. "There are lots of better looking people out there with better bodies and bigger dicks," he has said. "I couldn't be more surprised that I've been singled out. And I really have no idea why." In 1980, he started his own production and distribution company, Surge Studios.

He once said he would continue being Al Parker only so long as it was fun. After that, he said, "I'll count my money, burn my negatives, and slip quietly back into my private world."

PARKER, ALAN (b. 1944), film director. In 1978, Parker made *Midnight Express*, a film based on the prison experiences and escape of Billy Hayes, a young

Midnight Express (1978): The product of a self-admitted "boring heterosexual film director."

American incarcerated in Turkey for trying to smuggle hashish out of the country. However, Parker omitted one critical aspect of Hayes's experience that Hayes himself had always been quite open about: a homosexual relationship he'd had behind bars with a Swedish prisoner. Instead, Parker showed a scene where Hayes firmly rebuffs the Swede's advances.

Hayes called censoring the relationship "a cop-out," but director Parker defended himself to the press: "I don't know enough about New York gays to know how they'd feel about this scene, but I'm prepared to risk them. People elsewhere are not as sophisticated." Parker — who once called himself "a boring heterosexual film director" — also directed the 1980 film *Fame*, about a performing arts high school in New York City. That film was criticized for including just one gay character, and a sad and lonely one at that.

PARKER, DOROTHY (1893-1967), renowned American wit and writer, once described by critic Alexander Woollcott as "a blend of Little Nell and Lady Macbeth." Regarded by many gay men as one of the patron saints of the quotable — and sometimes savage — one-liner, Parker herself had several lesbian interests throughout her life, and her husband, writer Alan Campbell, was gay. A sampling of her legendary wit:

• At a party one night, she and long-time nemesis Clare Booth Luce happened to get to the door at the same moment to leave. "Age before beauty," Luce remarked snidely, motioning for Parker to go on ahead of her. "Pearls before swine!" Parker replied, sweeping past her and out.

• When told that Clare Booth Luce was always kind to her inferiors: "And where does she find them?"

• Asked at a Halloween party to join in with the others who were "ducking for apples": "Change one letter in that phrase, and you have the story of my life."

• On hearing that President Calvin Coolidge had died: "How can they tell?"

• She and her friends at the Algonquin Round Table often played a game in which they tried to invent imaginative sentences using unusual words. Asked once to use the word *horticulture* in a sentence, Parker thought for a moment, and then replied, "You can lead a horticulture, but you can't make her think!"

• On Katharine Hepburn's acting: "She runs the gamut of emotions all the way from A to B."

• On a notoriously oversexed London actress who had recently injured her leg: "How terrible! She must have done it sliding down a barrister — oh, I mean, bannister."

• When angrily confronted by *New Yorker* editor Harold Ross for spending an afternoon in a bar rather than in her office writing: "Someone else was using the pencil."

• Parker was married to Alan Campbell for fourteen years before they got a divorce in 1947. Three years after the divorce, they decided to re-marry. At the second wedding, Parker overheard a guest remark that most of the people there hadn't spoken to one another in years. "Including the bride and groom," Parker quipped.

- "If all the girls who attended the Yale prom were laid end to end — I wouldn't be a bit surprised."
- "A girl's best friend is her mutter."
- "I was the toast of two continents: Greenland and Australia."

PENIS, SIDE TO WHICH IT MOST OFTEN HANGS IN PANTS. Two studies have found that just over seventy-five percent of all men say their penis automatically hangs to the left side inside their trousers or underwear. Seventeen percent say it hangs to the right. The rest say it hangs to the left or the right, with no obvious preference for either side.

PENIS, THOUGHT-PROVOKING DESCRIPTION OF. "In terms of beauty, a penis is like a blender. You appreciate it when it's being used, sure, but when you're just looking at it from across the room, it looks real silly." — Journalist Rod Tannenbaum, in *The Village Voice*.

PENIS ENLARGEMENT, MOST BIZARRE TECHNIQUE. A seventeenth-century Chinese book, *Jou-pu-t'uan*, described a bizarre method for penis enlargement, which involved cutting off a male dog's erect organ, slicing it into small pieces, and then inserting the sections under the flesh of a human penis. "With luck," the book explained, "there will be a perfect grafting of man and dog." As with most attempts at penis enlargement, there is no validity to the technique.

PICASSO, PABLO (1881-1973), Spanish painter. When he was in his late teens, Picasso fell in love, and apparently had sex, with a sixteen-year-old gypsy boy, with whom he explored, for long periods, the mountains around Horta de Ebro in Spain. The two cemented their relationship by cutting their wrists and allowing their blood to flow together. However, the relationship ended abruptly when the boy pulled a knife on Picasso one night and exclaimed, "I love you too much, I must go away." The boy then disappeared completely, and Picasso never saw him again. His disappearance left Picasso extremely depressed.

During Picasso's early life in Paris, when he was trying to make a name for himself as an artist, most of his closest male friends were homosexual. One was the poet Max Jacobs, who worshipped the young Spaniard. Another was the famous art dealer, Pere Manyac. Manyac financially supported Picasso for a time, and introduced him to important contacts in the art world. The two lived together, until Picasso began to resent Manyac's possessiveness, and moved out.

Picasso's friendship with Max Jacobs, on the other hand, lasted for several decades. After Picasso abandoned Manyac, it was Jacobs who stepped in and became Picasso's new "guide" and protector in Paris. Jacobs supported him financially, and the two also lived together. To the shock and astonishment of many, however, when Jacobs was arrested many years later and interred in a Nazi concentration camp, Picasso was one of his only friends who would not help to try and get him released. Jacobs died in the camp.

Later in life, Picasso summed up his feelings about friendship and sex when he said, "I can't have friends if they're not capable of sleeping with me. Not that I require it of the women or want it from the men — but there should at least be that feeling of warmth and intimacy one experiences in sleeping with someone."

PICTURES AT AN EXHIBITION (1874), major piano composition by Russian composer Modeste Mussorgsky, later orchestrated by Maurice Ravel, and now one of the most popular works in the symphonic repertoire. The work was based on an exhibit of watercolors by the handsome young architect and painter Victor Hartmann, with whom Mussorgsky was apparently in love.

Hartmann's death in 1874, at the age of thirty-nine, devastated Mussorgsky. "What a terrible blow!" Mussorgsky wrote a friend. "Why should a dog, a horse, a rat live on — and creatures like Hartmann must die!" The composer — who was prone to long periods of dark depression and who, in times of stress, often drank himself to the point of physical collapse — seemed to go completely crazy afterward: he sold all his furniture and clothes and drank himself into one stupor after another. *Pictures at an Exhibition* was based on a memorial exhibit of Hartmann's watercolors in the summer of 1874, and was dedicated to him.

POLAROID FOUNDATION, non-profit arm of the Polaroid

Corporation. In 1978, the Foundation made a sizable financial grant to help "provide services for lesbian women," specifically to help provide legal counseling for lesbian mothers.

POLLS, U.S. PUBLIC OPINION ON HOMOSEXUALITY (1969-1988).

A Threat to the Nation

In a national poll conducted in 1965, 58% of the women and 82% of the men said that homosexuals represent a clear threat to the American way of life. Only two groups were seen as a worse potential threat: Communists and atheists. In recent years, Jerry Falwell, Pat Robertson, and others have preached that homosexuals represent a threat to the very fabric of American society. But to what extent has the general public actually shared that view?

• September 1969: Are homosexuals harmful to American life? (Lou Harris)
  Yes: 63%
  No: 26%
  Not sure: 10%

• August 1973: Do homosexuals do more harm than good in this country? (Lou Harris)
  Yes: 50%
  No: 50%*

• January 1974: Which of the following groups is likely to represent a threat to American society in the next two or three decades? (Roper)
  Percentage of people naming homosexuals: 13%

• January 1978: Which of the following groups is likely to present a threat to American society in the next two or three decades? (Roper)
  Percentage of people naming homosexuals: 17%

• June 1982: Do you think homosexuals are more likely or less likely to commit crimes than heterosexuals are? (Gallup)
  More likely: 23%
  Less likely: 36%
  The same/Don't know: 41%

Discrimination

However negatively the public may feel about homosexuality in general, polls have consistently shown that the majority of Americans favor laws outlawing discrimination against homosexuals in both housing and employment. But there are caveats. In a 1977 Louis Harris poll, for example, the public thought homosexuals should *not* be allowed to work as psychiatrists, social workers, youth counselors, priests, ministers, and rabbis. They were, however, comfortable with homosexuals being doctors, artists, factory workers, businessmen, store clerks, and television news reporters.

• June 1977: Do you favor a law outlawing job discrimination against homosexuals? (Lou Harris)

Yes: 54%
No: 28%
Not sure: 18%

• June 1977: Should a person who is openly homosexual be allowed to work as a policeman? (Lou Harris)

Yes: 48%
No: 42%
Not sure: 10%

• July 1977: Do you think it is wrong to deny a well-qualified person a job simply because he is a homosexual? (CBS News/ *New York Times*)

Yes: 61%
No: 20%
Not sure: 19%

• February 1978: To what degree do you think homosexuals are discriminated against in this country? (Gallup)

Great deal: 30%
Fair amount: 23%
Not much: 18%
Practically none: 15%
Don't know: 14%

• May 1981: Should fair housing and employment laws be extended to protect homosexuals and lesbians? (NBC/ Associated Press)

Yes: 48%
No: 38%
Not sure: 14%

• August 1983: Do you favor making it illegal to discriminate against homosexuals and lesbians in employment and housing? (Penn and Schoen, for Garth Analysis)

Yes: 51%
No: 36%
Don't know: 13%

The Presidency and Other Elected Offices

Would a well-qualified candidate for president lose the election if he publicly acknowledged he was gay? Should openly gay candidates be elected to *any* public offices? According to most polls, the public is not adverse to a congressman who is gay; but, despite some changes in attitudes over the years, they are not prepared to vote for a presidential candidate if he also happens to be a homosexual.

• June 1977: Should a man who acknowledges being a homosexual be allowed to hold public office as a U.S. congressman? (Lou Harris)

Yes: 53%

No: 36%

Not sure: 10%

• July 1978: Would you vote for a generally well-qualified candidate for president of the United States, if he were also a homosexual? (Gallup)

Yes: 26%

No: 66%

No opinion: 9%

• November 1985: Would you vote for a generally well-qualified candidate for president of the United States, if that candidate were also a homosexual? (Roper, for *U.S. News and World Report*)

Yes: 40%

No: 52%

• April 1983: Would you be likely to vote for a presidential candidate who received the endorsement of homosexual groups during the campaign? (CBS News/*New York Times*)

Yes: 47%

No: 50%

No opinion: 3%

• September 1983: If a well-qualified candidate for local office turned out to be a homosexual or a lesbian, would you be less likely to vote for that candidate? (*Los Angeles Times*)

Yes: 49%

No: 48%

Not sure: 2%

Homosexual Teachers

When Anita Bryant launched her crusade in the mid-1970s to "save America's children," the issue of whether gay people should be allowed to teach in public schools became fiercely emotional. But even before that it was hotly debated, and the issue still persists today.

• April 1973: Should an admitted homosexual be allowed to teach at a college or university? (National Opinion Research Center)

Yes: 47%

No: 48%

Don't know: 4%

• April 1988: Should an admitted homosexual be allowed to teach at a college or university? (National Opinion Research Center)

Yes: 57%

No: 39%

Don't know: 5%

• June 1977: Should an admitted homosexual be allowed to work as a school principal? (Lou Harris)

Yes: 33%

No: 58%

Not sure: 9%

• June 1977: Should homosexuals be hired as elementary school teachers? (Gallup)

Yes: 27%
No: 65%
No opinion: 8%

• October 1978: Would you vote for a ballot proposition allowing school boards to fire teachers who openly practice or advocate homosexuality? (Roper, for the Public Broadcasting System)
For: 54%
Against: 39%
Don't know: 8%

• May 1981: Should homosexuals and lesbians be allowed to teach in the public schools just like anyone else? (ABC News/ *Washington Post*)
Yes: 45%
No: 46%
Don't know: 9%

• November 1985: Would you vote for a law that allowed firing a homosexual from a job teaching school? (Roper, for *U.S. News and World Report*)
Yes: 33%
No: 61%

The Armed Forces

Polls have continually shown that the majority of Americans favor gay men or lesbians serving in the armed forces.

• June 1977: Do you think homosexuals should be allowed to serve in the armed forces? (Gallup)

Yes: 51%
No: 38%
No opinion: 11%

• July 1977: Would you vote for a bill that protected the rights of homosexuals to be in the army? (Yankelovich, Skelly and White, for *Time* magazine)
For: 60%
Against: 31%
Not sure: 10%

• September 1983: Should the U.S. military be able to discharge a soldier because he or she is a homosexual or a lesbian? (*Los Angeles Times*)
Yes: 40%
No: 50%
Not sure: 9%

Acceptance

Regardless of the strides gay people have made in the last ten years, has the general public grown more accepting of homosexuality as an alternative lifestyle?

• July 1983: Should homosexuality be considered an accepted alternative lifestyle? (Gallup, for *Newsweek* magazine)
Yes: 32%
No: 58%
Don't know: 10%

• September 1983: How sympathetic are you to the homosexual community? (*Los Angeles Times*)

Very sympathetic: 6%
Somewhat
sympathetic: 24%
Somewhat
unsympathetic: 17%
Very unsympathetic: 46%
Not sure: 5%

• July 1986: Do you think homosexuality has become an accepted alternative lifestyle? (Gallup, for *Newsweek* magazine)
Yes: 32%
No: 61%
Don't know: 7%

Legalization

Exasperated at public attitudes towards homosexuality, Christopher Isherwood once remarked, "What irritates me is the bland way people go around saying, 'Oh, our attitude has changed. We don't dislike these people any more.' But by the strangest coincidence, they haven't taken away the injustice; the laws are still on the books."

• October 1971: Should an individual be allowed to follow his own conscience, rather than the dictates of society, when it comes to having homosexual relations with another consenting adult? (Roper)
Yes: 39%
No: 48%
Don't know: 13%

• June 1977: Should it be legal for consenting adults to have homosexual relations? (Gallup)
Yes: 43%
No: 43%
No opinion: 14%

• June 1982: Should it be legal for consenting adults to have homesexual relations? (Gallup)
Yes: 45%
No: 39%
No opinion: 16%

• June 1986: (Asked shortly after the Supreme Court decision upholding the constitutionality of Georgia's sodomy laws) Should states have the right to prohibit certain homosexual acts between consenting adults in private? (Gallup, for *Newsweek* magazine)
Yes: 34%
No: 57%
Not sure: 9%

Miscellaneous Questions Asked Through the Years

• June 1977: Is homosexuality more prevalent today than it was twenty-five years ago? (Gallup)
Yes: 66%
No: 24%
No opinion: 10%

• June 1977: Can a homosexual be a good Christian or a good Jew? (Gallup)

Yes: 53%
No: 33%
No opinion: 14%

• November 1980: If your son or daughter became involved in a homosexual or lesbian relationship, how would you feel? (Research and Forecasts, for the Connecticut Mutual Life Insurance Co.)

Happy: 1%
Neutral: 17%
Unhappy: 30%
Very unhappy: 52%

• June 1982: Do you think homosexuals are likely to lead less happy, well-adjusted lives than heterosexuals? (Gallup)

Yes: 66%
No: 13%
Don't know: 21%

• September 1983: Do you think homosexuality is primarily something people are born with, or is it a matter of upbringing, or is it a matter of choice? (*Los Angeles Times*)

Born with: 16%
Upbringing: 25%
Choice: 37%
Not sure: 20%

• January 1987: Should gay couples be allowed to adopt children? (*Glamour* magazine reader opinion survey)

Yes: 41%
No: 59%

• April 1987: Would you favor removing from your public library a book by an admitted homosexual advocating homosexuality? (National Opinion Research Center)

Yes: 40%
No: 58%
Don't know: 2%

• April 1989: (Asked of residents of San Francisco) Are there too many gays living in San Francisco? (*San Francisco Chronicle*)

Yes: 25%
Somewhat too many: 24%
No: 39%

PORN STAR, GAY — FIRST AND MOST FAMOUS. Casey Donovan (1943-1987), gay porn star and actor, best known for his role in the 1971 film *The Boys in the Sand*. Born John Calvin Culver, in Canandaigua, New York, he sometimes referred to himself as "the godfather of gay porn."

Regarded as the first openly gay sex symbol, Donovan had a bachelor's degree in education and originally intended to become an elementary school teacher. He did teach school for several years, but spent his vacations acting in summer stock. Later, he appeared in two popular gay porno films — *Casey* and *Dragula* — and did a bit of hustling, before landing the role that propelled him to fame, in Wakefield Poole's *The Boys in the Sand*, in 1971.

Casey was brought into *The Boys in the Sand* after it had already started filming. He was originally slated to appear in only one scene, but when the film's original star demanded more money, director Poole expanded Casey's role and started reshooting the entire film with Casey as the lead. "The whole thing was just done for fun," Casey said later. "We never envisioned that thousands of people would see this home movie..." The "home movie" broke all box-office records for a gay porn film, was favorably reviewed in *Variety* (with the now-famous line, "There are no more closets"), and made Donovan a huge star within the gay community.

After that, Donovan unsuccessfully tried to break into mainstream movies. Asked once if he thought his career in porn films would hinder his future as a serious actor, he replied, "Not at all. Those days are gone forever. Not too long ago there were rumors about stars like Joan Crawford, Burt Lancaster, and Chuck Connors running around trying to buy up all of those fuck flicks they were supposed to have made way back when they were down and out. Today it wouldn't make any difference. Anybody can do what they want." However, despite a strong modeling career and much publicity surrounding his role in *The Boys in the Sand*, the closest Donovan ever came to appearing in a mainstream movie was in Radley Metzger's now-forgotten 1974 film about bisexuality, *Score*.

Through the years, even into his early forties, Donovan continued making porn films, including *The Other Side of Aspen* (1978), *L.A. Tool & Die* (1981), and *The Boys in the Sand II* (1984). He also appeared in several legitimate theater productions, and produced a revival of *The Ritz* on Broadway in 1983.

He died of AIDS in Inverness, Florida, on August 10, 1987. (See also *THE BOYS IN THE SAND*.)

PORNOGRAPHY, NINETEENTH-CENTURY — GAY EXCERPTS FROM. Only a fool would have mourned the passing of the Victorian era. It was an age when boys were sometimes castrated to prevent them from masturbating, and women were taught that the female of the species was incapable of orgasm. Prostitution flourished, as did venereal disease and unwanted pregnancies. It has been estimated that most prostitutes of the time lived only about four years once they entered the profession. The causes of their premature deaths were: venereal disease, complications from childbirth, murder, rape, starvation, unsanitary living conditions, and various non-venereal illnesses. Prudish and arbitrary censorship abounded, and doctors were thrown into jail for writing about contraceptives and birth control. By the time the Victorians got around to destroying Oscar Wilde, the age was, blessedly, in decline. Wilde and Queen Victoria died within two months of one another.

There were countercurrents to the madness. Pornography was quite popular, a curious but typically hypocritical development. Admittedly, the writing, publishing, and distribution of pornography were strictly underground affairs, and the authorities made various attempts at squelching it; but pornography thrived, and some enduring classics of erotic literature were written during this period.

Many of the major heterosexual erotic novels of the day included at least one explicit scene of male homosexual activity. Buried in all those pages of heterosexual bravado and sex-play were some stimulating treasures of homoeroticism.

The Power of Mesmerism (1891).

First published in Moscow in 1891, *The Power of Mesmerism: A Highly Erotic Narrative of Voluptuous Facts and Fancies* is the story of Frank Etheridge, a young man who learns the art of hypnotism and then applies it to his friends and his family, until all of them — even his mother and father — are enslaved to his sexual whims.

In one of his first introductions to the art of hypnotism, Frank, at college, spies through a keyhole to watch a headmaster secretly hypnotizing a young male student. Once the student is in a trance, the headmaster strips him, whips him, then uses him sexually:

"The master spoke to the boy, 'Raise your head, and take my prick in your mouth, and suck it till I spend.'

"The victim complied in a mechanical manner.

"The birching was now resumed, and as the master's excitement increased, the blows fell heavier, the boy's bottom becoming red and inflamed.

"He also commenced fucking the boy in the mouth, pushing himself backwards and forwards, when suddenly he dropped the birch and, seizing the boy's head, forced his prick within his mouth as far as he could ram it, spent, saying with spasmodic gasps, 'Swallow it all — my — spunk — shall — go down — your throat — if it — kills you.'

"When he withdrew his cock, the come was glistening in and around the boy's lips, but the boy had most undoubtedly swallowed nearly all but a few drops."

Later, after learning this mysterious art of "mesmerism" himself, Frank first experiments with it by putting his best friend, Harry, and the family's handsome stable boy, Thomas, into deep hypnotic trances. He then orders them to strip.

"He stripped himself, and ordered his two subjects to do the same, put a small box of cold cream under the pillow of the bed so as to be at hand, then contemplated and handled the young groom and his friend.

"Thomas was furnished with a lovely tosser, which swelled rapidly under Frank's touches as he uncovered the ruby head and gently pulled the foreskin backward and forward.

"'Now Thomas, keep yourself stiff by gentle frigging, but mind not to spend till I order you,' Frank said. Then he turned to the beautiful Harry Mortimer, who came to his side as soon as ordered. Harry was indeed an Adonis — splendidly shaped in every limb, delightfully plump and firm white flesh, rosy cheeks, sparkling blue eyes — but Frank was most engrossed with Harry's jewel of a prick, which was a perfect gem of the first water, nearly eight inches long when erect, as white and hard as ivory, yet of velvety softness to the touch, and set in a bed of soft, curly, golden-brown hair, which ornamented the roots and shaded the full bag of tricks in their receptacle below.

"Placing himself on the bed and sitting up with his back supported by a pillow, Frank ordered Thomas to straddle his lap. Taking up the box of cream, Frank first anointed the head of his own impatient priapus, then did the same to Thomas's fundament, working his two fingers well into it, which made the stable boy's prick throb and stiffen enormously. Then Frank adjusted his tool to the wrinkled orifice: in obedience to his mysterious influence, Thomas slowly impaled himself upon it, till his buttocks embraced the whole length of Frank's mancock."

Harry is then positioned so that Frank can suck *his* cock while continuing to fuck Thomas in the ass:

"Never had Frank experienced such ecstacy and erotic fury as this conjunction with his groom and his friend now caused him to feel; he thrilled from head to toe with voluptuous excitement as his spendings seemed to shoot from him again and again, with a very few seconds between each emission; Harry on his part deluged Frank's mouth and lips with the balmy juice of his virginity, and Thomas also flooded his own belly with convulsive jets of spunk — all of them being so young and vigorous they seemed almost inexhaustible."

The rest of the book is taken up with Frank unleashing the previously sublimated lusts of his hypnotized parents and his sister, until finally, by the book's end, everyone — including an aunt and some of the servants — are involved in one huge orgy.

The Romance of Lust (1876).

Published in London in 1876, *The Romance of Lust* recounts the sexual adventures of an unabashedly bisexual (and extremely well-endowed) young man, Charlie Roberts

Early in the book, Charlie is sent away to live with his uncle, an attractive, lusty doctor with a penchant for S&M, especially spankings and floggings. The uncle — "well-made, muscular, portly, handsome ... with a large well-filled pair of cods" — adores his husky, well-endowed nephew, and the two soon enter into a mutually satisfying sexual relationship:

"In an instant we were both stark naked. We threw ourselves into one another's arms and lovingly kissed each other. Our tongues met in a delicious sucking — our hands took each a prick, and we had a most exciting and loving embrace ... He then kissed my bottom-hole, making my prick stand and throb again with delight. Then spitting on his prick he quickly sheathed it in my glowing backside. After pausing to enjoy the exquisite pleasure of complete insertion, he stooped and, passing a hand round my belly, laid hold of my stiff-standing prick with one hand, while he gently pressed my ballocks with the other. We then proceeded to active measures. He soon made me spend, which I did with loud cries of delight, giving him the most exquisite pleasure by the pressures the act of spending made me exercise on his pleased prick. He soon resumed his thrusts, and eventually he spent in the most ecstatic joy."

With a little bit of instruction, Charlie eventually becomes accomplished in the fine art of fellatio, and begins servicing his uncle regularly:

"He took me in his arms and glued his lips to mine. Our tongues met. Both our hands wandered, his on my prick, which immediately responded to the touch, and my hand on his prick, which was only at half-mast. I rapidly unbuttoned him, and brought it forth, then kneeling, I took it in my mouth, and sucked it and fingered the root with my hand. Then, passing my other hand below, I sought to penetrate with my finger into the interior of his fundament. He rose to a full standing position to enable me to enter his anus more easily. His prick, standing fiercely now, showed how much I excited him. I ceased not until he was in an agony of pleasure — forcing my head on his prick

until it entered almost completely into my mouth, and then shooting his sperm right down my throat."

Not long afterward, a third young man, Dale, is coerced into joining their activities. The doctor seduces Dale under the pretense of administering a much-needed whipping to him. The doctor, who is already naked, orders Dale to strip, then commences with the whipping:

"He bent the boy's warm body over his brawny thighs — Dale's young stiffened cock rubbed against the naked thigh he lay on. The doctor now raised the rod ...

"Whack, whack, went the birch rod ... sufficiently stinging to cause the youth to move up and down, rubbing his cock against the doctor's thighs, and causing him such ecstacies as hardly to allow him to feel the blows. His warm soft flesh, too, rubbing against the doctor's large, stiff tool, soon put them both in a delirium of delight. The doctor then changed his position, and drew the boy more over his belly, so that his great prick could get between the boy's thighs, while the boy's cock rubbed against the doctor's belly ... The boy's bottom was now red with a glowing heat, and his cock was in a state of intense excitement, and the doctor's tool was as stiff and randy as possible... Almost at the same moment a delicious mutual spend was the result of their lascivious toyings."

Later, Dale is instructed to fuck Charlie in the ass, while the doctor watches and simultaneously administers a punitive whipping to Dale's thrusting rear-end:

"Whack — whack — whack — fell the strokes, sufficiently sharp to make Master Dale wince and wriggle his bottom to and fro. Quickly the exciting pleasure overcame all pain, and his lust rising, Dale thrust furiously in the channel he was operating in ... Dale began to thrust fast and furiously, evidently enjoying it to the utmost. I let him feel the full enjoyment of his new quarters, only telling him to lay hold of my cock and frig me ... Sensing that the final moment of crisis was coming on, the doctor had ceased his flogging and, wetting two fingers, gradually introduced them into the bottom-hole of young Dale and finger-poked him in unison with Dale's movements into me, so that the ecstacy was almost more than the poor boy could bear."

Several weeks pass, with the three enjoying a deeply satisfying sexual relationship. However, Charlie eventually decides it's time to leave his uncle's house and start life on his own. He is soon married — to his former boyhood governess — and he and his new wife, once settled, begin eagerly seducing their servants. One of the servants, "an admirable stallion" named Carl, has a smooth and beautiful body, and a muscular ass that Charlie finds irresistible:

"As a rule, I like to fuck a rough, hairy-arsed man, but I can all the same appreciate the delight in such an exquisite arsehole as Carl possessed. To me also it had the attraction of its first possession. When thus fully displayed to my delighted eye, I flung myself on my knees, kissed and tongued the exquisite and delicious orifice, and speedily got furiously lewd upon it; and rarely have I fucked an arse more deliciously incentive to sodomy."

The book ends, rather abruptly, with Charlie, approaching old age, having threesomes with his wife and their beautiful eighteen-year-old son.

The New Epicurean (1875).

Written as a series of letters to a number of imaginary ladies, *The New Epicurean, or The Delights of Sex* is usually attributed to Captain Edward Sellon, a former soldier and notorious nineteenth-century rake. Though virtually every erotic encounter in the book is heterosexually-oriented, the book is interesting for a single brief episode in which the narrator experiences a fleeting lust for another young man — a "little stallion," the boy is called — who is fucking his girlfriend in the woods when the narrator happens upon them:

"The sight was so exhilarating ... Now, whatever the ancients may have thought on the subject, I must confess I have never seen what the peculiar point of attraction could be in having beautiful boys, as they unquestionably did; yet when I saw that lovely young boy's bottom bounding up and down ... a strange dizziness seized me and I felt a lust, stronger than the lust for women, lay hold of me."

The sight immediately causes the narrator to orgasm — "a gushing stream" — and he is so turned on by the sight of the boy's thrusting buttocks, that he arranges to experience a similar episode, this time with a "young rascal" whom he hires to fuck a girl while he watches:

"His breeches were off, and his shirt was up above his waist. He fell upon her, and then — then at it he went in good style ... The sight was most fucktious. His beautiful bottom bounding up and down, its peach-like cheeks trembling from their very plumpness, his stiff little cock, now in, now out — I think you will admit that a lovelier picture could not well be conceived, and I would have given fifty guineas to have had Watteau here at that moment to paint the scene."

My Secret Life (1890).

Privately printed in 1890, *My Secret Life* is the detailed sexual autobiography of a man whose relentless appetite takes him into hundreds of sexual encounters — with maids, prostitutes, cousins, philandering wives, and others. Aside from being one of the most famous of all Victorian erotic novels, it is also, by far, the longest: when originally published, it ran to eleven volumes encompassing over four thousand pages.

Homosexual episodes are scattered throughout the entire narrative. In fact, the narrator is first taught to masturbate by a sixteen-year-old male cousin (who is also eager to try anal intercourse, though the narrator refuses), and his first sexual experiences — mutual masturbation — are with other boys. Several years later, one evening in Naples, the narrator is approached by a man who is selling the pleasures of two beautiful teenage boys. The narrator declines the offer, but adds:

"This set me thinking very much, and on reflection, though amusing one's self that way seemed to me most objectionable, if men liked it, it was their affair alone. A man had as much right to use his anus as he liked, as a man has to use his penis — that was the conclusion I came to. But it set me wondering if many men took their pleasure up other's backsides. Was it more pleasurable than fucking women? — Did the buggaree have pleasure like the buggerer? — and so on, till I thought I should like to try, but I never did. For a little time afterwards I thought over all I had seen, heard, and done with my own sex from boyhood to the present time. My curiosity on the matter was aroused, and the curiosity has become stronger since."

A short time later, as his interest in the subject grows, he engages in mutual masturbation with another man; but even that doesn't completely satisfy his curiosity, and he eventually pays a handsome, predominantly heterosexual young man to act the passive partner in anal intercourse:

"I put him in various attitudes and looked at his naked rigidity — feeling it, kissing it, glorying in my power — with my own prick upright. Then I placed him over the bed — his bum towards me, his head towards the looking glass — I stood back to look. There were his white buttocks and large white thighs. His prick was invisible, stiff against his belly ... I locked the door, I trembled, we whispered. I slabbered my prick and his hole with spit. His prick was still stiff. There was the small round hole — the balls beneath — the white thighs — I closed on him half-mad, holding him round one thigh. I pointed my prick — my brain whirled — I wished not to do what I was doing, but some ungovernable impulse drove me on. My rod with two or three lunges buried itself up him, and passing my hands round his belly I held him to me, grasping both his prick and his balls tightly. He gave a loud moan. 'Ohoo I shall faint,' he cried. 'Pull it out.'

"I recollect nothing more

distinctly. A fierce, bloody minded bawdiness possessed me, a determination to do it — to ascertain if it was a pleasure — I would have wrung his prick off sooner than have withdrawn for him, and yet felt a disgust at myself. Drawing once slightly back, I saw my prick half out of his tube, then forcing it back, it spent up him. I shouted out loudly and bawdily..."

He then masturbates the young man, and a few minutes later, still horny, they masturbate each other again. Afterwards:

"Immediately I had an ineffable disgust at him and myself — a terrible fear — a loathing — I could scarcely be in the room with him — could have kicked him. He said, 'You've made me bleed.' At that I nearly vomited — 'I must make haste,' said I looking at my watch. 'I forgot it was so late — I must go.' All my desire was to get away as quickly as possible. I left after paying him, and making him swear, and swearing myself, that no living person should know of the act."

Despite his disgust over the episode, the thought of sex with a man often gives him an uncontrollable erection afterward, and he sometimes indulges in masturbation with other men. He also — like many of the heterosexual men in these Victorian novels — savors and is turned on by the sight of another man's thrusting buttocks while a woman is being fucked.

PROSS, MISS, possible lesbian character in Charles Dickens's *A Tale of Two Cities* (1859). The devoted lady servant and protector of Miss Lucie Manette, Pross is a strong, brawny, and mannish woman. In fact, the reader is first introduced to her through the eyes of another character who silently muses upon meeting her, "I really think this must be a man!" Pross firmly believes that no male is good enough to marry her "darling" Lucie, and even thinks that Lucie's own father, the saintly Doctor Manette, is not worthy of such a daughter. Dickens points out that this disapproval is always heavily tinged with poignant jealousy. At the end of the book, Miss Pross is the only one "man enough" to finally defeat and kill the infamous Madame Defarge, whose machinations have set into motion much of the book's tragic story.

Other Dickens characters who have been interpreted as gay or lesbian can be found in

The Pickwick Papers and *Little Dorritt.*

PROSTITUTION, MALE — IN ANCIENT ROME. By the early part of the first century, male prostitution reached a kind of peak in ancient Rome. Not only was it not illegal, but the government collected a tax on it and gave boy prostitutes a legal holiday. In the Roman city of Pompeii, two brothers — both prostitutes — advertised their wares with a prominent sign showing a hugely hung young man weighing his cock against a stack of gold on a balance scales.

PSYCHOPATHICA SEXUALIS — CONTROVERSY OVER TRANSLATION INTO ENGLISH. First published in German in 1886, *Psychopathica Sexualis* was the groundbreaking scientific work by German neuropsychiatrist Richard von Krafft-Ebing that openly discussed homosexuality and other forms of sexual expression, including fetishism and sadomasochism. In 1893, the *British Medical Journal* ar-

Ancient Roman sculpture: What was he waiting for?

dently condemned the book's translation into English. A scathing editorial in the *Journal* not only questioned whether the work should have been translated, but added that, better still, it should have originally "been written entirely in Latin, and thus be veiled in the decent obscurity of a dead language."

RAMOS, OVIDIO. In March 1977, during Anita Bryant's campaign to overturn a gay-rights ordinance in Dade County, Florida, Ovidio Ramos — a 23-year-old gay Cuban-American described as "very artistic, extremely sensitive and nervous" — appeared with several friends on a local talk show on Miami's Spanish-language radio station to defend gay rights. After the group was interviewed, phone callers to the program barraged Ramos and his friends with threats, insults, and the not-unexpected misinformed remarks. Most of the group tried to take the remarks in stride, but Ramos seemed, according to a close friend, particularly despondent. For the next two days, Ramos sequestered himself in his apartment. On March 16, he watched a Phil Donahue segment in which Anita Bryant claimed that the Bible says homosexuals should be put to death. Immediately after the program, Ramos wrote a farewell letter to his parents, drank some whiskey — and then blasted his brains out with a revolver. "We opposed his participation on that radio program," his mother said later, "but it was out of our concern for him. His father and I knew very well that he was too sensitive a person to go through that experience without any serious consequences to his emotional well-being."

Another participant in the program later had his car torched and destroyed, and lost his job with the Spanish-lanuage edition of *Cosmopolitan.*

RANKE, LEOPOLD VON (1795-1886), renowned German historian, often called "the father of modern historiography." Ranke consistently blamed the decline of Renaissance Italy on homosexuality and syphilis.

Ronald Reagan: Playing it straight in *Dark Victory* (1939).

REAGAN, RONALD (b. 1911), U.S. film actor and president. Reagan had a small part as a listless male socialite in the 1939 Bette Davis film *Dark Victory*. The film's director, Edmund Goulding, who was himself gay, wanted Reagan to play the role as a gay man, in a slightly effeminate, foppish manner. Reagan adamantly refused, and later wrote of Goulding, "I had no trouble seeing *him* in that role, but for myself I want to think if I stroll where the girls are short of clothes, there will be a great scurrying about and taking cover."

REYNOLDS, BURT (b. 1936), U.S. film actor. Speaking of the extraordinarily good-looking male models currently used in some advertising, Reynolds openly acknowledged to interviewer Barbara Walters, "I could be bisexual for those guys." Reynolds has, however, denied for years that he is actually bisexual. Discussing his consistently poor health over the last several years, and the rumors he has AIDS, he told *Entertainment Tonight* in 1985, "That was the only disease I knew I could rule out." Burt supposedly once told Debbie Reynolds, "You're not famous until you've been accused of being homosexual."

SAGAN, CARL — HOMOSEXUAL ENCOUNTER WITH A DOLPHIN. In the 1960s, Sagan was visiting a dolphin research center on St. Thomas, when he became the object of a young male dolphin's sexual affections. Sagan was in a large indoor pool playing ball with the dolphin, named Peter, when the animal suddenly grazed him. "I felt some protrusion of Peter's lightly brushing my side as he passed," Sagan recalled in his book *The Cosmic Connection.* The dolphin persisted, and it quickly became apparent what the protrusion was, and what the dolphin wanted. "I felt," Sagan said later, "like some maiden aunt to whom an improper proposal had just been put." Despite the animal's cheerful single-mindedness, Sagan — though flattered — was in his words, "not prepared to cooperate."

SALO: THE 120 DAYS OF SODOM (1975), controversial film by Italian director Pier Paolo Pasolini, based on the book by the Marquis de Sade. The film — which graphically depicted acts of disfigurement, sadomasochism, and the eating of human feces — was declared obscene by the Italian courts, and its release was delayed for several months. In 1978, Scotland Yard's "Obscene Publications Squad" seized a print of the film from a London art cinema and charged the theater's management with "keeping a disorderly or bawdy house."

SARANDON, SUSAN (b. 1946), U.S. actress, best known for

her roles in *Atlantic City*, *Bull Durham*, and *The Witches of Eastwick*. Sarandon has been active in helping raise money for AIDS research, and in helping to increase public awareness of the disease. Her involvement began after she lost a close friend, actor Bobby Christian, to AIDS. "I remember early on," she once said, "when people were calling it a 'gay cancer,' I found myself in front of a march down to New York's City Hall, and I was the only woman there. I was stunned. That was years ago." She has since lost other close friends to the disease.

Arnold Schwarzenegger: You can look, but please don't touch.

Asked in 1989 if it was still difficult to get celebrities to lend their time to AIDS benefits, Sarandon replied, "There still aren't a lot of straight actors who will go out for benefits. Recently, someone called me for an AIDS benefit and said, 'We need a guy. We need someone from the real Hollywood community.' And they couldn't find anybody. There's still great prejudice. A lot of male actors are afraid that if they support AIDS fund-raising, they'll be known as gay and then they won't get work. The horrible thing is that it's a legitimate fear."

SCHWARZENEGGER, AR-NOLD (b. 1947), Austrian-U.S. bodybuilder and film actor. Although he has said he's glad he never accepted any of the propositions he received from homosexuals when he was starting out as a bodybuilder, he later wrote in his book *Pumping Iron*, "When a homosexual looks at a bodybuilder, I don't have anything against that. If I see a girl with big tits, I'm going to stare and stare. The same is true with the homosexual — he's looking at the bodybuilder and picturing what he would do with him."

SEAGULLS, LESBIAN. In 1977, researchers at the University of California at Irvine estimated that between eight and fourteen percent of southern California's female seagulls were lesbian. The estimate was based on a five-year study of 1,200 pairs of gulls on Santa Barbara Island. The study found that female seagulls form "homosexual pairs" and "exhibit all the courtship and territorial behavior used by heterosexually mated birds": they share the same nest, give birth to eggs (infertile), and protect their territory in the same way male and female couples do.

SEMEN, AMOUNT EJACULATED DURING ORGASM. The average ejaculation contains approximately four cubic centimeters — or one tablespoonful — of semen. According to a 1984 French study — in which semen was collected from 833 male volunteers, aged twenty-one to fifty — the largest volume of semen is ejaculated by men aged twenty-six to

thirty. Men aged forty-six to fifty have the lowest volume.

Whatever the age, the amount of semen ejaculated falls by as much as thirty percent if a man ejaculates on three successive days. "I think a man could probably have multiple ejaculations until he has a dry ejaculation," concluded one urologist. Some sexologists believe that men who orgasm once or more a day may enjoy the sensations less than those who wait a few days between orgasms. Research indicates that a larger volume of ejaculate plays a part in having more intense and pleasurable orgasms.

SEMEN, SPEED TRAVELING DURING EJACULATION. On the average, semen travels at about twenty-eight miles per hour as it ejaculates out of the penis.

SEMEN, TOTAL AMOUNT EJACULATED PER WEEK IN THE WORLD. Based on the United Nations statistic that there are 1,270,960,430 men in the world between the ages of fifteen and sixty-four, and assuming that each has at least one orgasm per week, the total semen ejaculated in the world per week (based on an average ejaculation containing four cc. of semen) is 4.96 million gallons, or enough to fill approximately thirteen Olympic-sized swimming pools every seven days.

"THE SEMIRAMIS BAR," short, autobiographical sketch by Colette, in which she described a turn-of-the-century gay bar, the Semiramis, in Paris, where she sometimes dined. Colette described the group who went there as a "crowd of long-haired young lads and short-haired girls." The gay men were "gentle and indolent and melancholy, like out-of-work prostitutes ... There's one who bestows upon himself the name of a genuine princess ... " And Colette confessed that, "while dining ... I enjoy watching the girls dance together ... I see only two graceful bodies united, sculptured beneath thin dresses by the wind of the waltz, two long adolescent bodies, skinny, with narrow feet in fragile slippers that have come without a carriage through the snow and the mud ... They waltz like the habitués of cheap dance halls, lewdly, sensuously..."

"THE SEXIEST MAN ALIVE," annual title bestowed on a male

Mel Gibson: The sexiest man alive?

public figure by the editors of *People* magazine. The four recipients thus far have been: Mel Gibson, Mark Harmon, Harry Hamlin, and John F. Kennedy, Jr.

"SEXIEST MEN IN AMERICA," annual list of ten men, deemed the sexiest in America, by the editors of *Playgirl* magazine. The list was particularly interesting in 1984: their number-one choice was Boy George. "With his cozy melodies, ever-changing wardrobe and *outre* makeup jobs, this is one good ole Boy to whom we gladly say: We'll tumble for ya." Second on the list that year was Mark Harmon. Third was Lee

Iacocca. Then, in order: California politician Willie Brown, former Olympic organizer Peter Ueberroth, actor Kevin Bacon, President Reagan's former Deputy Chief of Staff Michael Deaver, *Today Show* weatherman Willard Scott, Los Angeles Lakers coach Pat Riley, and, finally, rock star David Lee Roth. After reading the selections, one journalist wrote, "The list, we are assured, is not a satire."

Other choices that have appeared on *Playgirl's* list through the years: New York Governor Mario Cuomo, ABC newsman Ted Koppel, ex-quarterback-turned-congressman-turned-Bush-cabinet-member Jack Kemp, actor Don Johnson, former ballet star Alexander Godunov, and chubby comedian John Candy.

SEXUAL INVERSION (1897), pioneering study of homosexuality by British sexologist Havelock Ellis. The book was the first in Ellis's monumental seven-volume work, *Studies in the Psychology of Sex.*

In 1898, London social activist George Bedborough was arrested after he sold a copy of *Sexual Inversion* to a plainclothes detective from Scotland Yard. Bedborough was fined the equivalent of $200 and was told by the court, "So long as you do not touch this filthy work again with your hands and so long as you lead a respectable life, you will hear no more of this. But if you choose to go back to your evil ways, you will be brought up before me, and it will be my duty to send you to prison for a very long time." George Bernard Shaw later commented, "The prosecution of Mr. Bedborough for selling Mr. Havelock Ellis's book is a masterpiece of police stupidity."

Ellis's book was also banned for several decades from the shelves of the British Museum library, and was banned from sale to the general public in the U.S. until 1935.

SHAW, ROBERT, Chicago alderman who, during a Chicago city council debate on gay rights in 1988, waved a Bible at the crowd and shouted, "Sexual orientation is against everything in this book!"

SILKWORM MOTHS, HOMOSEXUAL BEHAVIOR IN. In the early 1930s, noted sexologist Magnus Hirschfeld was touring China, when he met a geneticist doing research into sexual behavior among male silkworm moths. "If you put the male insect with the female," Hirschfeld explained, in his book *Curious Sex Customs in the Far East*, "he immediately makes a rush at her and mounts her. But some few among the males behave quite differently. They crawl around the female ... and when placed right on top of the female, keep running away as fast as they can ... These males exhibit distinct feminine markings on their wings. Now if these males, having feminine characteristics, are put with other male specimens, their behavior becomes just as excited as it was sluggish when with the females ... But perhaps the most remarkable part of all is that the number of homosexual silkworm moths is three out of every hundred — exactly the same percentage that has been found to exist among humans."

SIPPLE, OLIVER (1942-1989), ex-Marine who thwarted a 1975 assassination attempt on President Gerald Ford. On the afternoon of September 22, 1975, 33-year-old Oliver Sipple was waiting with a crowd of several thousand other people for President Ford to make a brief appearance outside the St. Francis Hotel in San Fran-

cisco. Sipple, a retired Marine, had already been waiting with the others for over two hours for a glimpse of Ford. Finally, at 3:30, the president came out of the hotel to enter a waiting limousine; he hesitated for a moment, and waved to the expectant crowd. At that moment, Sipple saw a woman in front of him pull out a chrome-plated .38-revolver and take aim. Without thinking, he lunged at the gun. A shot rang out, followed by screams and chaos. President Ford, unhurt, was whisked away by secret service agents; thanks to Sipple's quick reaction, the bullet had missed him by five feet. "I was shaking so badly," Sipple said later, "that I couldn't light my cigarette." The would-be assassin — 45-year-old political activist Sara Jane Moore — was taken into custody by FBI agents.

Sipple didn't know it then, but that single instance of heroism was to have tragic consequences for the rest of his life. Within twenty-four hours he was a national hero, and his name was on the front page of every newspaper in the country. Eager to unearth more about him, the media soon learned that Sipple had once worked part-time in a San

Francisco gay bar, that he had actively campaigned for the election of openly gay candidate Harvey Milk to the San Francisco Board of Supervisors, and that he had been active in other gay-related activities in the city. In other words, he must be gay. The *Chicago Sun-Times* soon referred to him in one headline as the "Homosexual Hero." Other newspapers began referring to him as the "gay vet" or the "gay ex-Marine."

It didn't take long for the news stories to reach Sipple's mother, a lifelong conservative Baptist living near Detroit. Because of his family's religious beliefs, Sipple had never told them he was homosexual. His mother was at first confused by the reports of her son's sexuality, and then outraged: not at the press, but at her son. She went into seclusion. Eventually she broke off all communication with him and refused ever to speak to him again. The rest of the family — including his brothers and sisters — followed suit.

Three weeks later, Sipple filed a $15-million lawsuit against several national newspapers, charging them with invasion of privacy. The suit alleged that, in disclosing "that the plaintiff is homosexual in his personal and private orientation," the press had destroyed his relations with his family. The suit condemned the media's conduct as "unthinking, unfeeling, barbaric, and morbid."

Sipple's relations with his family never improved. In fact, when his mother died a few years later, the family didn't notify him until well after the funeral. His battle in the courts dragged on for the next five years, until finally, in 1980, a superior court judge dismissed the suit and ruled that Sipple had thrust himself into the public spotlight and had forfeited his right to privacy when he thwarted the assassination attempt on President Ford.

"The lesson of the Sipple case," his lawyer concluded, "is that if you have something to hide and if you ever find yourself standing next to Mother Theresa or Senator Cranston or President Bush and somebody takes a shot at them ... you'd better go the other way ... It's a horrifying lesson."

Shortly before his death, of an apparent heart attack in 1989, Sipple himself said, simply: "I have really hated all of this. I wish it would never have happened."

SKIN, national gay "fanzine" for uncircumcised men, or for men who like uncircumcised men, started by John Rowberry in January 1989. *Skin* contains personal ads, ads for videos and photo sets, and articles and stories related to "uncut" men. Information is available by writing Vidfile Inc., Box 14576, San Francisco, California 94114.

SMOLLETT, TOBIAS (1721-1771), English satirical novelist. In Smollett's 1748 novel *The Adventures of Roderick Random*, one of the characters, Lord Strutwell, predicts that homosexuality "gains ground apace and in all probability will become in a short time a more fashionable device than simple fornication" — a standard prediction uttered in almost every century of recorded history. It has, of course, never come to pass.

SODOMY, FIRST SONG ON BROADWAY TO CELEBRATE. "Sodomy," from the musical *Hair* in 1967. The song was a fifty-second paean to sodomy, fellatio, pederasty, and masturbation.

SOMERVILLE, EDITH (1858-1949) and **VIOLET MARTIN (1862-1915),** Irish writers. That Edith Somerville and Violet Martin adored one another was obvious to everyone who knew them. They themselves compared their relationship to a perfect marriage, and in an autobiographical sketch, Edith once described their personal and professional lives in terms of a romantic *pas de deux* performed by dancers. She called Violet her "faithfullest friend," and said that Violet had turned her life "into a song."

The two women were second cousins who originally met in 1882. Edith later compared that first meeting to "the colliding of stars," and said that it "lit for us a fire that has not faded yet." An artist by training, Edith was well-traveled, had had a college education (a rarity for a woman in those days), and was widely known for her sophisticated wit and humor. Violet was an expert hunter and horsewoman.

After their third meeting, the two women became inseparable companions and decided to write books together. Their first volume, *An Irish Cousin*, was published to glowing reviews in 1889. Other books — fourteen in all — soon followed, including a warmly praised novel, *The Real Charlotte*, in 1894, and a popular collection of short stories, which, like most of their work, examined Irish society with a warm and sympathetic eye.

They had been together for over thirty years when suddenly, in December 1915, Violet became violently ill; she died four days before Christmas. Edith was initially devastated by the loss, but the bond and harmony between the two women was so strong that apparently not even death could put a serious ripple in it. Violet, Edith decided, had merely passed from one plane of existence to another, and — in one of the more memorable and poignant claims of spiritualism in the early twentieth century — Edith informed her publishers that she was in regular communication with Violet's spirit, and that the two women would continue their renowned literary collaboration. Death, it turned out, was only a nuisance; at most, it meant there would have to be some changes in their working habits together.

Their ghostly collaboration produced sixteen more books. Edith never wavered from her contention that Violet had had an equal hand in writing them. What's more, she refused ever to refer to Violet in the past tense, and for the next thirty-two years she continued to faithfully celebrate Violet's birthday every June 11th.

Edith and Violet were finally reunited on the same "plane" on October 8, 1949, when Edith died at the age of ninety-one.

SPRINGSTEEN, BRUCE — ASS OF. In 1985, a picture of Bruce Springsteen's denim-covered ass on the cover of his album *Born in the U.S.A.* was dubbed by some critics "the ass that launched a million record sales." One gay commentator wrote, "Bruce Springsteen's *Born in the U.S.A.* album has now sold over five million copies worldwide, some of them to rim-freaks who have doubtless never even opened the record." Asked by *Rolling Stone* magazine why he put a picture of his ass, instead of his face, on the album, Springsteen replied, "We took a lot of different types of pictures, and in the end, the picture of my ass looked better than the picture of my face, so that's what went on the cover."

STONEWALL RIOT, ACTUAL NUMBER OF PEOPLE INVOLVED IN. According to eyewitnesses, the first Stonewall Riot on June 27, 1969 involved about four hundred people battling the police.

STUCKER, STEPHEN (d. April 13, 1986), U.S. actor who achieved his greatest fame for his campy roles ("Well, let's see — I can make a broach out of it, or a hat, or a pterodactyl ... ") in the films *Airplane* (1980) and *Airplane 2* (1982). Stucker was one of the first, and only, Hollywood actors to publicly acknowledge having AIDS while he was still seeking work. After the disclosure in July 1985 that Rock Hudson had AIDS, Stucker was interviewed about the disease on several national news broadcasts. He died in April 1986.

THE SUN ALSO RISES (1926), novel by Ernest Hemingway. In the novel — about expatriates in Paris — Hemingway apparently reflected his own feelings when he had the character Jake remark of homosexuals: "I was very angry. Somehow they always made me angry. I know they are supposed to be amusing, and you should be tolerant, but I wanted to swing on one, any one, anything to shatter that superior, simpering composure."

SUPREME COURT, U.S. — MAJOR GAY-RELATED ACTIONS BY.

1958: In 1955, a U.S. district court in southern California ruled that the gay publication *ONE Magazine* — devoted mostly to issues of homosexual rights — could not be distributed through the mails because it constituted obscene material. Although *ONE* had scrupulously avoided publishing anything that might be construed as immoral or obscene, the district court ruled that the "stories are obviously calculated to stimulate the lust of the homosexual reader." In 1958, the U.S. Supreme Court overturned the district court's ruling.

1967: The Supreme Court ruled that the Immigration and Naturalization Service could legally exclude homosexuals from entering the United States.

1976: The Court upheld, by a vote of 6-to-3, a lower court ruling that there was no constitutional right to engage in private homosexual activity. The case involved the sodomy laws of the state of Virginia. The three dissenting justices were William Brennan, Thurgood Marshall, and John Paul Stevens. It was later reported that Marshall was particularly outraged by the decision of the majority: he strongly believed that consenting adults should be protected in such matters, and that state sodomy laws were an abuse of governmental authority.

1976: The Court upheld the conviction of a Jacksonville, North Carolina man sentenced to one year in prison for committing an act of oral sex with a consenting male partner in the privacy of his home.

1977: By refusing to review the case of a Tacoma, Washington, schoolteacher fired because he was gay, the Court let stand an earlier Washington State Supreme Court decision that allowed the Tacoma School District to dismiss a teacher for being homosexual.

1981: The Court declined to rule on — and thus let stand — a 1980 New York Court of Appeals decision declaring that New York's sodomy law was unconstitutional.

1984: The Court rejected the appeal of a gay British businessman — a Texas resident for nineteen years — who had been denied U.S. citizenship, and who was ordered to leave the country, under a federal law excluding aliens "afflicted with ... sexual deviation."

1985: By refusing to hear the case, the Court in effect upheld a lower court decision banning the Detroit Metropolitan Community Church from holding group worship services in Michigan's prisons.

1985: The Court also upheld — again by refusing to hear the case — the firing of an Ohio high-school guidance counselor who lost her job after confiding to colleagues she was a lesbian.

1985: In a rare deadlock vote (4-to-4), the Court effectively upheld a lower court decision to strike down as unconstitutional an Oklahoma law prohibiting homosexuals, or those defending or promoting a homosexual lifestyle, from teaching in public schools.

1986: The Court, by a vote of 5-to-4, ruled that Georgia's anti-sodomy laws were constitutional. The case involved an Atlanta gay man, Michael Hardwick, who'd been arrested in his home while having sex with another man. The five justices who voted to uphold the anti-sodomy law were Warren Burger, William Rehnquist, Sandra Day O'Connor, Byron White, and Lewis Powell. The four dissenting votes came from Harry Blackmun, William Brennan, Thurgood Marshall, and John Paul Stevens. "To hold that the act of homosexual sodomy is somehow protected as a fundamental right," wrote Chief Justice Burger, "would be to cast aside millennia of moral teaching." A week after the ruling, the Court announced it would not review a similar challenge to the Texas anti-sodomy law, thereby leaving that law intact as well.

1987: The Court ruled that people with contagious diseases, including AIDS, are protected by federal anti-discrimination laws.

1987: The Court voted 7-to-2 to uphold the United States Olympic Committee's right to prohibit gays from using the word "olympics." The ruling came five years after the USOC first sued organizers of San Francisco's Gay Olympics, claiming that the name Gay Olympics infringed on the USOC's copyright.

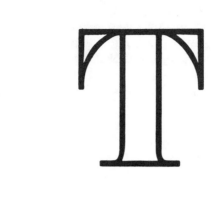

TESTICLES, LARGEST ON EARTH. The largest testicles of any known animal belong to the Blue Whale: its testicles measure approximately two-and-a-half feet in length, and weigh, on the average, about one hundred pounds each. By comparison, the average human testicle in only two-and-a-half inches long, and one-and-a-quarter inches wide. The largest human testicles occur in men afflicted with such diseases as elephantiasis, in which a testicle can become swollen to the size of a basketball.

THIRD PROVINCIAL COUNCIL OF LIMA, PERU (1583), religious council formed in the late sixteenth century to help the Catholic Church govern Spanish colonies in Latin and South America. The Council approved a prewritten sermon that priests were to give Indian converts on the subject of sodomy and homosexuality: "If there is any one among you who commits sodomy, sinning with another man, or with a boy, or with a beast, let it be known that, because of that, fire and brimstone fell from heaven and burned the fine cities of Sodom and Gomorrah and left them in ashes. Let it be known that it carries the death penalty under the just laws of our Spanish kings ... Let it be known that the reason why God has allowed that you, the Indians, should be so afflicted and vexed by other nations is because of this vice that your ancestors had, and many among you still have ... God will finish you, and he is already doing so if you will not reform. Take away drunkenness and feasts which are the sowing ground of these abominable vices, remove the boys and men from your beds, do not sleep mixed up like pigs, but each one of you by himself, do not sing or say dirty words, do not entice your flesh with your hands, because this is also a sin and deserving death and hell."

TIPTON, BILLY (1914-1989), U.S. jazz musician discovered at the time of his death to have actually been a woman. Tipton died at his Spokane, Washington home of a bleeding ulcer in January 1989. One of Tipton's adopted sons immediately called paramedics who, upon examining the body, informed him that the corpse in the living room was that of a woman, not a man.

"I'm just lost," one of Tipton's three sons told the press. "He'll always be Dad. But I think he should have left something behind for us, something that would have explained the truth." Tipton, who gained renown as a saxophonist and piano player, and who founded the Billy Tipton Trio, apparently changed her sexual identity so she could have a career as a jazz musician during a time when jazz musicians were almost exclusively male. The Trio's drummer, Dick O'Neil, later recalled how members of the audience had occasionally commented on Tipton's unusual baby face and high singing voice.

TOFFLER, ALVIN (b. 1928), author of the bestselling book *Future Shock*. In 1980, Toffler predicted, "We are never going to move back to the pre-1970s condition of homosexuals or blacks or any other group in society. We are not going to have an Anita Bryant or John Briggs world, although we will — and *should* — have pockets or subcultures in which their values prevail. The same will be true for gays. Both groups are likely to come to terms with each other eventually, or each will move off to a different part of the turf and ignore the other. One way or another, they will coexist."

TOLSTOY, LEO (1828-1910), renowned Russian author. When Tolstoy was in his early eighties, his wife, Sonya, became so jealous of the intense relationship he had with his disciple Vladimir Chertkov that she openly accused the two of being homosexual lovers. "He has developed a revolting senile crush on Chertkov," she wrote in her diary. "Falling for men was more in his line as a boy! And now he is absolutely at that man's beck and call." Her jealousy of Chertkov became so blinding that she once ran out of the house half-naked screaming, "I'm going to kill Chertkov!" (She was later found babbling incoherently and lying face-down in some wet grass on the estate.)

Sonya felt rejected and usurped as Tolstoy's wife, and she finally confronted him with her suspicions one night. "You and Chertkov are writing secret love letters to one another!" she cried. (Actually, they'd been exchanging letters on the terms of Tolstoy's will, which left sole control of Tolstoy's manuscripts to Chertkov.) As further proof of the alleged homosexual liaison, Sonya brandished part of a diary entry Tolstoy had written six decades earlier, when he was twenty-three. "I have never been in love with a woman," the entry read, "but I have quite often fallen in love with a man ... I fell in love with a man before I knew what pederasty was ... Beauty has always been a powerful factor in my attractions; there is D——,

for example. I shall never forget the night we left Pirogovo together, when, wrapped up in my blanket, I wanted to devour him with kisses and weep. Sexual desire was not totally absent, but it was impossible to say what role it played ... "

Confronted with her accusations, Tolstoy simply ran into his room and locked the door on her. "Tell her, that if she's trying to kill me," he told a friend, "she'll soon succeed." Sonya began repeating her suspicions that Tolstoy and Chertkov were lovers to everyone around her and she began poring obsessively over all of Tolstoy's writings for confirmation that he was — indeed had always been — a "pederast." Chertkov still came to visit at the house; but whenever he did, Sonya snatched up her binoculars and spied on his and Tolstoy's every move as they walked about the estate together talking.

Her accusations finally caused Tolstoy to leave her. "My position in this house," he wrote her, "is becoming — has already become — intolerable." "Lyovochka, my darling," she wrote him back, "come back home, my beloved, save me from turning to suicide again. Lyovochka, companion of my

Tommorrow's Man: Cover and layout from a 1959 issue.

whole life, I'll do anything, everything you want, I'll give up every kind of luxury, your friends will be mine, I will take care of myself. I will be mild and gentle. My darling, my darling, come back, you have to save me." Her entreaties went unheeded, and Tolstoy died less than a month later, having never seen her again.

TOMORROW'S MAN, popular physique magazine of the 1950s and 1960s, subtitled "The International Magazine of Bodybuilding." It began publishing in 1952.

Tomorrow's Man — which, like other physique magazines, stressed muscular develop-

ment, health, and self-discipline — featured photos of professional bodybuilders, readers "training at home," and international male models, as well as the usual photos by some of the best physique photographers of the period, including "Bruce of Los Angeles" (later "Kensington Studios"), and Don Whitman of Western Photography Guild in Denver.

Amid the photos of beautiful eighteen-year-olds shirtless in tight jeans or posing straps — typically subtitled, "Tony has made a good start on the road to healthy shape and strength" or "Tom has reaped the rich rewards of training with barbells" — were articles on masturbation, circumcision, and other sexual matters, as well as questions from readers ("I am very embarrassed over the size of my penis. I am a university student. I have noticed, when in the showers, that mine is smaller than most. Could I have a deficiency some- where?"). There were also the expected, perfunctory tips on diet, exercise, and good sleep- ing habits.

A legal disclaimer accompa- nied almost every issue: "NO- TICE: From time to time we receive requests asking for in- formation on where nude or undraped photos can be ob- tained. In answer, TM wants these facts to be known: The sale or publication of such ma- terial is unlawful and anyone dealing in it is liable to punish- ment by law. TM is therefore unable to advise anyone on the sources or availability of such material." The disclaimer could sometimes be found right next to ads touting "private" photo sets of some of the magazine's most popular models.

In 1983, gay porn star Rich- ard Locke spoke for many of his generation when he said that Tomorrow's Man was one of his favorite magazines to mastur- bate to when he was growing up.

Prescott Townsend: An up-front activist even in the 1940s.

TOWNSEND, PRESCOTT (1894-1973), early gay activist, sometimes called the "Grand- daddy of Gay Liberation" in Boston. By the time he died at the age of seventy-eight, Townsend had become a legend in Boston's gay community. Post-Stonewall activists knew him as an elderly, bearded par- ticipant at gay pride parades, anti-war rallies, and other events. But his activism actu- ally extended far back, long before any of that.

He was born into an elite Boston family. His early years were spent doing experimental theater; he also worked as a doorman at a gay bar, and remained an outspoken social activist. In 1944, he was arrested on a morals charge. Legend has it that when the judge asked him if he cared to make a statement before being sentenced, Townsend replied, "So, what's wrong with a little cocksucking on the Hill?"

Townsend was always open about his homosexuality. "I was thrown out of the Social Register the same year as Barbara Hutton," he would tell friends. "And for the same reason." He was the first openly gay person to appear on Boston's radio talk shows, and the first to lobby the state legislature to "legalize love." In the 1950s, he organized a group of a dozen people into the Boston Mattachine Society. Then, in the early 1960s, he formed a new group with similar aims: the Boston Demophile Society.

In his later years, Townsend kept his hair long and grew a long beard. He became somewhat less active politically, but, by some accounts, more active sexually.

TRAITS OF HOMOSEXUALS, EXPERTS' OPINIONS ON. Ever since homosexuality became a concern of medicine, various "experts" have claimed they can spot "inverts." Their motives, of course, have usually been destructive: if you can identify homosexuals, then you can eradicate or "treat" them. Through the years, these "experts" have listed various surefire traits by which homosexuals can be readily identified.

The Clue of the Dog-Shaped Penis

Author: A. Tardieu, leading French writer on forensic medicine in the nineteenth century

Date: 1857

Where Written: *Etude medicolegale sur less attendant aux mouers*, a book

How to Spot Inverts: Homosexuals who take the active role in anal intercourse are easily identified by their skinny, underdeveloped penises, which are shaped and tapered like a dog's. Homosexuals who take the passive role can be identified by their unusually smooth rectums.

The Fat Fag Theory

Author: Dr. William Lee Howard

Date: 1906

Where Discussed: Address to the American Association of Medical Examiners in Boston

How to Spot Inverts: All homosexuals have "morbid, introspective, and suspicious"

personalities. Also, "muscular exercise is repugnant to them, hence at about forty years of age we find them with fat, flabby bodies."

The Tell-tale Cat

Author: Dr. W.C. Rivers

Date: 1920

Where Written: "New Male Homosexual Trait," an article in a U.S. medical journal

How to Spot Inverts: Rivers revealed what he thought was a newly discovered, characteristic trait of most male homosexuals: they have an inordinate fondness of cats. He had begun to notice that many homosexuals were breeders or exhibitors of cats, or had strong attachments to them. "If fondness for cats be entitled to a place among male homosexual traits," he wrote, "the reason will be that it is a woman's taste."

The Poor Whistler

Author: Dr. John Meagher, a New York psychiatrist

Date: 1929

Where Written: "Homosexuality: Its Psychobiological and Psychopathological Significance," an article in a U.S. medical journal

How to Spot Inverts: Homo-sexuals are characterized by their fondness for "pleasant artistic things and music." "Their favorite color is green." Homosexuals, he said, are also notoriously poor whistlers.

The Effeminacy Syndrome

Author: Albert Koor

Date: 1930

Where Written: *Degeneracy*, a book

How to Spot Inverts: Homo-sexuals are uniformly characterized by having a very broad pelvis, "a characteristic feature of 100% of all the homosexuals." Other homosexual traits: a taste for flashy wearing apparel; a tendency to high-pitched voices; a languid look in the eyes; and feminine poise, movements, and actions. "They show a preference for knitting, embroidering, and other feminine occupations," he added.

"Whatever else, just don't trust them"

Author: Dr. La Forest Potter, New York physician

Date: 1933

Where Written: *Strange Loves: A Study in Sexual Abnormalities*, a book

How to Spot Inverts: Among the dozens of "scientific" conclusions Potter discussed in his book were: homosexuals have a peculiar swinging motion of the hips due to an anatomical defect in the spine and pelvis; they also have abnormally wide hips, feminine buttocks, and hairless chests; they possess thick, luxuriant hair and soft delicate skin; their shoulders are sloped; and they have large, easily aroused nipples. Potter also claimed that homosexuals were "thoroughly unscrupulous and absolutely untrustworthy."

The Fifth Sense

Authors: Jack Lait and Lee Mortimer

Date: 1951

Where Written: The book *Washington Confidential.*

How to Spot Inverts: Homosexuals are "uneasy with masculine men," and "recognize each other by a fifth sense immediately." More importantly, the cycle of unnatural desire is easily spotted in a homosexual individual: it closely follows "the menstrual period of women."

Pouting and Clingy

Author: Brother Aquinas Thomas, F.S.C., a noted sociologist

Date: Early 1960s

Where Discussed: A briefing on homosexuality for the Metropolitan Law Enforcement Conference in New York City

How to Spot Inverts: "They do not like games of body contact, yet they may display some skill in events of individual co-ordination. They are usually helpless in a combative sense and are seldom known to fight. Yet they are known to flash rank to squelch smaller adversaries, and these outbursts of rage often take on the pattern of a tantrum ... They are usually quite jealous, especially when there is competition for their particular friend. They develop noticeable crushes and, like a clinging vine, seem to need the approval and supportive strength their particular friend affords them. In this company they develop signs of sophistication, but if frustrated, easily pout."

The Effeminacy Syndrome — Again

Author: Dr. Lawrence J. Hatterer, a New York psychiatrist known for his book *Changing Homosexuality in the Male*

Date: July 1975

Where Written: "How to Spot Homosexuality in Children," an article in *Harper's Bazaar*

How to Spot Potential Inverts:
According to Dr. Hatterer, signs of potential homosexuality in a boy include: if your son has no really close friends of the same sex; if he plays exclusively with dolls, or dresses up like a little girl; if he exhibits a reluctance to engage in rough and tumble play; if he shows excessive passivity or submission, or is afraid of expressing assertive or aggressive behavior with his peers; if he moves around in a way that would normally be identified as feminine. "Recognizing these signs as a cry for help," Hatterer concludes, "and reacting to your child with acceptance and love instead of with anger and disapproval could be the first step toward understanding."

A More Modern Theory

Author: Unknown

Date: 1977

Where Discussed: *National Lampoon* magazine

How to Spot Inverts: In a now-classic satire of Anita Bryant — "Hi, I'm Anita Bryant. And I Can Cure Homosexuality In Just 10 Days!" — the *National Lampoon* listed what it called "The Seven Deadly Signs of Homosexuality." They were:

1. Carrying your books funny 2. Wearing short-sleeved shirts 3. Spending too much time with girls 4. Wearing your wristwatch backwards 5. Being careful with your parents' car 6. An interest in yoga 7. Being polite to policemen

TRANSSEXUALS, MALE-TO-FEMALE — DETAILS OF OPERATION. Gender-reassignment surgery usually begins with hormone therapy, a series of as many as one hundred or more hormone injections lasting over a period of about a year-and-a-half. In male-to-female transsexuals, the hormone is estrogen, which softens the skin, redistributes body fat (such as around the hips and waist) into a more feminine pattern, and encourages the growth of feminine breasts. Hormone therapy usually produces noticeable changes within three months. During this phase, electrolysis — to remove unwanted body hair — may also be sought. Patients require, on the average, about two hundred sessions with an electrologist.

After the initial hormone therapy phase, reconstructive surgery on the genitals is performed. According to Stanford University, only about one in four who begin the program go on to actual surgery. The surgery involves amputating the penis and removing the testicles from the scrotal sac. The scrotal skin is then used to create the lining of a vagina, which is inserted just above the rectum. Skin transplants, usually from the thighs, may also be needed. In some cases, physicians simply turn the penis inside out, like the finger of a glove, to create the vaginal walls. Plastic surgery, to create the normal external appearance of female genitalia, is also performed, and some surgical re-arranging of internal body structures may be necessary to permit the insertion of the new vagina.

Because the body's natural tendency is to treat the recently created vagina as a surgical "wound," the transsexual must constantly dilate the opening of the canal so that it does not heal closed. Even with dilation, it may eventually close up completely, necessitating follow-up surgery to re-open it. And because the newly formed vagina has no ability to produce its own lubricating secretions, medications and ointments must be used to keep it pliable. Weekly dilations of the urethra may also be needed, to keep it

from becoming constricted as a result of the accumulation of scar tissue.

As an adjunct to the actual genital surgery, some transsexuals also seek plastic surgery on their face, neck, Adam's apple, and hands, to create a more distinctly feminine appearance.

Although male-to-female transsexuals would seem, from a physiological standpoint, incapable of orgasm — they have no clitoris, and the erotic sensitivity of the new vagina is limited — many report having achieved orgasm on a regular basis. This has led researchers to re-examine the whole nature of orgasm, and to re-define the role emotional factors, rather than physical stimulation, play in attaining orgasm.

Total cost of the gender-re-assignment procedure is usually about $10,000.

TRANSSEXUALS, MALE-TO-FEMALE — NUMBER IN U.S. Because of some lingering secrecy surrounding the subject, and because of confidentiality involving patients' records, an exact number is difficult to come by. However, some experts estimate that there are between 15,000 and 20,000 post-operative male-to-female transsexuals currently living in the U.S.

TREE-CUTTING, FAMOUS HOMOPHOBIC INSTANCE OF (1969).

Residents of the Forest Hills neighborhood in Queens, New York had always enjoyed the small residential park that lined the nearby Grand Central Parkway. The park was heavily wooded with cherry trees, dogwoods, and other greenery, and it was, in the words of one local resident who always ate her lunch there, "a safe, pleasant place." It remained a safe and pleasant place — until the morning of June 22, 1969, when neighbors woke up to discover that the entire area had been leveled by someone using axes and chainsaws. Not a single tree was left standing; all that remained were stumps oozing sap.

The leveling, it turned out, was the work of a local anti-homosexual vigilante committee, which had been trying for weeks to rid the park of gay men who often met there late at night. Asked by a reporter if the committee was in fact responsible for the vandalism, the group's spokesman, lawyer Myles Tashman, tersely replied, "Use your own imagination."

The committee consisted of about forty local men, and had first been organized several weeks earlier to "harass fags" who came to the park. Using walkie-talkies and high-powered flashlights, the men searched the park every night, surrounded suspected homosexuals, and then ran them out of the area. The committee members were, according to Tashman, "concerned for the safety of women and children" — to which one local woman later responded, "Nonsense. What mothers and children are out at one o'clock in the morning?" When the harassment efforts failed, the men turned to their axes and chainsaws.

Some local residents called the police while the tree-cutting was in progress; but when a squad car finally arrived, the police merely chatted with the anti-homosexual vandals for a few minutes, laughed, and then left without making arrests. One woman and her boyfriend drove by the scene and stopped to complain directly to the vandals, but the two of them were threatened with an axe and told to drive on.

The entire episode made the front page of *The New York Times*, and there were calls for a complete investigation. The local police precinct at first de-

HAD YOUR ASIATIC FLU SHOTS?

Trim magazine does its bit for world health (c. 1960).

nied that any officers had ever been called out to investigate the incident, then later acknowledged that a squad car had been sent to the park; the officers had reported that everything was "normal" there. Meanwhile, Myles Tashman — apparently baffled at all the negative publicity his committee was generating — told the press that his group's harassment of homosexuals had been conducted entirely "with police consent."

Several weeks after the van-

dalism, police investigators concluded there were "no clues" as to who had leveled the parkway, or why. When questioned about whether or not there would be an investigation of the incident, a spokesman for the mayor's office told the press, "Why stir up a hornet's nest?"

TRESTRAIL, MICHAEL (b. 1930), former personal bodyguard to Queen Elizabeth II of England. Trestrail was forced to resign his position in 1982,

French actor Jean-Louis Trintignant: He loves playing "villains, perverts, fetishists, murderers."

after it was publicly revealed he was gay: a former boyfriend reportedly approached a London newspaper with an offer to tell all about his and Trestrail's affair. In announcing the resignation, Buckingham Palace described Trestrail as "a close and trusted companion of the queen." Later, there were reports that Margaret Thatcher intended to make a major public issue of homosexuals working inside the Palace; it was said that a quick and fiercely angry phone call from the queen herself forced Thatcher to relent.

TRIM, popular physique magazine of the late 1950s and early 1960s. First published in 1957, the magazine sought "to help improve the general fitness and health consciousness of America's young men." *Trim* featured the work of Bob Mizer (of the Athletic Model Guild), and other male photographers, as well as the work of various gay artists.

TRINTIGNANT, JEAN-LOUIS (b. 1930), French actor, best known for his role as the investigating judge in the 1969 political thriller *Z*. In 1965, Trintignant played a bisexual veterinary student in *The Sleeping Car Murders*. "I love to play villains, perverts, fetishists, murderers," he said at the time. "I like to get inside this kind of mind. I follow the accounts of such people in the newspapers with great interest."

TURNER, LANA (b. 1920), U.S. actress. In 1975, Turner angrily denounced a homophobic article in *The Los Angeles Times*, which attacked her large gay following; the article characterized Turner's gay fans as "forty-year-old creatures, tired old drag queens, fighting and bitching each other." "In all the years I have been in public life," Turner said

Lana Turner: In 1975, she came to the defense of her gay fans.

in a public statement, "this is the first time that my audience has been so cruelly maligned." Turner's own daughter, Cheryl Crane, is a lesbian. (See also *CRANE, CHERYL.*)

U V

UMBRELLAS, BANNED AS EFFEMINATE BY U.S. ARMY.

In 1983, the U.S. Army banned men in uniform from carrying umbrellas, on the grounds it would present an effeminate image. "They feel it is an artificial affectation that Army officers need not have," said a Pentagon spokesman. One anonymous officer remarked scornfully, "Can you imagine a guy in war fatigues walking around a base carrying an umbrella?!"

UNDERARM HAIR, SIGNIFICANCE OF.

According to some researchers, the purpose of armpit hair on humans is probably roughly similar to the purpose of spectacular coloring on certain flowers or the mating calls of certain animals: to invite sexual activity and increase reproduction. Researchers believe that the hair collects and traps hormone secretions, as well as the natural body odor, which may then have an aphrodisiac effect on potential sexual partners. It is believed that pubic hair may serve the same purpose.

"UP STAIRS LOUNGE,"

popular gay bar in the French Quarter of New Orleans. The bar was gutted by fire in 1973, killing thirty-two people: the largest death toll of any fire in recent New Orleans history. Though the fire was clearly the work of an arsonist, authorities never found a suspect.

According to eyewitnesses, the fire started at around eight o'clock on the night of June 24, 1973, during the bar's Sunday evening beer bust. An investigation later revealed that someone poured lighter fluid on the stairway leading up to the bar and then ignited it. Although some people managed to escape through a back exit, others were trapped and burned to death behind security bars on the second-story windows.

"The most difficult thing for me," said one of the survivors, "was the fact that I had to go to work the next day, and I had to shield the grief because I wasn't out of the closet." A pastor at a local Episcopal church held a memorial service for the dead; afterwards, he received hostile phone calls, death threats, and a chastisement from his superiors. "Do you think Jesus would have kept these people out of his church?" he said later. "I got into a lot of trouble over that service, but I didn't care." For several years, on the anniversary of the tragedy, flowers were laid at the site of the old bar. To this day, the building remains empty and gutted, and the mystery of who started the fire, and why, remains unsolved.

VASELINE PETROLEUM JELLY — DEVELOPMENT OF. *Vaseline* was first developed in the 1860s by a young U.S. chemist, Robert Augustus Chesebrough. Originally marketed as a medicinal aid to help heal cuts and burns, it is manufactured by distilling off the lighter portions of petroleum and then purifying the residue. Dozens of uses — from keeping rust off garden furniture to removing white rings from mahogany tables — have since been discovered, including the various obvious uses for gay men. Chesebrough himself claimed to have swallowed a spoonful of it every day "for my health." Perhaps it worked: he died at the age of ninety-six, in 1933.

VATICAN, AS REPOSITORY FOR WORLD'S LARGEST PORNOGRAPHY COLLECTION. Most authorities believe that, contrary to widespread popular belief, the Vatican does not have the largest collection of pornography in the world, nor even a collection of pornography that would be regarded as substantive in comparison with other modern collections. However, because of the Church's secrecy on the matter, a definitive inventory of its holdings is not known. What the church *does* hold is an exhaustive collection of art by Michelangelo, Raphael, and others (some of which, depending on the definition, might be considered erotic), file copies of all books on the Vatican's *Index of Forbidden Books* (most of which were forbidden because of blasphemy and heresy, not obscenity), and many rare and priceless books (some of which may be pornographic in nature) from the Renaissance and other periods.

Actually, the world's largest collection of pornography is probably housed at the famous Kinsey Institute in Bloomington, Indiana. The Institute owns over 100,000 pieces of erotica, including books, photographs, films, paintings, sculptures, and other art works, many of which are homosexual in nature. For years the Institute has been a repository for the usually unseen, explicitly erotic works of many famous modern artists. A substantial number of new pieces are acquired by the Institute every year.

VIDAL, GORE — ON THE AIDS EPIDEMIC. In 1987, Vidal was asked by *Playboy* magazine if he thought AIDS was Mother Nature's way of weeding out certain segments of the population. Vidal replied that if that were true, it would prove "what an ironist mother nature is. The one group that does not add to the population and, therefore, is in the truest sense altruistic is the one group to get knocked off. It should obviously be the heavy breeders that get the plague if nature was looking out for our best interests. People who did not make babies would be preserved, and the baby makers would die. I'm afraid Mother Nature doesn't really like the human race, but then, why should she?"

VIM, popular physique magazine of the 1950s, first published in 1954. Subtitled "The Magazine for Vigorous Living," *Vim* featured physical culture photography by the Athletic Model Guild, Spectrum Films, the Western Photography Guild, and other notable male photographers of the time. Articles included such topics as "In Defense of Nudism," "Are Bodybuilders Oversexed?" and "How to Develop a Low He-Man Voice." One memorable article — on the do's and don'ts of bathing — began, "If you are building a handsome body remember that the classic Greeks — glorifiers of the body beautiful — invented the bath as we know it, and ever since then

Vim magazine of 1956: It debated the ethics of showing models in G-strings, and other pressing issues of the day.

bathing has been a true mark of culture. A lot of suds have dribbled down the drain since ancient Rome, where public pools let 3,000 bathers dunk together ... " Other features debated the propriety of showing male models in G-strings — some readers found it offensive and immoral, others wanted complete nudity — or criticized other physique magazines for their lack of integrity and the introduction of "undesirable elements" (ie. homosexual overtones) in their editorial content.

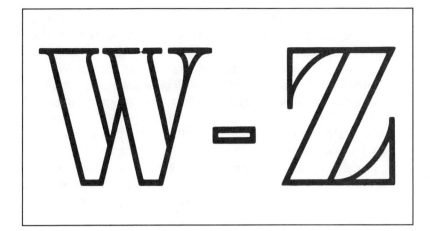

WALDENBOOKS, REMOVAL OF GAY MAGAZINES BY. In 1985, Waldenbooks, the largest chain of franchise bookstores in the country, ordered its retail outlets to remove all gay men's magazines from their shelves; the stores were directed to stop stocking such publications as *Mandate*, *Honcho*, and the like immediately. "This is not an optional decision," stated a confidential memo distributed to all stores. The stores would, however, be allowed to continue carrying *Playboy*, *Playgirl*, *Penthouse*, and other heterosexually-oriented "skin" magazines.

At the same time, several Waldenbooks outlets began a policy by which no one under twenty-one could buy any book dealing with homosexuality, regardless of whether it was a sociological study or a novel by Gordon Merrick. An acceptable I.D. would be required in all questionable cases. No such restrictions existed for the purchase of such books as *Valley of the Dolls* or *Lady Chatterley's Lover*. Some Waldenbooks later eased this policy.

THE WALT WHITMAN BRIDGE. In 1955, the Delaware Port Authority announced it would name a new bridge between Philadelphia and Camden, New Jersey, after American poet Walt Whitman. After all, Whitman had been Camden's most illustrious resident, and he was, arguably, the greatest poet the U.S. ever produced. It soon became apparent, however, that not everyone approved of the decision: shortly after the Port

Authority made its announcement, a local Catholic diocese cited what it called Whitman's "objectionable" personal life and demanded that a less disreputable American be found to name the bridge after. To bolster its position, the diocese initiated a massive letter-writing campaign — mostly from students at local Catholic schools — also asking that the bridge be named after someone else. Finally, however, after publicly reporting they could find no conclusive evidence that Whitman was a practicing homosexual, the Port Authority announced it would go ahead with the name as planned.

WARHOL, ANDY (1928-1987), U.S. "pop art" innovator and professional celebrity. Warhol once said of sex, "The most exciting thing is not doing it. If you fall in love with someone and never do it, it's much more exciting." On another occasion, he remarked, "Truman [Capote] says he can get anyone he wants. I don't want anyone I can get."

WARNER, LUCIUS (1960-1988), 28-year-old New Orleans man murdered by his nephews because he was gay.

On the night of May 31, 1988, Patrick Govan and his brother Clarence, both in their twenties, broke into the house of their uncle, Lucius Warner, with a plan to forcibly strip him, tie him up, and then throw him out on his porch, as a way of publicly humiliating him because he was gay.

The two nephews, accompanied by a sixteen-year-old friend, first cut the wires in an outside fuse box on Warner's home, then went through the front door to the living room, where Warner was asleep on a sofa. After waking him, they tried to tie him up. But because he kept crying out and pleading with them not to hurt him, they started beating him. One of Warner's next-door neighbors later said she heard him screaming, "Oh God, oh God, please don't take my life!" She didn't call police because she thought he was "over there listening to gospel music" and praying.

Warner died of internal hemorrhaging as a result of the beating; he lost large amounts of blood from a ruptured spleen. The sixteen-year-old accomplice in the murder eventually pleaded guilty to manslaughter, in exchange for his testimony. The two nephews, Patrick and Clarence Govan, were found guilty of second-degree murder.

WASHINGTON STATE UNIVERSITY SURVEY ON HOMOSEXUALITY (1969). A 1969 Washington State University study of the university's students and of residents in the Spokane area found that both students and the general population ranked homosexuality second only to murder in seriousness as a crime. Respondents ranked homosexuality a more serious offense than armed robbery, income-tax evasion, drunk driving, stealing, and perjury. Washington State Superior Court judges, given the same survey, ranked homosexuality as tenth on their list, below armed robbery, drunk driving, perjury, and income-tax cheating.

WEICKER, LOWELL (b. 1931), former U.S. senator, Republican from Connecticut. He was first elected to the Senate in 1970.

A National Gay and Lesbian Task Force study of the voting records of U.S. senators during the 1987-1988 session found that Weicker, along with Illinois Democrat Paul Simon, had the best voting record on gay-rights issues. In fact, Weicker made

Senator Lowell Weicker, Jr.: A Republican who voted far better than most Democrats.

what the NGLTF considered the "correct" vote one hundred percent of the time, on thirteen critical bills. Weicker also fought, unsuccessfully, for an AIDS anti-discrimination plank in the Republican Party platform in 1988.

Because of Weicker's liberality on gay rights and other issues, national conservatives, including William F. Buckley, launched a major campaign to defeat him when he ran for reelection in 1988. Buckley and others openly campaigned for Weicker's Democratic opponent, who was seen as more conservative on social issues.

The campaign was successful, and the 1987-1988 session of Congress was Weicker's last.

WESTHEIMER, DR. RUTH (b. 1928), German-U.S. sex therapist. Speaking of her early clinical experience in sexuality in the U.S., she told *Playboy* magazine, "Charles Silverstein, the one who wrote *Joy of Gay Sex* and *Family Matters*, saw me at a seminar and said, 'Look, if you want to volunteer your time at the Institute for Human Identity' — that's a counseling service for homosexuals and bisexuals — 'we will give you supervision.' I said, 'Great.' He said, 'You have to be supervised by a lesbian in order to learn about the lifestyle.' There I had a few nightmares, because I said, 'My gosh.' I was very naive. I thought they were going all over New York City to find a lesbian with a whip and boots to train me."

Westheimer's openness about sexual issues, and her outspoken liberality on homosexuality in particular, have repeatedly drawn fire from conservative and religious groups in the country. Typical of the outrage was an angry letter to *U.S.A. Today*, after the newspaper ran a cover story on Westheimer in 1984. A woman from northern California wrote: "Living in the San Francisco Bay area where there is a high rate of AIDS makes me concerned when she advises young men that the homosexual lifestyle is as normal as apple pie. They are dying at the rate of almost one per day in San Francisco. Is Dr. Westheimer giving young teenage males the kiss of death when she leads them into that lifestyle ... She is a menace and an unfortunate guide to our young people."

WHALE, JAMES (1896-1957), British-U.S. film director, best known for some of Hollywood's finest horror films: *Frankenstein* (1931), *The Old Dark House* (1932), *The Invisible Man* (1933), and *The Bride of Frankenstein* (1935).

Throughout his career, Whale was known as a demanding, sometimes bitchy man, widely admired, but often intolerant of people who got in his way or who didn't share his perfectionistic temperament. Elsa Lanchester — who starred in the title role of *The Bride of Frankenstein* — remembered him as a "bitter" person, enormously gifted and witty, but at times acrimonious.

Director James Whale touches up Boris Karloff's make-up on the set of *The Bride of Frankenstein* (1935).

Whale first came to Hollywood in 1930 from a career in the theater. He was "imported" by Universal Studios to direct a film version of *Journey's End*, a play he had successfully directed on the London stage. He decided to stay in Hollywood, mostly because of the money; in fact, he told another British expatriate, actor Charles Laughton, "You will love it here in Hollywood, Charles. I'm pouring the gold through my hair and enjoying every minute of it."

Whale loved money. For one thing, he came from a poverty-stricken family. A talented artist, he had originally wanted to be a newspaper cartoonist. However, as a young lieutenant fighting in the first World War, he was captured by the Germans, and it was in a POW camp (where the prisoners often staged amateur theater productions) that Whale first became interested in acting. After the war, he entered the theater first as an actor, then as a set designer and stage manager, and finally as a director. He was thirty-four when he arrived in Hollywood.

After completing *Journey's End*, Whale directed *Waterloo Bridge*, a 1931 sentimental romance starring Mae Clarke and Bette Davis. That same year, he was approached about doing a film version of Mary Shelley's vintage horror fable *Frankenstein*. Whale handpicked Boris Karloff for the role of the monster in the film, and invested the entire production with an enormous amount of pathos and humor, far beyond what the original script called for. (The film's best-remembered scene, for example — the monster's encounter with an innocent girl who teaches him to float daisies on the water of a lake — was entirely conceived by Whale.) The resulting film, now a classic, was a tremendous success with both the critics and the public, and Whale emerged as a kind of hero at Universal Studios, where he was allowed to work with almost complete creative independence for the next five or six years. During that time, he made *The Old Dark House*, a literate, perverse, and funny horror film starring Charles Laughton and Boris Karloff; *The Invisible Man*, with Claude Rains; *The Bride of Frankenstein*, with Ernest Thesiger and Elsa Lanchester; and the 1936 version of *Show Boat*. Aside from *Show Boat*, he made several other non-horror films during the period, most of them distinguished by his interest in innovative camera-movement, or by his attention to period detail, or by the sophisticated touches he invariably brought to sometimes prosaic scripts.

Shortly after *The Bride of Frankenstein*, Whale was assigned to direct *The Road Back*, a sequel to Erich Maria Remarque's famous World War One novel, *All Quiet on the Western Front*. The story, about post-war life in Germany, was strongly anti-war and, in a not-so-subtle way, anti-German. Whale finished the film in 1937, but the German consulate objected to the final cut and put pressure on the studio (including a threatened German boycott of all Universal pictures) to make major changes in the final print. The consulate was particularly concerned about anything that might be construed as an insult to Adolph Hitler.

The studio not only acceded to German demands, but also shot new footage (under a different director) and re-edited the entire movie into a bizarre mixture of heavy-handed melodrama and previously unscripted slapstick comedy. The result, according to a review in *The New York Times*, was that,

"Universal has narrowed and cheapened it and made it pointless ... as though it were dealing with a routine comedy of the trenches."

Whale was understandably infuriated — and deeply depressed — by the hatchet job performed on his work, and the episode marked the beginning of the end of his Hollywood career. He made several films for other studios, but by 1941 he and Hollywood had reached an impasse of temperaments, and he retired to his Pacific Palisades home, which he shared with his lover, producer David Lewis. Whale increasingly devoted much of his time to another lifelong passion, painting. He was lured out of retirement briefly, in 1949, to make the short film *Hello Out There*, but it was never released.

In 1957, Whale committed suicide by throwing himself head-first into the shallow end of his swimming pool. He had recently suffered a series of debilitating strokes that left him physically impaired and mentally confused. "I have had a wonderful life," he wrote in his suicide note, "but it is over, and my nerves get worse and I am afraid they will have to take me away ... no one is to blame."

In recent years, many critics (most notably, Vito Russo) have speculated that Whale's homosexuality — and the sense of irony and the capacity for empathy that accompanied it — played an important part in the driving creative force that helped Whale to achieve his unique artistic vision. Discussing Whale's ability to find unexpected depth in some of his material — especially in his horror films — Elsa Lanchester wrote in her memoirs: "The poet Shelley has written that poetry turns all things to loveliness; it exalts the beauty of that which is beautiful, and it adds beauty to that which is most deformed. James Whale seemed to carry out this thought, giving his monsters spiritual beauty and pathos, over and above the horror."

WHO'S AFRAID OF VIRGINIA WOOLF?, landmark 1962 play by U.S. playwright Edward Albee. In 1984, Albee was forced to threaten legal action to cancel an all-male production of the play at a community theater in Arlington, Texas; he complained to the producers that he never intended the cast to be all men. For years, Albee has adamantly denied the charge that the electrifying drama is really a "gay" play in straight drag.

WILDE, DOLLY (1899-1941). The niece of playwright Oscar Wilde, Dolly shared many traits with her famous uncle, including an extravagant wit, a literary talent expressed in brilliant conversation — and a taste for members of the same sex. "I am more Oscar-like than he was like himself!" she once declared. According to contemporaries, she even looked like her famous uncle. "Her face," wrote Bettine Bergery, "is exactly like Aubrey Beardsley's drawing of Oscar Wilde."

Born Dorothy Ierne Wilde in London in 1899, Dolly was the daughter of Oscar Wilde's older brother, Willie, a failed writer and an alcoholic who drank himself into an early grave just months before she was born. His death left the family financially impoverished, and for years they had to rely on the charity of others to survive. When she was eighteen, Dolly ran away from home to become an ambulance driver behind the front lines in World War One. After the war, she settled in Paris, where she became part of Natalie Barney's famous circle of lesbians, artists, and celebrities.

On first meeting her, most people were struck by the astonishing physical resemblance between Dolly and her famous uncle, Oscar. She had a long, heavy, rather horse-like face, with warm and gregarious but somehow poignant features. On one occasion, she attended a masquerade ball dressed as Oscar; she arrived, according to one eyewitness, "looking both important and earnest." However, after Dolly was introduced to Radclyffe Hall and her lover, Lady Una Troubridge, in 1929, Troubridge remarked that of Oscar and Dolly, Dolly was easily "the better man."

The similarities to Oscar did not end there. She became renowned as an acidic wit and brilliant conversationalist. One of her most frequently repeated quips came after she went with writer Virginia Woolf to a performance of *Hamlet*. Dolly, like much of Paris, idolized Woolf, and when in the middle of the play Dolly caught an unexpected glimpse of Woolf yawning, she felt compelled to look away. "It was," she later remarked, "as if I had caught God in a domestic moment of relaxation."

"When Dolly was in a room," said one acquaintance, "it became charged with her vivid aliveness. Her positive personality dominated any place she was in, dispelling dullness... " Not everyone, however, was captivated by her: F. Scott Fitzgerald, in Paris in 1929, became furious with her and publicly insulted her after she made a pass at Zelda Fitzgerald at a party.

There was, according to friends, a dark side to her, and she remained, despite her sparkling personality, for the most part discontented and aimless. She was, one friend observed, "half in love with death." She drank heavily, was addicted to opium for a time, and also took up cocaine-sniffing. For ten years, she maintained a tumultuous on-again, off-again love affair with Natalie Barney, an affair that drove her twice to attempt suicide, once by slitting her wrists, another time by swallowing an entire bottle of sedatives. It was an unhappy relationship for both of them, and Natalie eventually convinced Dolly to return to London. "I am still haunted," Barney wrote many years later, "by the twitch in her smile at our parting."

Back in London, Dolly learned she had cancer. When conventional therapy failed, she made a desperate pilgrimage to Lourdes hoping for a miraculous cure. There was none: the cancer progressed, and she died in London the following year, at the age of forty-one. Summing up her short and rather tragic life, Gertrude Stein eulogized, "Well, she certainly hadn't a fair run for her money."

WILDE, OSCAR — DIRECT DESCENDANTS STILL LIVING. There are two direct descendants of Oscar Wilde still living today: a grandson, Merlin (through Wilde's son Cyril), and Merlin's son, Lucian, Oscar Wilde's great grandson. Both live in London.

WILLIAM II RUFUS (1056-1100), son of William the Conqueror, and king of England from 1087 to 1100. Rufus was regarded as a blasphemer, contemptuous of the Church and almost everything to do with it. He surrounded himself with effeminate favorites, and popularized certain controversial fashions — such as long hair and flowing, feminine garments — for men. He was, however, known as a ruthless warrior.

Many years after his death, the tower of Winchester Cathedral, where Rufus was buried, collapsed on top of his remains. For years, this was seen as a

William Rufus: There is no strong evidence he was homosexual, but the rumors abounded.

sure sign of God's displeasure towards homosexuals.

WILLSON, HENRY (1911-1978), Hollywood agent. One of the most successful agents in Hollywood history, Willson is best remembered today as the man who "discovered" Rock Hudson. At one time or another, he also managed the careers of Lana Turner, Julie London, Robert Wagner, Troy Donahue, and Natalie Wood. He was openly gay at a time when most Hollywood insiders were firmly entrenched in the closet, and he rarely went anywhere without a large coterie of extraordinarily handsome would-be actors around him. "Willson was notorious," said one director, "for having around these good-looking guys who couldn't do anything but be good-looking." The sight of this raised a few eyebrows in Hollywood, especially since Willson himself was short, pudgy, and rather ugly.

He had been born and raised on the East Coast before coming to Hollywood in the 1930s to seek his fortune. An impressive talker and a shrewd manipulator, he soon found work as a talent agent for producer David O. Selznick. Later, after the Selznick studios were disbanded, Willson started his own agency.

He often said it wasn't talent per se that he was looking for in a potential client, but malleability: someone who could be remodeled, from the bottom up, in the image of a star. He was tough, hard-working, and unscrupulous — it was widely rumored he had Mafia connections — and actor George Nader later recalled that he "exuded evil."

Willson launched the successful careers of a dozen popular performers. He was also personally responsible for some of the most famous and ostentatious name changes in Hollywood history: Merle Johnson became Troy Donahue, Arthur Gelien became Tab Hunter, Francis McGowan became Rory Calhoun, Robert Moseley became Guy Madison (Willson supposedly hit on the name after glancing at a billboard for Dolley Madison snack cakes), and Julia Mildred Turner became, simply, Lana Turner.

In 1947, Willson "discovered" a tall, fresh-faced Illinois farmboy, Rock Hudson. When Hudson heard there were some casting openings at the Selznick Studios, he left his photograph there and was called for an appointment the next day with Willson. "Can you act?" Willson allegedly asked when they first sat down. Hudson said no, and rose to leave. "Good. Sit down," Willson quickly added. "I think I can do something for you." Willson remained Hudson's agent for fourteen years until, in 1962, Hudson became dissatisfied with the arrangement — he felt Willson was just coasting along on Hudson's fame — and sought new representation.

In later years, Willson suffered heavy financial losses and became an alcoholic. His health and influence deteriorated, and in 1978, at the age of sixty-seven, he died at the Motion Picture Country Hospital in Woodland Hills after a lengthy, undisclosed illness.

Ironically, Willson's greatest public recognition came after Rock Hudson's death from AIDS in 1985. At the time, some newspapers and magazines tried to rationalize Hudson's recently revealed homosexuality by blaming it on Willson's influence. One newspaper ran a story of Willson's career under the screeching headline, "The Man Who Led Rock Into Evil." "The path that led AIDS-ravaged Rock Hudson to his deathbed," said the article, "began many years ago, when he fell into the clutches of a gay agent who introduced him to Tinseltown's tarnished twilight world of homosexuals." Another article referred to Willson as the head of a so-called "Lavender Mafia," a supposed group of power-hungry, ruthless homosexuals who allegedly ruled Hollywood from behind the scenes.

WINDSOR, WALLIS WARFIELD (1894-1986), duchess of Windsor, famous as the woman for whom Edward VIII abdicated his throne in 1936.

Noel Coward, though a friend of hers, once acidly referred to her as "a fag hag to end all," and her numerous friendships with homosexual men aroused comment among her contemporaries and evoked jealousy from the duke. In fact, he finally complained to her about the number of male homosexual guests she kept inviting to their dinner parties. Annoyed, she retorted, "You should listen to them, because they're much brighter than you are!" On another occasion, when he complained to her again, she replied, "Where am I going to find stray men in Paris? If you want to fill out the table, you've got to invite the pansies!"

Her close friendship with Woolworth's heir Jimmy Donahue led to gossip that she and Donahue were romantically involved and that her marriage to the duke was falling apart. Actually, Donahue — the grandson of Woolworth's founder, Frank W. Woolworth — was unabashedly gay. He'd once deeply humiliated his mother by showing up in drag to a dinner party for her good friend Francis Cardinal Spellman, and he'd had several brushes with the law due to his predilection for male prostitutes. When the duke went out of town on business, Donahue took his place and escorted the duchess everywhere. The long friendship ended when the duke, notorious for his homophobia (he called gay men "those fellows who fly in over the transom"), finally threw Donahue out of the house one night and forbade the duchess from ever seeing him again. Several years later, in 1966, Donahue committed suicide, at the age of fifty-one.

When the duchess died in 1986, it was revealed she had left the bulk of her estate, including her jewels, to the Institut Pasteur in France. By the time of her death, the Institut had become renowned as a center for AIDS research. However, the duchess had drafted her will long before that, and according to one of her attorneys, "She did not, as has been reported, leave the bequest to AIDS research. At that time, we hadn't heard of AIDS."

WITTGENSTEIN (1973), biography of the great German-English philosopher Ludwig Wittgenstein (1889-1951), by Stanford scholar W.W. Bartley III. The work included several pages about Wittgenstein's sex life, specifically about his homosexuality. Amid generally fine reviews, there were academic critics who took vehement exception to the notion that Wittgenstein was gay, or that he'd even had any kind of sex life at all. One reviewer denounced the book as "a farrago of obscenity and lies," another called it "foul." And still another — in an age-old homophobic ploy—insisted that "sensuality in any form was entirely foreign" to Wittgenstein. A letter-writing campaign was launched by various Wittgenstein scholars to have Bartley "drummed out" of the international academic community, and even Wittgenstein's estate — which was in possession of explicit evidence of Wittgenstein's homosexuality — threatened legal action to halt further distribution of the book.

WYCOFF, DEAN, spokesman for a northern California chapter of the Moral Majority. "I agree with capital punishment," Wycoff said in 1980, "and I believe homosexuality is one of those crimes that could be coupled with murder and other sins." He made the remarks as he and other fundamentalist leaders were launching a $3-million adver-tising campaign to attack homosexuals. The campaign — targeted primarily at San Francisco, which Wycoff called the "Sodom and Gomorrah of the nation" — was to include billboards and print advertisements designed to build anti-homosexual feelings in the community. "If they think they have a chance in San Francisco," said openly gay San Francisco Supervisor Harry Britt, "they don't know this town."

YALE UNIVERSITY, AS "GAY" SCHOOL. The August 4, 1987 issue of *The Wall Street Journal* contained an editorial by Yale graduate Julie Iovine who claimed that, "Yale has a reputation as a gay school." Iovine — now married to a Yale faculty member — speculated that one out of every four students at the university might be gay, and quoted a Yale undergraduate who told her, "It's just a matter of your friends being blond, brunette, gay or straight. No big deal. It probably depends on what part of the country you're from, whether or not you're going to be surprised by two women making out in the library."

Yale's president, Benno C. Schmidt, immediately condemned the article as "journalistic drivel," and sent an urgent letter to the university's alumni saying he was "outraged that the *Wall Street Journal* would publish such an article." Iovine, however, stood by the piece and told the Associated Press, "I think the reaction has been really extreme. I'm not saying that Yale is overrun by gays, which, by the way, what's wrong with that?"

YMCA, FIRST U.S. The first YMCA in the U.S. was founded in Boston in 1851. The use of YMCAs as a meeting and cruising place for gay men has been documented at least since 1914.

YOKEL'S PRECEPTOR; OR MORE SPREES IN LONDON (c. 1850), offbeat and often satirical London travel guide that directed out-of-towners to where they could see, among other things, male homosexuals in the city. "The Quadrant, Holborn, Fleet Street and the Strand are full of them," it noted. "Not so very long ago signs and bills were hung in the windows of respectable hotels in the vicinity of Charing Cross with the notice: 'Beware of paederasts!' They usually gather near the picture shops, and are recognisable by their effeminate appearance, fashionable clothing, etc. ... The Quadrant is visited by a great number of the most notorious, who parade there in search of their 'prey,' just like so many feminine prostitutes."

YUGASIE, Ute Indian brave living in western Colorado in the late nineteenth century. After he refused to take part in a battle against a U.S. cavalry unit in 1878, the other male members of the tribe ostracized him and decreed that he should be forced to dress, live, and work as a woman for the rest of his life. Yugasie lived for another sixty years, in a state of enforced transvestism. Although many Indian tribes tolerated or even revered transvestism, and although some Indian men lived a homosexual or quasi-female existence, Yugasie was offered no choice.

YUSSOUPOV, PRINCE FELIX (1887-1977), Russian prince who engineered the assassination of Rasputin in 1916.

Yussoupov — heir to one of the largest fortunes in Russia — was a bisexual and a transvestite. Just before his birth, his mother prayed that having borne three sons already, her next would be a girl. That it turned out to be another boy seemed only a minor inconvenience: she raised him as a female anyway and kept him in beautiful dresses — with his hair long and elegantly coiffed — throughout his childhood and adolescence. "My mother's caprice," Yussoupov said later, "was to have a lasting influence on my character." He became a part-time transvestite, and even as an adult he sometimes went strolling in public dressed as a woman, often in his mother's own lavish gowns, jewelry, and wigs.

By his late teens, Yussoupov had developed into a slender and extraordinarily handsome young man; in fact, he was called "the most beautiful young man in Europe." He became a favorite of various Russian army officers, who often invited him to spend an evening in their private dining rooms at the most fashionable restaurants. Yussoupov soon acquired a somewhat shaky reputation and was publicly admonished for his so-called "aesthetic tastes." "His favorite author is Oscar Wilde," noted one contemporary. "His instincts, countenance, and manner make him much closer akin to Dorian Gray than

Brutus."

When he was twenty-nine, Yussoupov (like many other members of the aristocracy) became increasingly concerned that the notorious monk Rasputin wielded too much power over the tsar and tsarina. Rasputin, he declared openly, was destroying the monarchy and had to be killed. (Some people later claimed that Yussoupov actually despised Rasputin because the monk had once rebuffed his sexual advances.) Yussoupov and four co-conspirators decided on a plan to kill the monk, and invited him to a late party at Yussoupov's home on the night of December 29, 1916. Their intention was to poison him.

Cyanide — "enough to kill several men instantly" — was baked into cakes for the occasion, and the wine was also poisoned. Rasputin, who arrived around midnight, at first refused to eat or drink anything; but, after much cajoling, he finally ate two of the cyanide-laced cakes. The conspirators watched expectantly, but there were no adverse effects. Rasputin then downed two tall glasses of the poisoned wine, also with no effect.

After two hours of this, Yussoupov — who had been trying

to remain calm as he entertained the monk with guitar-playing and singing — broke into a panic and ran upstairs to get his gun. When he returned, he immediately shot Rasputin in the back. (According to one of Yussoupov's servants, the five conspirators also raped Rasputin, then took out a hunting knife and hacked off the monk's penis and testicles.) It took three more shots before the conspirators were convinced Rasputin was finally dead. They bound the monk's seemingly lifeless body in heavy chains and threw it into the icy Neva River.

Amazingly, however, Rasputin was still alive when they tossed him into the water; when his body was found several days later, it was obvious he had struggled partly free of his chains, and his right hand was frozen in the sign of the cross. His lungs were full of water: a sign he had ultimately died of drowning.

When the Tsar learned that Yussoupov had engineered the murder, he immediately sent the young prince into internal exile. Shortly afterward, with revolution flaring across the country, Yussoupov fled to Paris, taking with him a fortune in jewels and paintings. He died there in 1977.